D1613279

A Whole-System Approach to High-Performance Green Buildings

A Whole-System Approach to High-Performance Green Buildings

David Strong
Victoria Burrows

ARTECH
HOUSE

BOSTON | LONDON
artechhouse.com

Library of Congress Cataloging-in-Publication Data
A catalog record for this book is available from the U.S. Library of Congress.

British Library Cataloguing in Publication Data
A catalog record for this book is available from the British Library.

ISBN-13: 978-1-60807-959-9

Cover design by John Gomes
Image: Green School, Stockholm, Sweden. (*Source:* 3XN Architects, reproduced with permission.)

© 2017 Artech House
685 Canton Street
Norwood, MA 02062

10 9 8 7 6 5 4 3 2 1

Contents

CHAPTER 3

Designing for the Future: Design Quality and Future Proofing, Intelligent Buildings, Whole Life Value, and Closing the Performance Gap

CHAPTER 4

CHAPTER 5

CHAPTER 7

CHAPTER 8

CHAPTER 9

CHAPTER 10

Preface

In his famous treatise *De Architectura* (circa 20 B.C.), the Roman architect Marcus Vitruvius Pollio asserted that a well-designed building must have three key attributes: *firmitas, utilitas,* and *venustas*—solid, useful, and beautiful. Given the extraordinary growth in population during the past 60 years, rapidly diminishing natural resources, declining biodiversity, and the impacts of climate change, Vitruvius, if writing today, might well include a fourth and essential attribute: *sustineo*—sustainability.

Delivering a genuinely sustainable built environment will not be achieved by incremental change—radically different ways of thinking and working are required to deliver buildings that are not only beautiful but also in every sense sustainable. The world is changing and we must adapt to secure the future for generations to come.

The definition of a genuinely sustainable building has been the subject of considerable worldwide debate. Regrettably, objectivity and technical fact often become obfuscated by "greenwash," which is designed to give the impression of a green building, but does not deliver all of the potential benefits.

Many countries have adopted building standards or building assessment and certification schemes in an attempt to objectively validate the environmental impact of new buildings and refurbishment projects. We will explore these in later chapters. Assessment schemes enable some degree of objectivity and independent scrutiny to be applied to the "green" performance claims. They have enormous potential to drive the sustainable development agenda and to stimulate a market pull for sustainable buildings, as clients, agents, and tenants become increasingly aware of the environmental performance of the buildings they own or occupy. Furthermore, a growing body of evidence supports the assertion that premium rents and higher resale values are being commanded by buildings that achieve the highest green building assessment scores. However, it is a sad fact that many of the first generation of green buildings have failed to fully deliver, with the energy requirements of the building often being considerably higher than expected, and in some cases occupant satisfaction has been poor.

Genuinely sustainable buildings are about much more than achieving zero-energy (or carbon)—it is essential that they not only result in ultra-low CO_2 emissions, but that they also need to be healthy, productive, resilient, and comfortable for the occupants. Experience shows that simplicity tends to work in the built environment and complexity tends to fail. Sustainability is a complex web of interrelated issues and success is highly dependent on a whole system approach to design, construction, commissioning, and operation. Collaborative, integrated multidisciplinary teamwork is critical to success. Profoundly different ways of working are required to "unlock" and realize the huge savings in energy and reduced environmental impact. The combination of "whole system thinking" based on intelligent architecture and effective engineering offers improvements in resource efficiency of between 4 and 10 times (i.e., achieving the same result but using up to 1/10 of the resources).

This book's goal is to help close the gap between design intent and the practical reality of delivering genuinely sustainable buildings. The book explores how natural systems can significantly reduce the requirements for energy to heat, cool, ventilate, and illuminate our buildings. Nature can also provide the inspiration for more efficient structures, use of new materials, and radical reductions in waste. Architects and engineers now have access on their desktops to the latest generation of low-cost (or free) computer software. These tools enable modeling and analysis of design options at a level of sophistication inconceivable at the dawn of the green building revolution, only 20 years ago. The guidance provided in this book aims to help deliver the next generation of sustainable buildings—fit not only for the planet but for the people who occupy them.

Acknowledgments

Many people have helped to make this book possible. In particular, I would like to thank my coauthor, Victoria Burrows, for her invaluable and extensive contribution to the book, and in particular for writing Chapter 8, Construction Phase Opportunities, and for compiling the case studies.

This book would not have been possible without the involvement of many eminent contributing authors—I am extremely grateful to them for generously sharing their invaluable expertise. My thanks also go to Aileen Storry, senior commissioning editor at Artech House for her guidance and support.

I am much indebted to my friend Huston Eubank who, from book inception through to final review, has unstintingly shared his wealth of "green building" knowledge and provided sage and much good-humored advice. It was Huston who at a critical juncture reminded me that Winston Churchill once said, "Writing a book is an adventure. To begin with it is a toy and an amusement. Then it becomes a mistress, then it becomes a master, then it becomes a tyrant. The last phase is that just as you are about to be reconciled to your servitude, you kill the monster and fling him to the public."

Finally, my grateful thanks to my wonderful wife Tan, who, with much forbearance, has sustained and encouraged me over the past two years of manuscript production! I dedicate this book to my children Edward and Elizabeth (Lillie), since it will be upon the shoulders of the next generation that the burden will largely fall to secure a genuinely sustainable and much less profligate future.

David Strong
December 2016

CHAPTER 1

Scope and Scale of the Challenge

We shape our buildings and afterwards, our buildings shape us.
—Winston Churchill

1.1 Impact of the Built Environment

The buildings we occupy have a profound impact on our lives. We spend over 80% of our time within buildings and they directly affect our health, happiness, and sense of well-being. Furthermore, the energy we use within them is a major contributor to global carbon emissions (see Color Plate 1).

In most developed countries the CO_2 arising from the energy we use to heat, light, ventilate, cool, and operate equipment within our buildings accounts for between 40% and 50% of total national emissions. In addition, in the United Kingdom CO_2 emissions arising from the manufacture and distribution of construction products are estimated to be equivalent to 19% of the CO_2 emitted in-use over the building's life cycle [1].

With the built environment accounting for 40% of the materials and about a third of the energy consumed by the world economy [2], it is not surprising that buildings have become the focus of so much national and international attention. During the past 20 years many countries have introduced new regulatory requirements associated with reducing the energy demands of new and existing buildings.

There has also been a growing realization that in addition to energy usage (and the associated CO_2 emissions), the impact of the built environment is much greater than these issues alone. This has led to the adoption of environmental rating and assessment methods for buildings that assess not only the energy demand, but also the impact of other factors such as land use and biodiversity, water consumption, pollution, and access to daylight.

Waste arising from construction activity and the production of building materials is enormous—in many countries accounting for 25% to 35% of total waste [3]. Typically, about 15% to 20% of all new construction material is sent to landfill as a consequence of over ordering, damage resulting from poor site storage, or inefficiencies in the construction method. Given the scale and scope of the challenge presented by waste arising from construction (and building material extraction and production), many countries have put in place ambitious targets to reduce to zero the amount of construction waste going to landfill and/or introduced fiscal measures such as landfill taxes to address the issue.

- Humans spend over 80% of their lives within buildings, with the internal environment having a profound impact on:
  - Health,
  - Happiness,
  - Productivity, and
  - Well-being.
- Typically 40% to 50% of total national CO_2 emissions (in developed countries) are derived from energy used within buildings. The extraction and production of construction materials adds a further 19%
- Construction accounts for 25% to 35% of total waste. 15% to 20% of new construction material is sent to landfill.

The evidence associated with the positive benefits of good design is overwhelming. A Royal Institute of British Architects research paper [4] concluded the following:

- "Well-designed homes and neighbourhoods create better and healthier places to live and build strong communities; they can reduce crime and provide homes that keep their value.
- Well-designed schools support teaching and learning and have a positive impact on students' behaviour.
- Well-designed hospitals aid speedier recovery and result in more efficient and contented staff.
- Well-designed offices lead to a more valued and productive workforce and profitable premises.
- Good-quality public spaces help create healthy communities, desirable properties and can revitalise run-down neighbourhoods."

1.2   The Emerging Market Drivers and Demand for Sustainable Buildings

At the root level, there have been three primary drivers for the development of green building awareness. In order of relative impact and importance these are as follows:

1. The passion of thought-leaders and early adopters (see Section 1.3),
2. Growing market demand (see Section 1.4), and
3. Government regulation (see Section 1.5).

While governments have the important responsibility of steering the boat, it is the thought leaders who initially lead the way for others (including government) to follow.

The past decade has seen the introduction of a number of push-and-pull factors that are having a profound impact on the market demand for sustainable buildings by providing the "carrots and sticks" to stimulate demand and improve delivery.

More demanding building regulations, codes, and standards are providing the "sticks" with mandatory energy labeling of buildings together with environmental assessment and certification of buildings being the "carrots."

1.3   Thought Leadership and the World Green Building Movement

The past 20 years have seen a profound shift in attitudes to "green" buildings. The World Green Building Council (WorldGBC) is a global member network of Green Building Councils enabling green building and sustainable communities through thought leadership and market transformation. The WorldGBC aim is "to make all building and communities sustainable, enabling us to thrive on our planet today and in the future."

Evidence of the new market drivers for sustainable buildings is the rapid growth in green building councils (GBCs) around the world. In 2006 only 6 countries had green building councils affiliated with the WorldGBC; by 2016 this number had increased to 75.

Thought leadership has also been provided by a growing number of green building champions and innovators: architects, engineers, property clients, owners/ developers, builders, researchers, manufacturers, and component suppliers, all of whom have contributed to the mainstreaming of more sustainable buildings.

1.3.1   Building Environmental Assessment Methods

Green building assessment methods have gained remarkable traction during the past 15 years, with demand for certificates as statements of a building's credentials increasing rapidly. Most of the environmental assessment systems owe their origin to the U.K. Building Research Establishments Environmental Assessment Method (BREEAM), the development of which started in 1989 (based on an original sustainability framework proposal by John Doggart). A prototype was trialed in 1990, with the first practical commercial version, "BREEAM for Offices," being launched in 1998. It is noteworthy that it was the property sector (U.K. developers: Stanhope, Greycoat, Olympia and York, and retailer Sainsbury's) who initially funded the creation of BREEAM. Their motivation was to differentiate their buildings and to create a "market pull" for more sustainable commercial office buildings. Developed by a consortium of industry experts, it later evolved into the first formal BREEAM scheme. Many other schemes soon followed: LEED in the United States, Greenstar in Australia, Green Mark in Singapore, CASBEE in Japan, and so on (see Figure 1.1).

Increasingly, building environmental assessment methods are being adopted in countries without formal building regulations as de facto construction standards. While adoption is largely driven by market pull, it is providing an effective mechanism for reducing energy demand. Concerns have been raised, however, regarding compliance enforcement and consistency. There is also a risk that the assessment process will become little more than a "tick-box" exercise undertaken by assessors who become adept at manipulating the scoring method. Despite these concerns, it is clear that environmental assessment of buildings, building components, and construction materials is becoming a key driver for building designers,

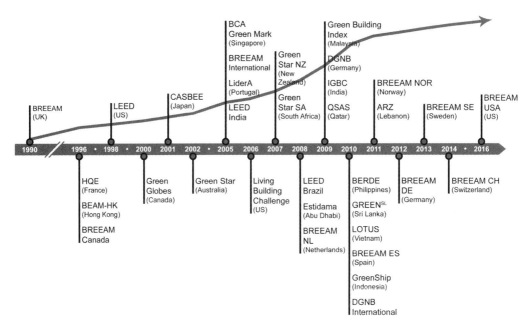

Figure 1.1   Worldwide growth in building environmental assessment schemes.

contractors, developers, and occupiers worldwide, resulting in beneficial change and improvement.

Early assessment schemes focused primarily on design rather than actual "in-use" performance. This approach risked intelligent design decisions being overruled by assessors "chasing" credits with little regard for in-use performance. This has led to numerous examples of buildings with poor energy performance or poor user experiences being certified with high BREEAM or LEED ratings. However, most schemes now address this issue by certifying both the design and in-use stages. The trend toward performance-based assessement is increasing and new initiatives such as *arc* by the U.S. Green Building Council and Green Business Certification, Inc., will accelerate the trend towards a focus on actual, rather than theoretical, performance [5].

1.3.2   Trends

With nearly 100 GBCs having been established around the world (see Color Plate 2), over 25 of them have either adopted (or adapted) existing rating schemes such as BREEAM or LEED or have developed their own national schemes. The schemes have many similarities, but their emphases vary from country to country. What most have in common is a confusing plethora of acronyms! The timeline in Figure 1.1 shows the launch dates of the major and regional green building assessment systems (based on first scheme launch for whole building sustainability issues for new buildings). The "boom" in development of new systems occurred between 2005 and 2010. Most schemes are now well established and have been developed for application in other countries to maximize reach.

Global green building rating schemes tend to follow a similar assessment process, with slight variances across the schemes. A set of performance criteria, specific for a building stage (i.e., new construction, refurbishment, interiors) or building type (i.e., commercial, retail, housing, neighborhoods), is identified through reference guides or manuals detailing the intent, requirements, and documentations required to demonstrate compliance. For certification, a nominated person (usually a trained and certified assessor, accredited professional, or project team member) coordinates the submission of design documentation to the certifying body for external audit. Formal certification is based on "as-built" verification of compliance, often involving a site audit.

A further trend supporting the rapid development and uptake of the certification schemes is the increasing stipulation of certification as part of development permits or planning permissions. For example, LEED and BREEAM certifications are required for many government, federal, and state developments. For example, since 2010 all new buildings in Abu Dhabi must achieve a minimum rating of 1 Pearl, with new government-funded building having to achieve at least 2 Pearls; and in Singapore, as well as minimum requirements for new and refurbished buildings, projects built in selected strategic areas must achieve minimum certification levels, for example, Green Mark Platinum in Marina Bay.

The focus of these schemes has also shifted from "design intention" statements through to validation on completion of construction—and further still into verification through in-use performance. Buildings must now prove they deserve the accolades, requiring design teams to take greater ownership of how the building performs.

1.3.3   Common International Assessment Methodology

Developing or adapting an assessment scheme specific to a particular country or region provides the opportunity to adjust criteria to suit prevalent climatic, social, and cultural needs, for example, by placing greater emphasis on particular issues or introducing context-specific credits.

There have been many calls for international standardization of building rating schemes to enable some degree of comparability between the schemes and to ensure they are based on tangible, measurable metrics. As a minimum, it is likely that common metrics will be developed and adopted internationally, which could enable a common language to emerge associated with assessing the sustainability of buildings (including social factors such as internal environmental conditions and comfort).

Within Europe two decades of collaboration and deliberation by the European Committee for Standardisation (CEN) TC 350 has resulted in the publication of EN 15978, a standard for the assessment of the environmental performance of buildings. EN 15978 was developed to remove technical barriers of trade in the construction sector. It claims to offer a standardized, comparable, and technology-neutral way to measure long-term carbon emissions arising from design and construction choices. The approach requires a detailed life cycle analysis based on carbon footprint (see Figure 1.2). The key features of EN 15978 are as follows:

- Entirely based on physical properties (no weighting),
- Calculated for the service life required by the constructor,

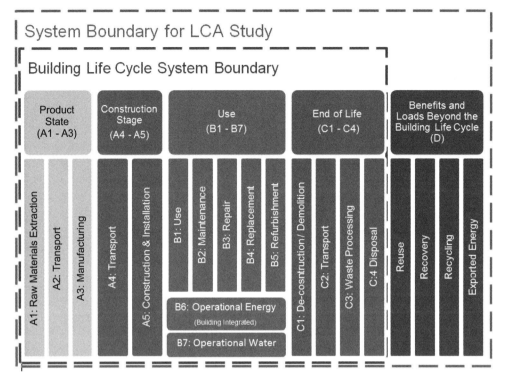

Figure 1.2 Standard EN 15978 key analysis requirements. (Image courtesy of eTool.)

- Covers the full life cycle, cradle to grave,
- Lists specific requirements for input data quality and coverage, and
- Bases building energy consumption primarily on dynamic energy simulation, and only secondarily on the construction code.

1.3.4 Differences Among Schemes

An international comparison of sustainable rating tools undertaken by Richard Reed et al. in 2011 [6] has been updated and built on to determine the features of the most commonly used schemes and those more focused toward holistic processes (see Table 1.1). Generally, the scope of assessment is similar and reflective of local priorities. Scheme variations may have slightly different scope, scoring, and certification fees. Schemes are regularly updated to bring the criteria in line with new interest areas and to promote continuous improvement beyond code or regulation baselines, and a step-change toward exemplary performance levels. Projects that target, for example, "the first Platinum in x country" or under a new scheme version may find their ambition is beyond the market's ability to deliver, resulting in a more expensive product, which can reflect poorly on the intention of such systems.

The main difference between the various assessment systems is the weighting they apply to different environmental categories. These naturally follow the main environmental and social issues for that region, which results in rating systems tailored to account for climate and local culture. For example, Japan's CASBEE is

Table 1.1 Comparison of Major Building Environmental Assessment Methods

Scheme (Dominant Country)	Certifying Body	Launch Year	Schemes	Ratings	Assessment Categories	Prerequisites
BREEAM (U.K.)	Building Research Establishment (BRE)	1990	Various; specific to building type, new/existing and neighborhoods	Pass (≥30%); Good (≥45%); Very good (≥55%); Excellent (≥70%); Outstanding (≥85%)	1. Management 2. Health and well-being 3. Energy 4. Transport 5. Water 6. Materials 7. Waste 8. Land use and ecology 9. Pollution 10. Innovation	Mandatory performance requirements in key performance areas, such as energy and water performance, contractor practices, materials sourcing and ecological impact
CASBEE (Japan)	Institute for Building Environment and Energy Conservation (IBEC)	2004	Housing, new construction (separate schemes for schools and interiors), urban and city scale	Poor C (0–0.5); Slightly poor B– (0.5–1); Good B+ (1–1.5); Very good A (1.5–3.0); Superior S (≥3.0)	1. Energy efficiency 2. Resource efficiency 3. Local environment 4. Indoor environment	Real estate only
DGNB (Germany)	German Sustainable Building Council (DGNB)	2009	Specific schemes for most new and existing building types	Bronze (≥35%); Silver (≥50%); Gold (≥65%); Platinum (≥80%)	1. Environmental quality 2. Economic quality 3. Sociocultural and functional quality 4. Technical quality 5. Process quality 6. Site quality	Minimum performance index applies for each certification level for key areas
Green Mark (Singapore)	Building Construction Authority (BCA)	2005	Various; specific to building type, new/existing and "beyond buildings"; parks, infrastructure, and districts	Certified (50–<75 points); Gold (75–<85 points); GoldPLUS (85–<90 points); Platinum (≥90 points)	1. Energy efficiency 2. Water efficiency 3. Environmental protection 4. Indoor environmental quality 5. Other green features and innovation	Envelope thermal performance and ventilation simulation requirements for higher rating levels

Table 1.1 (continued)

Assessment Process	Assessment Fee[a]	Certified Buildings	Assessment Information	Other Information/Distinguishing Features
Project teams engage a BREEAM accredited professional (AP) as a third party or as part of the design team to advise on credit criteria. A BREEAM assessor assesses documentation, submits at design and/or the post-construction stage for certification by the BRE	GBP £1,520–5,000[b] (USD $2,000–6,500)	Over 600,000[c]	Estimator tools are freely available, guidance manuals only to training assessors via the BREEAM projects	Category scores apply weightings developed in consultation with industry. Therefore, credits do not carry the same percentage values. BREEAM has been developed over many iterations to improve governance and alignment with regulatory standards. Adapted international versions include BREEAM Netherlands (NL), Spain (ES), Norway (NOR), Sweden (SE), Germany (DE), and Austria (AT).
An application for certification is accompanied by assessment results provided by a CASBEE accredited professional for buildings	JPY 400,000–1,000,000 (USD $3,964–9,910)	530	Technical manuals and assessment software freely available in Japanese and English	The rating is based on the Building Environment Efficiency (BEE) metric: The greater the ratio of Q (environmental quality) to L (environmental load) the higher the score. Since 2008, CASBEE has included Lifecycle CO_2 ($LCCO_2$) assessment, which evaluates CO_2 emissions during the entire building life cycle from construction and operation to demolition and disposal.
The project submission is coordinated by a third-party auditor to DGNB	3,000–28,080 (USD $3,338–31,250) (new offices 2014) (discounts for DGNB members)	625	Manuals and tools available only to members	The first certification system for sustainable buildings to consider social and economic sustainability as well as ecological aspects. Can be applied or adapted for every country; currently active in 20 countries outside Germany. A relevance factor is applied as a weighting process for each credit scored.
Green Mark assessor conducts design and documentary reviews to verify if the building project meets prerequisite credits and credit criteria. Site verification conducted upon project completion, including operational energy data (for GoldPlus and Platinum), and face-to-face audit.	SGD $15,390–35,790 (USD $11,496–26,735) (May 2016)	2,700 (May 2016)	Assessment scheme criteria manuals, score calculators, and guidance manuals available online; BCA Green Mark Portal provides further resources (requires Singapore residency)	Certified Green Mark buildings are required to be reassessed (under existing building criteria) every 3 years to maintain the Green Mark status. BCA Green Mark scheme has expanded beyond Singapore to 71 cities in 15 countries.

Table 1.1 (continued)

Scheme (Dominant Country)	Certifying Body	Launch Year	Schemes	Ratings	Assessment Categories	Prerequisites
Green Star (Australia)	Green Building Council Australia (GBCA)	2003	Every building type can be assessed under four life cycle schemes: communities, design and as-built, interiors, and performance (O&M)	One Star (10–19 points) Two Star (20–29 points) Three Star (30–44 points) Fourth Star (45–59 points) Five Star (60–74 points) Six Star (75+ points)	1. Management 2. Indoor environment quality 3. Energy 4. Transport 5. Water 6. Materials 7. Land use and ecology 8. Emissions 9. Innovation	
LEED (US)	Green Building Certification Institute (GBCI)	1998	Various; specific to building type, new/existing and neighborhoods	Certified (0–49 points) Silver (50–59 points) Gold (60–79 points) Platinum (≥80 points)	1. Sustainable sites 2. Water efficiency 3. Energy and atmosphere 4. Materials and resources 5. Indoor environmental Quality 6. Innovation and design process 7. Regional priority credits	Each of the performance categories has mandatory measures
Living Building Challenge (US)	International Living Future Institute (IFLI)	2006	Living Building Challenge	Certified	1. Site 2. Water 3. Energy 4. Health 5. Materials 6. Equity 7. Beauty	Net-zero energy, net-zero water, net-zero waste - performance over 12 continuous months of occupancy
Pearl Rating System (Abu Dhabi)	Estidama	2010	Every building type can be assessed using the community, building or villa schemes; operational rating system in development	1 Pearl (mandatory credits) 2 Pearl (≥60 points) 3 Pearl (≥85 points) 4 Pearl (≥115 points) 5 Pearl (≥140 points)	1. Integrated development process 2. Natural systems 3. Livable buildings 4. Precious water 5. Resourceful energy 6. Stewarding materials 7. Innovating practice	Mandatory credits within each category (except innovation) include energy and water performance, hazardous materials elimination, protection of natural systems and IDP process

Table 1.1 (continued)

Assessment Process	Assessment Fee[a]	Certified buildings	Assessment information	Other information / distinguishing features
Documentation is submitted to GBCA, reviewed by an independent panel of sustainable development experts and an overall score is assigned	AUD $17,500–40,000[d] (USD $13,361–30,500)	1,314	Submission guidelines are free to GBCA members, $600 per manual to purchase; tools available freely	Projects receive certification only for four stars or higher, representing better than best practice. Six stars represents world leadership. Scheme also used as a basis for Green Star South Africa (SA) and Green Star New Zealand (NZ).
Project teams submit documentation to GBCI for technical review and certification; LEED accredited professionals (AP) may support the process	USD $2,750–27,500+ (discounts for US-GBC members)	Over 96,000[e]	Tools are freely available	Scheme developments include extensive industry consultation and pilot credits. Version 4 is due for launch October 2016. Also developed into subsidiary country-specific versions including: LEED Brazil, LEED Canada, LEED India, LEED Emirates, LEED India, and LEED Mexico, adapted to suit local climatic and political conditions.
Independent third-party auditors review the documentation submitted by a project seeking certification and conduct a site audit; a preliminary audit may be conducted on project completion	USD $2,500–25,000+	44	Manuals and tools freely available; petal handbooks only to members	Focusing on regenerative development, can be applied to any building, regardless of scale, location, or age. Petal certification recognizes compliance with the petal criteria, without total net-zero performance.
The Pearl Qualified Professional (PQP), a member of the design team, facilitates the Pearl rating assessment for design and construction stages and coordinates the submission. A Pearl assessor at Estidama reviews and assesses the documentation for certification			Assessment guides and calculation tools are freely available.	For example, the water and energy sections carry the most credits. Estidama is the first rating scheme to introduce IDP as a core (and mandatory) element.

a Rates based on per gross floor area (GFA) of new building; valid as of July 2016 unless otherwise stated.
b Dependent on net floor area (NFA) and complexity.
c Includes certificates for homes.
d Based on contract value.
e Includes certificates for homes.

most concerned with land use, whereas, not surprisingly, Estidama stresses the importance of water conservation; and Singapore's Green Mark scheme has minimum system efficiency requirements for chilled-water plants.

In some of the systems, a building has to score against all the criteria, so a client or designer cannot select the assessment criteria. So if a building is weak in one category, it will be penalized for not earning a credit. Often the assessment of a building cannot be separated from its local environment. For example, a building will be marked down on its sustainability if local health and educational systems are weak or nonexistent. The rigor of the schemes for necessary governance and comparison often limits flexibility to adapt to contextual circumstances.

The introduction of prerequisite credits to most schemes brings credibility to the achieved rating levels—a criticism of earlier versions. These serve to set minimum performance standards or to require feasibility studies for features or processes that may not have previously been considered in order to encourage holistic approaches.

1.3.5   Certification—Barrier or Enabler for Integrative Design?

Green building certification schemes are often very linear, with the credits being viewed in silos such that synergies between the performance areas are not adequately addressed. The rise in the incorporation of integrated design process (IDP) credits is recognizing the undeniable benefits of collaboration and whole system approaches, and building on the awareness that rating schemes have created into a focus on actual in-use performance beyond utility bills.

For example, Green Mark's 2015 version, due for launch in mid-2016, has had a major overhaul from early versions. A broader range of prerequisites and introduction of new credits are promoting a more holistic approach to development, focusing on four core elements:

1. Climatically contextual design woven into the early thinking of building design,
2. Building energy performance in totality,
3. A life cycle approach toward resource use within a building, and
4. The livability of the indoor environment.

To get the most value from a green building assessment rating scheme, the following "golden rules" must be followed:

1. Choose the right scheme for the right reason. It is very easy to assume that setting a target to achieve certification will be a catch-all and you will definitely end up with a sustainable building. Know what schemes are available for application and evaluate the implications of each.
2. Embrace the step change. Updated certification scheme versions continuously raise the bar beyond standard practice. Sometimes, a lower rating can mean a better (and more cost-effective) building.
3. Widen your perspective. Understand the scope of the scheme being used, and do not limit sustainability initiatives to those that will only score points.

4. Identify synergies. Evaluate each feature or initiative for impacts (both positive and negative) on the wider stakeholders beyond the project team, to ensure they provide long-term value. An integrated strategy (such as a water management, harvesting, and reuse system) may earn credits in multiple sections.

5. Remember the weightings. One credit does not always equal one point. This will affect cost/benefit calculations.

6. Do not forget the paperwork. The documentation aspect of achieving certification must not be underestimated, particularly if more than one scheme is being used.

7. The devil is in the details. Do not be caught out by assumptions of compliance. Most schemes have accompanying guidance manuals detailing the minutia of criteria. Engage an expert.

For rating schemes to have the greatest impact, it is important that they encourage an integrated approach to the design process and the adoption of low pressure loss engineering solutions—these issues are vital if the targeted energy performance and operational cost savings are to be fully realized. These issues are addressed in the following chapters.

1.3.6 Pushing the Boundaries

A number of schemes have been developed that seek to go beyond the requirements of the main established assessment methods. Of particular note are the two schemes discussed next.

Living Building Challenge

The Living Building Challenge (LBC) is a building certification program that claims to define the most advanced measure of sustainability in the built environment today. Administered by the International Living Future Institute, LBC goes beyond BREEAM and LEED; for example, net-zero energy and net-zero water are minimum requirements. The idea behind LBC is that buildings, like trees and flowers, should be designed to exist within the natural "budget" of where they are built. They adapt according to the world around them rather than the world adapting to accommodate them. When you build from this perspective, there is less emphasis on codes and baselines—in nature, the sun provides the energy and the rain provides the water and buildings function more like ecosystems. See Chapter 10 for case studies of certified LBC projects.

One Planet Living

The One Planet Living (OPL) framework developed by the sustainability charity Bioregional, is a way of organizing progress toward sustainable development, based on the premise that most of humanity is living as if it had several planets at their disposal. One Planet Living uses 10 principles (see Figure 1.3) as the basis for planning the transition toward sustainability. The principles cover all of the key sectors

☺	**Health and happiness**	Encouraging active, social, meaningful lives to promote good health and wellbeing
🤝	**Equity and local economy**	Creating safe, equitable places to live and work which support local prosperity and international fair trade
👥	**Culture and community**	Nurturing local identity and heritage, empowering communities and promoting a culture of sustainable living
🦋	**Land and nature**	Protecting and restoring land for the benefit of people and wildlife
💧	**Sustainable water**	Using water efficiently, protecting local water resources and reducing flooding and drought
🍎	**Local and sustainable food**	Promoting sustainable humane farming and healthy diets high in local, seasonal organic food and vegetable protein
🚲	**Travel and transport**	Reducing the need to travel, encouraging walking, cycling and low carbon transport
🌳	**Materials and products**	Using materials from sustainable sources and promoting products which help people reduce consumption.
♻	**Zero waste**	Reducing consumption, re-using and recycling to achieve zero waste and zero pollution
⚊	**Zero carbon energy**	Making buildings and manufacturing energy efficient and supplying all energy with renewables

Figure 1.3   One Planet Living framework. (*Source:* Bioregional.)

involved in sustainability, including those that are most human-centric. The central proposition is that stakeholders involved in projects of all kinds should work together to draw up action plans based on the 10 principles, setting out actions under each of them with specific targets and key performance indicators and covering a period of one or more decades (see Case Study 10.4 in Chapter 10).

1.4   Creating a Market Pull for Sustainable Buildings

In 2000 the prevailing view was the "Vicious Circle of Blame" (see Figure 1.4a), which resulted in a perception that seemingly insurmountable barriers were associated with creating a market demand for sustainable buildings. During the past 15 years, however, the barriers have largely disappeared and there is a much more optimistic view of the opportunities associated with green buildings. Demand from owners and occupiers is increasingly stimulating market pull with agents and architects responding to the new drivers (see Figure 1.4b).

1.4.1   Responding to Client and Occupant Requirements

Anecdotal evidence started emerging in the early 2000s of enhanced resale value and rental premiums associated with green buildings. Skeptics were unconvinced and there was a pressing need for good data to validate the claims. The first robust

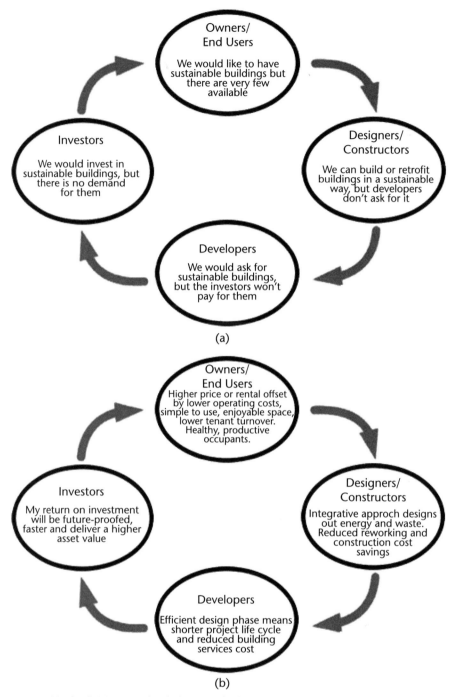

Figure 1.4 (a) The "Vicious Circle of Blame"—the barriers to sustainable buildings as perceived in 2000 (after [7]). (b) The "Virtuous Circle of Opportunity"—the positive drivers for sustainable buildings in 2016.

study based on objective data was published by Jones Lang LaSalle/CoreNet Global in 2007 [8] (see Figure 1.5). Key conclusions from the study included the following:

- "2007 represented a tipping point in occupier attitudes towards sustainability. Momentum will gather further and faster in 2008.

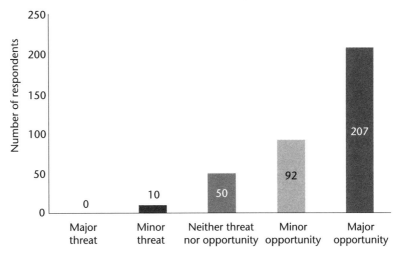

Figure 1.5   Sustainability—an organizational threat or opportunity (*Source:* Jones Lang LaSalle [8].)

- A survey of over 400 occupiers globally identified that there is clear occupier demand for sustainable real estate solutions.
- Occupiers are prepared to pay a premium to secure sustainable real estate but the ability of the supply side to provide sustainable solutions is currently viewed by occupiers as sporadic."

1.4.2   Growing Awareness That "Green" Buildings Pay

Other studies followed that provided further evidence of the growing demand for sustainable buildings:

- A study by CoStar Group published in March 2008 [9] found that sustainable "green" buildings outperform their peer nongreen assets in key areas such as occupancy, sale price, and rental rates, sometimes by wide margins.
- The Royal Institution of Chartered Surveyors published a research report in March 2009 that provided an analysis of the financial performance of green buildings in the United States [10]. The report concluded:
  - "There is indeed, a premium for the rents that 'green' buildings with the Energy Star rating can command.
  - The aggregate premium for the whole sample is on the order of 3% per square foot compared with otherwise identical buildings
  - When looking at effective rents—rents adjusted for building occupancy levels—the premium is even higher, above 6%.
  - The researchers were also able to look at the impact on the selling prices of green buildings, and here the premium is even higher, on the order of 16%. This really is quite significant—what it implies is that upgrading the average non-'green' building to a 'green' one would increase its capital value by some $5.5 million."

- In 2013 the Institute for Market Transformation and Appraisal published a report [11] that stated:
  - "In many markets, rental premiums are emerging in green buildings as many of today's best tenants are increasingly willing to pay a premium for green spaces. For these tenants, leasing green space is an opportunity to demonstrate a commitment to sustainability, attract the best employees, and improve productivity."
  - Rental premiums of between 4% and 27% were reported for commercial office buildings in the United States.

Other research reports [12, 13] provided additional evidence of the increasing demand and awareness within the sector associated with the commercial opportunities offered by green buildings. There was also a growing awareness of the corporate social responsibility (CSR) and brand equity implications (positive and negative) associated with environmental rating and/or energy label attached to buildings occupied by major corporations.

The most definitive study to-date regarding the business case for green buildings was undertaken by the WGBC [14]. This 2013 report provides a comprehensive review of the costs and benefits for developers, investors and occupants. Key findings included:

- Building green does not necessarily need to cost more.
- Buildings with better sustainability credentials enjoy increased marketability.
- Green buildings have been shown to save money through reduced energy and water use and lower long-term operations and maintenance costs.
- Green design attributes of buildings and indoor environments can improve worker productivity and occupant health and well-being, resulting in bottom line benefits for businesses.

The interest in sustainable/low-energy buildings was further enhanced in the U.K. with the introduction of requirements for pension funds to report the carbon emissions arising from their real estate portfolios.

1.5 Compliance Drivers

Following the thought leadership and example set by early adopters, governments around the world have responded by introducing building codes aimed at reducing the energy demand of new buildings. In some countries measures have also been introduced that require the energy consumption of existing buildings undergoing major refurbishment or substantial modification to be minimized.

In the United States, ANSI/ASHRAE/IES Standard 90.1 (2013) has been modified eight times since 1975, with the design energy targets being made more demanding at nearly every revision. On the basis of an energy use index (with the index being set at 100 in 1980), the index now stands at 50—implying a 50% reduction in the design energy use intensity for an office building to about 110 kWh/

m^2 per year (see Figure 2.8 in Chapter 2) over a period of 40 years. The ASHRAE 90.1 standard is not federally mandated; however, it is referenced/required in a number of state efficiency laws. It is increasingly being adopted for nearly all new buildings being designed in the United States, often mandated by the client as a minimum requirement. Demonstrating compliance with ASHRAE 90.1 is a paperwork exercise. Essentially, designers demonstrate compliance by submitting the results via their model and attesting that their design complies.

In Europe the Energy Performance of Buildings Directive (EPBD) required all current 28 European Union member states to ensure that minimum energy performance standards/regulations were introduced by 2006 together with the introduction of building energy labeling. Setting high-level targets and an achievable timeframe afforded member states the opportunity to develop step-change action plans appropriate to their specific context. The EPBD is deemed to have had a dramatic impact on building energy performance in Europe, and the introduction of building energy labeling has helped to stimulate market interest and demand for low-energy buildings.

A harmonized methodology for assessing the energy requirements of buildings was developed by the European Committee for Standardisation (Comité Européen de Normalisation or CEN). This was based on an unprecedented level of cooperation between experts and governments across all member states. The CEN methodology has been adopted by most European countries as the basis for assessing the energy performance of new (and in some cases existing) buildings with an instantly recognizable energy ratings chart that was previously used for white goods and is now applied to your new home or office. Other countries have also introduced regulatory requirements to minimize energy demand with the U.S. Department of Energy DOE2 model being used as the basis for assessment in some countries.

Figure 1.6a shows a U.K. Display Energy Certificate (DEC). These are required for all public owned and operated buildings visited by the public such as hospitals, universities, and local authority buildings (libraries, town halls, etc.). They are based on building type, function, and actual energy consumption and occupied floor area. The certificates should be updated annually, with any changes in energy usage being displayed. (The certificate in Figure 1.6a shows a steady improvement in performance over a number of years.) The midpoint on the A to G scale (100) is the benchmark/average performance of a building of the same type, function, and occupancy. DECs are sometimes referred to as "operational" ratings because they are designed to provide an indication of the actual performance of the building in use.

The Energy Performance Certificate (EPC) for a new commercial building is shown in Figure 1.6b. EPCs are known as *asset ratings* and are based on a standardized methodology that assesses the theoretical energy rating of the building based on an assessment of the thermal characteristics of the building, standard hours of occupancy, plant and equipment, etc. In the United Kingdom new dwellings are assessed and rated using the Standard Assessment Procedure (SAP) with existing houses being rated using a reduced dataset version of SAP. Nondomestic buildings are assessed and rated using a National Calculation Method (NCM). In the United Kingdom a Simplified Building Energy Model and/or government-approved Dynamic Simulation Model (DSM) is used to generate the data for the EPC. EPCs are required to be provided to the prospective purchaser or tenant of

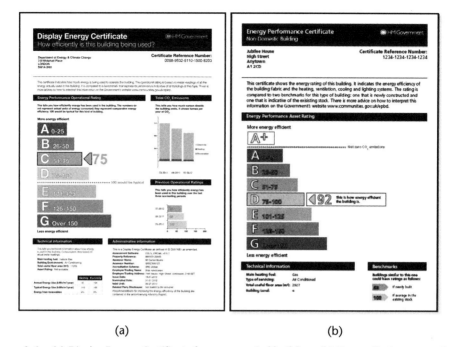

(a)   (b)

Figure 1.6   (a) Display Energy Certificate for an occupied building. (b) Energy Performance Certificate for a new building. (*Source:* U.K. government, Open Parliament Licence v3.0.)

any domestic or nondomestic building in the United Kingdom. Similar labels exist in all 28 member states of the European Union, although the way the certificates are produced and their specific design and content vary from country to country.

1.5.1 Zero-Energy and Nearly Zero-Energy/Carbon Buildings

The 2010 recast of the EPBD required that "Member States shall ensure that by 31 December 2020 all new buildings are nearly zero-energy buildings; and after 31 December 2018, new buildings occupied and owned by public authorities are nearly zero-energy buildings." Member States shall furthermore "draw up national plans for increasing the number of nearly zero-energy buildings" and "following the leading example of the public sector, develop policies and take measures such as the setting of targets in order to stimulate the transformation of buildings that are refurbished into nearly zero-energy buildings."

A nearly zero-energy building is defined in the EPBD recast as "a building that has a very high energy performance. The nearly zero or very low amount of energy required should be covered to a very significant extent by energy from renewable sources, including energy from renewable sources produced on-site or nearby." Again, subsidiarity allows member states to implement these requirements in different ways and it is not yet clear how the specific requirements associated with achieving "nearly zero-energy buildings" is to be defined and/or implemented in each country.

It is likely that other countries will follow the EU lead in introducing regulations associated with achieving zero-carbon or nearly-zero energy buildings. Clearly, practical difficulties exist and the targets will be more difficult to achieve in some climatic regions and for some building types and functions than in others.

However, the trends are clear; governments around the world are putting in place increasingly demanding requirements associated with reducing the energy demand of buildings. This will further stimulate demand for sustainable buildings and the focus is already starting to shift from the theoretical demands of achieving the more onerous requirements at the design stage, to the practical reality of operating a building in-use to achieve nearly zero net energy use.

1.6   Whole System Thinking

As we have identified, achieving genuinely sustainable development cannot be addressed either by a "broad brush" or single-issue approach. Success is not easy and is highly dependent on collaborative interdisciplinary teamwork from inception to occupation and beyond.

The traditional approach to design, construction, commissioning, and operation (where experts work in professional silos) has to be replaced with an exceptional level of team integration. Adopting an integrated approach to design based on whole system thinking (WST) can deliver significant savings in capital (CAPEX) and operational (OPEX) costs and also provides a more effective way to achieve the ambitious performance targets previously outlined without compromising the future of the building.

WST requires a high level of architectural intelligence and engineering skill; however, the prize in terms of lower CAPEX, OPEX, and environmental impacts are well worth the effort. The following chapters explore the opportunities and how to realize them.

Ten Key Methods for Achieving Sustainable Design and Operations Outcomes

Jerry Yudelson, from *The World's Greenest Buildings: Promise vs. Performance in Sustainable Design* [15]

1. Goals: Set Big Sustainable Audacious Goals (BSAGs) for your next building project. Some key element(s) of the project should push the boundaries for key design outcomes. This could include but must not be limited to setting goals for building certification at the highest levels of recognized rating systems.

2. Energy use objective: The site EUI for building design should be less than or 80–100 kWh/m^2/year (25,000–30,000 BTU/ft^2/year) for a typical office; less for school or college before considering the contributions of onsite or purchased renewable energy. More ambitious projects will aim at 100 kWh/m^2/year source energy use, including energy used to power the building.

3. Carbon emissions: The project should be carbon neutral in terms of site energy use, either through using on-site renewable power generation, biomass CHP systems, geothermal or geo-exchange systems, or purchased renewable energy.

4. Sustainable key performance indicators (KPIs): sustainability KPIs should include energy, carbon, water use, and waste minimization. Each should be committed to at the outset of the project.

5. Cost management: Despite the "stretch" BSAG goals, the overall building cost should be equal or close to regional averages for similar building types and sizes.

6. Commitment: Every building team member must strongly commit to the desired outcome(s) before being selected to participate in the project. This should be similar to the "contract" signed by building teams engaged in integrated project delivery. This commitment would extend to the team's willingness to provide consulting time during post-occupancy evaluations at the one-year and three-year anniversaries.

7. Collaboration: An integrated design process should be employed and seen by all building team members as essential to the success of the project, and all building teams would need to learn how to make this process work.

8. Commissioning process: Building commissioning should begin during the design phase and continue through the first year of operations, to ensure that all key energy and comfort systems are operating as designed and are understood by building operators and occupants.

9. Cloud-based monitoring: Each project should incorporate and commit to a cloud-based performance monitoring system for at least the first five years of operations, to ensure that sustainable outcomes are in fact achieved.

10. Communications: Each project must include onsite and online publicly available information displays that should how well the project is meeting its commitments to sustainable operations. Cloud-based systems can provide these reports as a matter of course to building operators and occupants, while lobby displays for visitors (showing energy used vs. produced onsite, for example) add to the commitment.

References

[1]   U.K. Department of Business Innovation and Skills, *Estimating the Amount of CO_2 Emissions That the Construction Industry Can Influence*, Autumn 2010, https://www.gov.uk/government/uploads/system/uploads/attachment_data/file/31737/10-1316-estimating-co2-emissions-supporting-low-carbon-igt-report.pdf (July 2016).

[2]   Rees, W. E., "The Built Environment and the Ecosphere: A Global Perspective," *Building Research & Information Journal*, Vol. 27, No. 4–5, October 2010, pp. 206–220.

[3]   http://www.ukgbc.org/resources/additional/key-statistics-construction-waste (July 2016).

[4]   Royal Institute of British Architects, *Good Design—It All Adds Up*, https://www.architecture.com/Files/RIBAHoldings/PolicyAndInternationalRelations/Policy/Gooddesignitalladdsup.pdf (July 2016).

[5]   "Platform Will Drive Building Performance Within the Green Industry," *U.S. Green Building Council Press Release*, Oct. 2016, http://www.usgbc.org/articles/gbci-announces-new-technology-orangization-arc.

[6]   Reed, R., et al., "A Comparison of International Sustainable Building Tools—An Update," paper presented at 17th Annual Pacific Rim Real Estate Society Conference, Gold Coast, 16–19 January 2011, http://www.prres.net/Proceedings/..%5CPapers%5CReed_International_Rating_Tools.pdf (July 2016).

[7]   Cadman, D., "The Vicious Circle of Blame," in *What About Demand? Do Investors Want Sustainable Buildings?*, M. Keeping (ed), London: RICS, 2000.

[8]   Jones Lang LaSalle/CoreNet Global, *Global Trends in Real Estate: An Occupier's Perspective*, 2007, http://www.joneslanglasalle.com/ResearchLevel1/Global_Trends_in_Sustainable_Real_Estate_-_Feb_2008_EN.pdf (July 2016).

[9]   Burr, A. C., "Demand in Marketplace for Sustainabiliy Creates Higher Occupancy rates, Stronger Rents and Sale Prices in 'Green' Buildings," *CoStar*, March 2008.

[10]   Eichholtz, P., N. Kok, and J. Quigly, *Doing Well by Doing Good? An Analysis of the Financial Performance of Green Office Buildings in the USA*, Research Report, March 2009, Royal Institution of Chartered Surveyors.

[11]   Institute for Market Transformation and Appraisal, *Green Building and Property Value—A Primer for Building Owners and Operators*, 2013, https://www.appraisalinstitute.org/assets/1/7/Green-Building-and-Property-Value.pdf (July 2016).

[12]   Taylor Wessing LLP, *Behind the Green Façade: Is the UK Development Industry Really Embracing Sustainability?*, 2009.

[13]   CB Richard Ellis/EMEA Research, *Who Pays for Green? The Economics of Sustainable Buildings*, 2009.

[14]   World Green Building Council, "The Business Case for Green Building: A Review of the Costs and Benefits for Developers, Investors, and Occupants," http://www.worldgbc.org/files/1513/6608/0674/Business_Case_for_Green_Building_Report_WEB_2013-04-11.pdf. Last accessed October 2016.

[15]   Yudelson, J., and U. Meyer, *The World's Greenest Buildings: Promise Versus Performance in Sustainable Design*, 2013, New York and London: Routledge.

CHAPTER 2

Whole System Approach

Making the simple complicated is commonplace; making the complicated simple, awesomely simple, that's creativity.

—Charles Mingus

The design, construction, and maintenance of any major building is a highly complex and multifaceted undertaking. Most new buildings are unique and, in this respect, every one is a prototype. In manufacturing there are opportunities for a prototype to be refined, improved, and enhanced. In many sectors, a process of continuous improvement enables redundancy and inefficiency to be reduced (or eliminated)—leading to significant enhancements in resource efficiency. The prototypes of the building sector, however, do not lend themselves as readily to refinement.

As a consequence of the protracted nature of the design and construction process, the building sector has generally been very poor at learning from its mistakes! The absence of effective feedback mechanisms results in opportunities for innovation and performance enhancement being significantly reduced or often missed altogether.

New initiatives such as Soft Landings (see Section 3.5 in Chapter 3) have sought to address this issue and there are promising signs that the sector is starting to recognize the importance of effective feedback and the significant opportunities that are associated with reducing the capital expenditure (CAPEX) of major projects, together with the operational costs (OPEX).

The CABE Guide for Clients, Creating Excellent Buildings [1], identifies four key requirements associated with delivering a sustainable building:

1. Include sustainability objectives in the outline brief.
2. Define the parameters for sustainability and set firm, auditable targets.
3. Police these sustainability indicators with the same rigor as cost issues.
4. Define a process and specify the advisers you need to make informed decisions and evaluate them.

2.1   What Is "Whole System Thinking"?

A whole system approach to building design requires all aspects of construction, operation, and maintenance to be addressed at the design stage. Conventional approaches to building design do not generally enable a holistic approach to be adopted, with building client and key members of the design team often operating in isolation based on specialism or professional discipline.

Integration of the design and delivery team is an essential component of a whole system approach. Traditional building procurement often results in the design and construction team working in sequence rather than in parallel. Major savings in CAPEX and OPEX can be achieved by bringing design, construction, and building maintenance/operation skills together at an early stage.

2.1.1   Integrating the Design Process

Many practitioners have found it impossible to produce a genuinely sustainable building if a conventional approach to building design, construction, commissioning, and operation is adopted.

Learning the lessons from best practice of what works (and what doesn't) suggests that delivering a high-performance building is critically dependent on a collaborative, multidisciplinary approach, with a shared vision and holistic understanding of the key objectives. This approach is often referred to as an integrated design process (IDP), in which the impact of every design decision on other aspects of the building is considered and continually reviewed.

The roadmap for the integrated design process [2] states that IDP is:

- "an iterative process, not a linear or silo-based approach;
- a flexible method, not a formula;
- different each time, not predetermined; and
- an iterative process with ongoing learning and emergent features, not a pre-ordained sequence of events."

IDP represents a profoundly different way of working. The key differences are highlighted in Table 2.1. The conventional design process often results in:

- Insufficient stakeholder engagement,
- Lack of clarity in the initial brief,
- Value engineering changes with an uncoordinated reappraisal of design,
- Lack of monitoring during construction and commissioning, and
- Incorrect operation and management of the building.

The collaborative, multidisciplinary integrated team working with an integrated design process delivers:

Table 2.1   Key Differences Between IDP and a Conventional Approach to Design

Integrated Design Process	*Conventional Design Process*
Inclusive form the outset	Involves team members only when essential
Front-loaded—time and energy invested early	Less time, energy, and collaboration exhibited in early stages
Decisions influenced by broad team	More decisions made by fewer people
Iterative process	Linear process
Whole-systems thinking	Systems often considered in isolation
Allows for full optimizations	Limited to constrained optimization
Seeks synergies	Diminished opportunity for synergies
Life-cycle costing	Emphasis on up-front costs
Process continues through post-occupancy	Typically finished when construction is complete

Source: Busby Perkins+Will and Stantec. Reproduced with permission.

- Synergistic solutions that address and resolve multiple problems and issues simultaneously;
- Significant reductions in the requirements for energy-intensive building services plant and equipment by identifying and exploiting the opportunities offered by nature to ventilate, heat, cool, and illuminate our buildings for some, or all of the occupied hours;
- Social, human, environmental, and economic benefits;
- Forensic attention to detail, which improves efficiency and designs out waste; and
- Robust life cycle costing, which enables more rational decisions to be made regarding the whole-life performance of the building envelope and the building services plant and equipment.

2.1.1.1   Phases of an Integrated Design Process

Too often sustainability is only considered as a "bolt-on" during the final design stage, but this is far too late in the process to optimize the design and deliver a genuinely sustainable outcome. There is an adage that "all the really important mistakes are made on the first day of the design process." Figure 2.1 compares design team involvement during a conventional design process with IDP. The figure also demonstrates how the opportunities to influence sustainability diminish during the design process. Two important considerations result from this:

- Adding sustainability features becomes increasingly difficult, costly, and suboptimal as the design approaches the construction phase.
- The best time to consider sustainability is during the concept design and schematic design phases—this provides the best opportunity to deliver a sustainable building at the lowest CAPEX and OPEX.

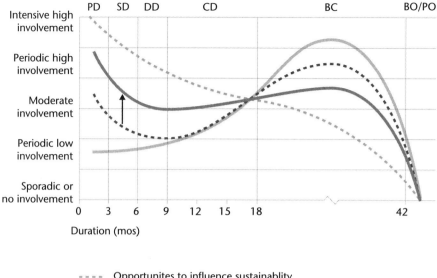

Figure 2.1 Key differences between a conventional approach to design and IDP. (*Source:* Busby Perkins+Will and Stantec. Reproduced with permission.)

- Clients need to recognize that the fees associated with IDP and earlier design team involvement will be higher than a conventional approach (and will be incurred earlier). However, any additional fees will be recouped many times over as a consequence of greater optimization, leading to significantly lower CAPEX and OPEX.

According to the roadmap for IDP [2], seven phases make up the integrated design process, as summarized below:

1. Predesign (PD): Looks at the relationships between the project and its surrounding environment to explore possibilities for the site, the users, and the owner. The scope of the project is determined and the design team is coordinated.

2. Schematic design (SD): Investigates technologies, new ideas, and new applications while laying the foundation for the project's goals and objectives. Preliminary analyses are conducted with respect to finances and energy consumption.

3. Design development (DD): Results in a schematic design concept being selected and approved by the client. Architectural, mechanical, and electrical systems are considered.

4. Construction documentation (CD): Finalizes all design development documents including calculations and specifications.

5. Bidding, construction, and commissioning (BC): This begins when the main design plans have been realized. By the end of this phase, the team will

have achieved a finished, fully functional, and well-commissioned building, ready for occupancy.

6. Building operation (BO): Transitions the building from the design team to the building occupants. At this stage, final building commissioning has occurred and building operators have been fully trained on the efficient operation of their new building.

7. Post-occupancy (PO): Efforts continue to monitor and maintain, measure and verify, recommission and evaluate. Postconstruction provides an opportunity for feedback loops, facilitating continuous building optimization.

2.1.2   IDP Design Team Organization

Adopting IDP requires profoundly different ways of working. The conventional hierarchical approach is replaced by a core team that must include the client, who takes an active role during the design process.

Of particular importance is the key part played by the IDP facilitator—this position is akin to that of the conductor of an orchestra. He/she does not need to be a technical specialist, but does need to have the facilitation, organizational, and interpersonal skills to manage the IDP process and to ensure that conflicts are quickly and harmoniously resolved.

If the individual has the relevant skills and expertise, the facilitator can also undertake the role of sustainability champion for the project; however, this role is sometimes undertaken by one of the other core team members. Figures 2.2 and 2.3 highlight the key differences between the conventional and IDP approaches. The conventional design team organization is shown in Figure 2.2. In this case the client's primary contact is the architect, who coordinates the activities and inputs from other team members in a hierarchical manner.

In contrast, Figure 2.3 illustrates the organizational arrangement for a typical IDP. In this case the team is expanded to include the main contractor, IDP champion/facilitator, and a cost consultant. The team is closely interlinked, with support from specialist consultants being called on when required.

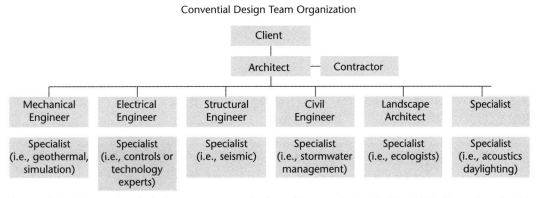

Figure 2.2 Conventional design team organization. (*Source:* Busby Perkins+Will. Reproduced with permission.)

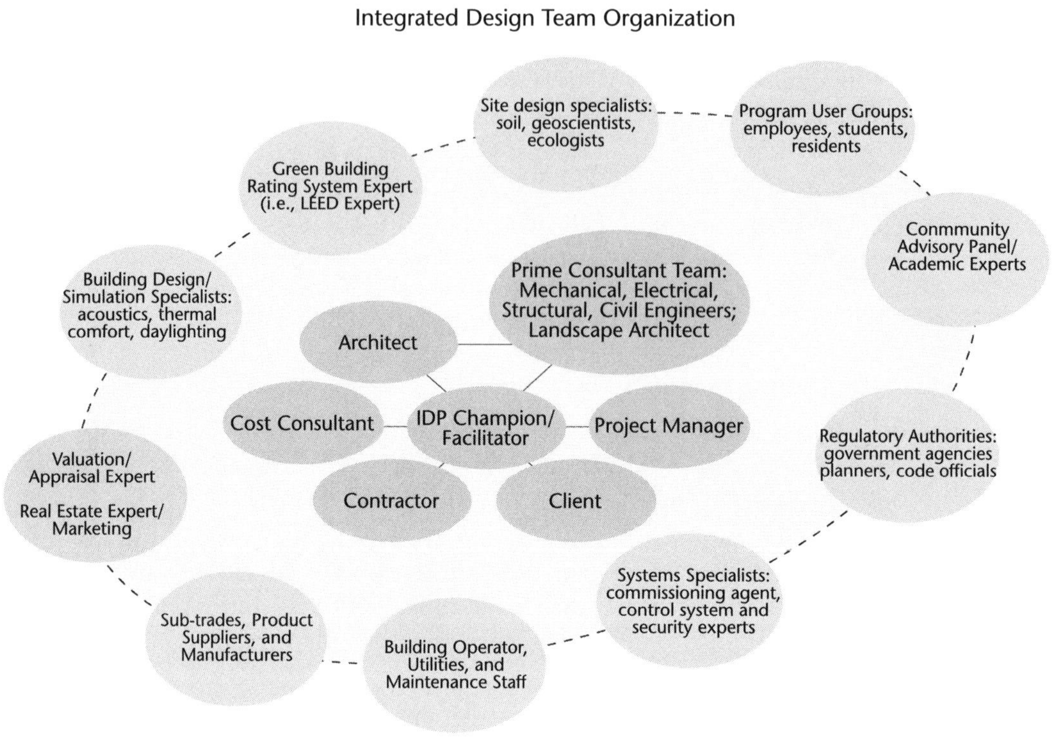

Integrated Design Team Organization

Figure 2.3   Integrated design team organization. (*Source:* Busby Perkins+Will. Reproduced with permission.)

2.1.3   Benefits of Integrative, Collaborative, Multidisciplinary Design Team Engagement

Demonstrable benefits accrue from collaborative working, particularly when sustainability issues are addressed during the early stages of design. Buildings designed in this way not only have significantly lower environmental impact, they also deliver major social sustainability benefits in terms of enhanced occupant health, productivity, and well-being. Although difficult to quantify in financial terms, these additional benefits often result in buildings with significantly higher rental and resale value (see Section 1.4.2). The key benefits are summarized in Table 2.2.

Furthermore, closer attention to detail during the early stages of design often identifies significant construction cost savings by "designing out" requirements for costly and complex building services plant and equipment (see Chapter 5).

2.2   Identifying and Exploiting the Opportunities for CAPEX and OPEX Reductions Offered by a Whole System Approach

In their book The Integrative Design Guide to Green Building [3], the 7Group and Bill Reed provide a compelling example by asking the question "How does the selection of paint color for interior walls impact the size of the heating, ventilating, and air-conditioning (HVAC) system?"

The connection between paint color and building services equipment CAPEX and OPEX may not be immediately self-evident. However, the example shows how

Table 2.2   Key Benefits of IDP

Integrated Design Principle	Benefits of Successful Integrated Design	Net Benefits
Broad, collaborative team from outset	Early formation of a broad, interdisciplinary team ensures necessary expertise is present when opportunities for impact are greatest. Collaboration harnesses the team's best effort and collective wisdom.	Realization of challenging goals and objectives.
Well-defined scope, vision, goals and objectives	Investing time up-front ensures common understanding and "buy-in."	Realization of high-performance (sustainable) buildings.
Effective and open communications	Transparency builds trust and increases team's best effort and enthusasism.	Realization of more optimally integrated solutions.
Innovative and synthesis	Fostering open-mindedness and creativity leads to innovation and synthesis, which allow the team to achieve the complex requirements of a high-performing building.	Maximized benefits and quality.
Systematic decision making	A clearly defined and understood decision-making process can lead to better choices. Tools like life cycling can foster the type of holistic and long-term thinking necessary for sustainable design.	Minimized costs.
Iterative process with feedback loops	Providing opportunities for feedback along the way allows lessons to be learned form start to finish.	Good team relationships that may result in lasting partnerships for future projects.

Source: Busby Perkins+Will and Stantec. Reproduced with permission.

the light reflectance value (LRV) of the paint selected by the architect (or interior designer) has a direct impact on the number and distribution of light fittings. Reducing the number of light fittings by selecting paint with a high LRV reduces the HVAC cooling load, since a smaller number of luminaires can be specified to provide the same level of lighting. This not only saves operational energy and costs associated with lighting and HVAC, but also saves CAPEX associated with lighting equipment, wiring, HVAC ductwork, and plant.

The example goes on to identify the absence of dialogue between the lighting engineer and the person tasked with specifying the paint. Similarly, HVAC engineers tend to use rules of thumb associated with lighting loads when sizing HVAC plant—often resulting in significantly oversized plants that are not based on the actual installed lighting load. This results in significant and unnecessary CAPEX and inefficient HVAC operation under part-load conditions, leading to higher OPEX.

Many such examples of dis-integrative specification exist that can only be identified and addressed by effective design team integration and the avoidance of key specifiers operating in isolated silos.

Arguably, the single greatest opportunity for achieving substantial savings in CAPEX and OPEX is associated with the specification of the building envelope. The façade design and specification have a major bearing on CAPEX, OPEX, and the sustainability of the building (see Section 5.2). In a conventional design process, however, this critical element is often specified by the architect (as a key aesthetic element) at the concept design stage, with limited (or no) input from other members of the design team.

Some building codes/regulations and/or environmental assessment methods, such as Singapore's Green Mark, impose stringent requirements associated with the thermal performance of the envelope. This ensures that some consideration is given to this critical issue, but opportunities for performance enhancement and greater savings associated with the following are often poorly addressed:

- Optimization of solar gains to avoid (or reduce) cooling loads and/or provide a useful contribution to any space heating demand.
- Exploiting daylight to reduce the demand for artificial lighting (while avoiding glare and excessive solar gains resulting in a requirement for mechanical cooling), with major benefits such as:

  - Enhanced occupant health, productivity, and well-being (see Section 2.4);
  - Reduced electrical demand for artificial lighting;
  - Reduced (or no) requirement for HVAC equipment;
  - Smaller, ducts, pipes, pumps, fans, transformers, switchgear, etc.; and
  - Significantly lower operational and maintenance costs.

In countries with building codes (or environmental rating systems), the specification of the façade envelope is all too often only considered in detail during the final stages of detailed design, when the compliance assessor is told to "do what it takes to achieve (or fix) compliance." Again, this is far too late in the design and specification process to make meaningful changes or to identify and exploit the opportunities for achieving the multiple benefits that can be derived from optimizing the façade.

2.2.1 Tunneling Through Cost Barriers

Engineers are trained to identify the point at which spending more results in only marginal savings—this is often referred to as the point of diminishing returns (e.g., increasing the thickness of insulation or specifying double- rather than triple-glazed windows). Although this approach may be valid for optimizing individual components, it often masks much greater savings if the building is considered as a whole system.

The benefits of tunneling through cost barriers are identified by Paul Hawken, Amory Lovins, et al., in their seminal book Natural Capitalism [4]. A key message is "Optimizing components in isolation tends to pessimize the whole system—and hence the bottom line. You can actually make a system less efficient while making each of its parts more efficient, simply by not properly linking up those components. If they're not designed to work with one another, they'll tend to work against one another." The approach proposed in Natural Capitalism requires the following: "A well trained engineer will be guided by the following three precepts:

- The whole system should be optimized.
- All measurable benefits should be counted.
- The right steps should be taken at the right time and in the right sequence."

PassivHaus Standard

The PassivHaus Standard (PHS) was developed by the German PassivHaus Institute and has resulted in thousands of ultra-energy-efficient buildings having been constructed in Europe and North America. The PHS requires the new building to be considered as a whole system and a number of key performance metrics to be achieved. A rigorous independent certification process ensures compliance that the metrics shown in Table 2.3 are achieved prior to a PassivHaus certificate being issued.

PassivHaus provides a very compelling example of how considering the building as a whole system enables much greater savings to be achieved than consideration of individual components would deliver. Adopting the PHS for buildings constructed in Northern Europe (where space heating is normally required) allows the following benefits to be achieved by tunneling through cost barriers:

- As a consequence of the ultra-high levels of thermal insulation, avoidance of thermal bridging, and airtightness a conventional heating system is not required, resulting in significant cost savings associated with:
  - The elimination of the boiler, radiators and/or underfloor heating system, pipes, pumps, motorized valves, control system, etc., and
  - No requirement for connection to a gas supply.
- Major OPEX savings are also realized:
  - No fuel cost for space heating,
  - No maintenance costs associated with the space heating system, and
  - No requirement for annual safety certification for gas or oil-fired systems.
- The airtightness standard results in a draught-free building with mechanical ventilation with heat recovery delivering:
  - Significant savings in space heating by recovering over 90% of the heat from the stale exhaust ventilation air. (If required, the small residual space heating demand can be met by heating the fresh ventilation supply air.)

Table 2.3   Key PassivHaus Requirement

Space Heating Demand	Not to exceed 15 kWh annually or 10 W (peak demand per square meter of usable living space
Space Cooling Demand	Roughly matches the heat demand with an additional, climate-dependant allowance for dehumidification.
Primary Energy Demand	Not to exceed 120 kWh annually for all domestic applications (heating, cooling, hot water, and domestic electricity) per square meter of usable living space
Airtightness	Maximum of 0.6 air changes per hour at 50 Pascals pressure (as verified with an onsite pressure test in both pressurized and depressurized states).
Thermal Comfort	Must be met for all living areas year-round with not more than 10% of the hours in any give year over 25°C.

Source: PassivHaus Institute.

- Exemplary standards of indoor air quality.
- Buildings designed to be compliant with the PHS achieve excellent comfort conditions, being warm in the winter and cool in the summer. (Note: It is a common misconception that PH buildings do not have openable windows—this is untrue–windows can be opened and are important in enabling the building to remain cool in the summer.)

The adoption of the PHS standard implies levels of insulation, elimination of thermal bridging, and airtightness and indoor air quality not normally required by the building regulations/codes of most Northern European countries, which provides an excellent example of how exceeding minimum regulatory requirements provides an opportunity to tunnel through cost barriers to deliver an exemplary building.

2.3 Avoiding Pitfalls

2.3.1 Risks of Relying on Overly Complex Technologies

A number of perverse incentives often result in the specification of unnecessarily complex and costly building technologies, including the following:

- Architects' and/or engineers' fees are often linked to the overall construction cost. This has the potential to introduce a very unhealthy and perverse incentive. Tunneling through cost barriers to design out systems that are not really required entails greater innovation and intelligent whole system thinking. Inevitably this brings with it a fear of more design work, but a lower fee and greater perceived risk. All too often the status quo prevails, overly complex systems continue to be specified, and opportunities to substantially reduce both CAPEX and OPEX are not realized.
- There are huge commercial vested interests in selling complex construction systems and building services plant and equipment. It is self-evident that there is no commercial value in selling nothing! However, intelligent whole system design often results in the elimination of systems, making buildings simpler to manage, own, and operate.

In their book The World's Greenest Buildings: Promise Versus Performance in Sustainable Design [5], Jerry Yudelson and Ulf Mayer state the following in answer to the question "What is the biggest problem in green buildings?":

Unmanageable complexity is the biggest problem of all. Most buildings are too complicated for the people who must run them. There's too much technology that's trying to do too much, there's not enough resources devoted to running the buildings properly, and often designers seem to think that one size fits all. But it doesn't.

A key lesson from a detailed examination of exemplar sustainable buildings reveals an important principle: In the built environment, simple technologies tend to work, complexity tends to fail.

2.3.2   Benefits of Adopting an Eco-Minimalistic Approach to Design

Between 1985 and 2010, many first-generation sustainable buildings were very technology reliant with most architects and engineers specifying technically complex and overly sophisticated systems. These buildings often displayed their sustainability with passive ventilation stacks, microwind turbines, heat pumps, photovoltaic panels, and green roofs and facades, etc., being on display as overt public symbols of the building's "green" credentials (see Figure 2.4). Some of the technologies specified might have made a valid contribution to delivering a sustainable outcome, however, all too often the technologies proved to be no more than a tokenistic visual symbol and in some cases actually added to the energy requirements (e.g., building-mounted microwind turbines, which in most urban locations turned out to be net consumers of energy [6]).

Many clients still expect to see technologies being specified as the starting point for a green building and some clients have difficulty accepting the proposition that "designing out plant" will not have negative consequences regarding comfort or functionality (e.g., a market barrier to the early adoption of PassivHaus in Europe was the lack of a conventional space heating system [7]).

When considering the thermal performance and energy systems to be incorporated, it is essential for a hierarchical strategy to be adopted based on a "fabric first" approach (see Section 5.1.2 in Chapter 5 for further details). This will ensure that the thermal performance and air permeability of the building are optimized prior to the specification of the plant and equipment and/or to the incorporation of any renewable energy technologies. The fabric first approach lies at the heart of eco-minimalism, by ensuring that the most important and critical aspects of the building are considered prior to the specification of the building services and/or any renewable energy technology "bolt-on." This minimizes the size and cost of any heating, cooling, and ventilation plant, while ensuring that the owning and operating costs are also minimized. The decisions associated with the key building elements (insulation, façade, glazing, airtightness, etc.) result in a sustainability legacy and operational cost implications that can last for decades (or until the building is refurbished or demolished).

Eco-minimalism is all about doing more with less—this requires intelligent joined-up thinking at the design stage. Further details are provided in Chapters 5 and 6.

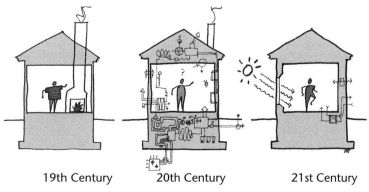

| 19th Century | 20th Century | 21st Century |

Figure 2.4   The evolution of housing from the 19th century to PassivHaus. (*Source:* John Tittmann AIA, Albert, Righter, Tittmann Architects, www.architects.com. Reproduced with permission.)

2.3.3 Closing the Performance Gap

Very few of the first generation of low-energy buildings are achieving the energy savings (or operational costs) that the designers expected and the client was promised. This performance shortfall has led to a number of initiatives to close the gap between design intent and actual performance in use.

Color Plate 3 shows the results from coheating tests undertaken in 30 new homes to determine the difference between the design whole building heat loss (W/K) and the actual measured whole heat loss [8]. Over half of the houses tested had an unacceptably high variation between the design and actual performance. In many cases the new houses were not even compliant with the building regulations and in some cases the actual measured heat loss was over twice the design value. The four dwellings with the smallest discrepancy were all designed to achieve the PassivHaus standard, demonstrating the benefit of exceptional attention to detail and the avoidance of thermal bridging.

Given the potential for litigation, liability risks, consequential loss, and reputational damage, the performance gap is an issue that many engineers, architects, and some building owners and operators would rather not address. However, given the increasing adoption of energy and environmental labeling of buildings, it is an issue that is likely to grow in an importance, with building clients increasingly asking the question "Is my building performing in the way I was promised and, if not, who pays?"

The important issues associated with the performance gap are not new. More than 20 years ago, in their paper "Building Design, Complexity and Manageability" [9], Adrian Leaman and Bill Bordass looked at "complexity in office buildings and the consequences, desirable and undesirable." Their key conclusions were:

> …many office buildings do not function as well as their designers originally intended. They are frequently uncomfortable for their occupants, especially in the summer and sometimes make people chronically ill. This results in lower human productivity, a substantial hidden cost to many organisations. Their energy consumption is often excessive and consequently the related emissions of carbon dioxide.

There is a growing awareness and interest in the post-occupancy assessment of buildings to determine objectively what works and what doesn't. Building performance evaluation (BPE) protocols and processes have been developed in a number of countries to analyze how a building operates and compare its in-use performance against design targets and benchmarks (see Section 9.1 in Chapter 9).

BPE is a powerful methodology that allows for the detailed investigation of building performance to identify problems that need to be rectified to enable optimum performance. BPE generally considers inter alia occupancy times and patterns, energy and water usage, comfort conditions achieved (temperature, humidity, indoor air quality, etc.), acoustic performance, daylight, etc. In his paper "Do Our Green Buildings Perform as Expected?" [10], Mark Gorgolewski stated:

> Buildings are complex entities that rely on both technical systems and human behaviour to create appropriate environments with optimal use of resources. There

are often significant gaps between predicted [or expected] performance and measured performance in areas such as energy use, carbon emissions, water use, indoor environmental quality and comfort.

Discrepancies arise for many reasons such as modeling inaccuracies, or envelope and systems integration problems. Quality issues, occupancy changes, commissioning, operational issues, and motivation of occupants can lead to additional costs for building owners, reduced occupant productivity and buildings that fail to live up to their potential.

Figure 2.5 shows that in most cases actual energy use intensity (EUI) is higher than the predicted value.

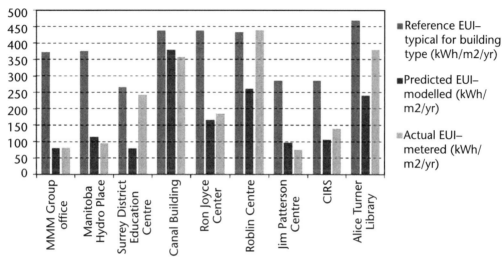

Figure 2.5   Comparison of EUI in kWh/m2·yr of nine Canadian buildings (reference, predicted, and actual). (*Source:* M. Gorgolewski et al. [11].)

Portcullis House

Costing over £245 million (USD $390 million), Portcullis House has the distinction of being one of the most expensive office buildings (per square meter) constructed in Europe. The 20,720-m² (net internal area) building provides offices for 210 members of the U.K. Parliament and 400 staff, together with select committee meeting rooms, restaurant, and cafeteria. The design brief required the building to achieve a BREEAM Excellent rating and deliver an EUI target of no greater than 90 kWh/m2·yr. Biomimicry guided the initial design concept, with the cooling and ventilation approach being inspired by the natural systems found in a termite nest (see Color Plate 9b). This ground-breaking building incorporated many innovative systems including cooling (without chillers) being provided by water from an aquifer coupled to a displacement ventilation system. The 10 distinctive passive ventilation chimneys are the "terminals of a sophisticated, energy efficient ventilation system" [12].

In addition, there is a ventilated façade with full heat recovery; the thermal mass of the building is used to control the indoor environment. The engineers "estimated a saving of almost two thirds in annual energy cost compared with a prestige air conditioned office" [13]. Given the ambitious energy target for the building, there was considerable interest in how the building performed in practice. An initial report by the U.K. National Audit office stated that "in the first twelve months since Portcullis House opened in September 2000, the total energy consumption was equivalent to 413 kWh/m^2 per annum" (i.e., over 4.5 times the original target). It wasn't until display energy certificates became mandatory in 2006 that the true performance became clear—the latest certificate shows a building that is operating at marginally above the average energy performance for a mixed-mode office building with mechanical ventilation (100 on the A-G scale = typical) with an EUI in 2015–2016 of 185 kWh/m^2·yr. On the basis of 721 occupants, each occupying the building for an average of 2,000 hours per year the energy required per occupant = 2.66 kW, placing the building well into the "needs improvement" category (see Figure 2.8).

Portcullis House Key Lessons

The most likely cause of the poor energy performance is unmanageable complexity. The designers adopted an approach that resulted in a multitude of complex active and passive energy systems. Controlling the various systems to deliver both a comfortable environment and low energy consumption proved impossible. Designers and specifiers can learn some important lessons from this building. A large budget does not guarantee success, and although biomimicry can be a useful source of inspiration, it has to be translated into an efficient functioning building with considerable care. Arguably, the most important lesson is that the greater the complexity of the energy systems (even when they are designed to provide "free" cooling and ventilation), the greater the risk that the building will perform worse than expected.

2.4   Delivering Buildings Fit for People and the Planet

2.4.1   Human Health, Productivity, and Well-Being

For many years there has been a growing body of anecdotal evidence that "green" buildings often provide conditions that have a positive impact on the health, productivity, and well-being of occupants. Until recently, definitive, objective data has been difficult to obtain. However, a number of recent studies have demonstrated beyond all reasonable doubt that "There is overwhelming evidence which demonstrates that the design of an office impacts the health, well-being and productivity of its occupants" [14].

There is an often quoted ratio of 1:5:200 which purports to relate office construction cost = 1, to maintenance cost (including energy) = 5, to the business operating cost (including staff costs) = 200 over a period of 25 years [15]. This ratio may well be open to challenge and will clearly vary substantially between building type and function. Despite these reservations, the ratio serves as a useful reminder that the initial construction cost is generally a very small proportion of the lifetime owning and operating costs and how in commercial buildings the staff employment costs will be by far the largest element over 25 years.

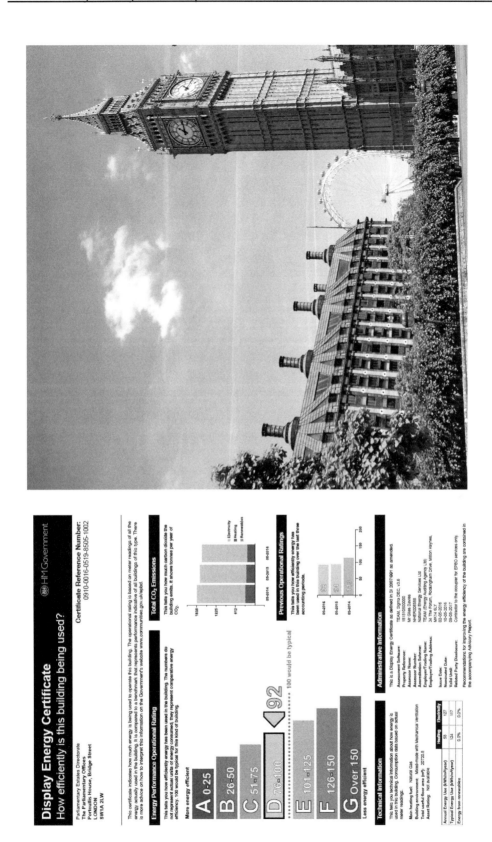

Figure 2.6   (a) Portcullis House display energy certificate. (*Source:* U.K. Open Parliament Licence v3.0.) (b) Portcullis House, London (on left, photo by David Strong); see also Color Plate 4.

Given that a small increase in staff productivity can yield very significant commercial gain, it is surprising that the importance of designing buildings to maximize health, productivity, and well-being has received comparatively little attention. You do not need to look very hard in our towns and cities to find plenty of examples of buildings constructed during the past 50 years that do not provide optimum working conditions, for example, summer overheating (and/or too cold in winter), poor use of natural light (with overreliance on artificial light and/or with the daylight causing glare and discomfort), and poor ventilation or acoustics [16]. Indeed there are examples of buildings that have won sustainability awards where the internal environment is far from ideal (e.g., a school where the acoustic environment is so poor the learning outcomes are severely compromised [17]).

A building that makes claims to being sustainable, but does not provide superb working (or living) conditions for the occupants cannot claim to be genuinely sustainable—optimizing the productivity, health, and well-being of occupants is a key social sustainability objective and every bit as important as the environmental, or economic sustainability considerations.

The World Green Building Council report [14] stated:

Staff costs, including salaries and benefits, typically account for about 90% of a business' operating costs [as Figure 2.7 shows]. It follows that the productivity of staff, or anything that impacts their ability to be productive, should be a major concern for any organisation. Furthermore, it should be self-evident that small differences can have a large effect. What may appear a modest improvement in employee health or productivity can have a significant financial implication for employers. This equation is at the heart of the business case for healthy, productive offices.

The key conclusions of a worldwide review [17] found that:

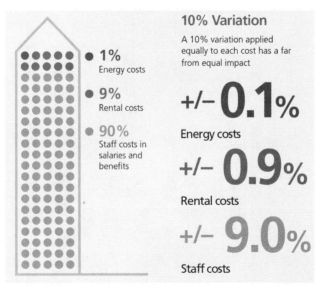

Figure 2.7 Typical business operating costs. (*Source:* World Green Building Council.)

Physical elements in the school environment can be shown to have discernible effects on teachers and learners. In particular, inadequate temperature control, lighting, air quality and acoustics have detrimental effects on concentration, mood, well-being, attendance and, ultimately, attainment.

The research evidence is clear and consistent—whatever the building type and function the following five design considerations are associated with achieving exemplary standards of health, well-being, and productivity:

1. Thermal comfort (see Section 5.3.2),
2. Visual comfort (see Section 5.3.3),
3. Indoor air quality (see Section 5.3.4),
4. Acoustic environment (see Section 5.3.5), and
5. Biophilia (integrating the building with the natural world; see Section 4.2).

2.4.2   Daylight

The lead author produced a report [18] that provides a comprehensive summary of the benefits provided by daylight penetration into buildings and an ability to establish a visual link with the natural world outside. The key findings are summarized below.

Numerous research studies have demonstrated that daylight has profound implications in terms of human health, happiness, and productivity, including:

- Quality of life, happiness, and a sense of well-being;
- Health (and healing);
- Ability to learn in educational establishments;
- Productivity while at work; and
- Profitability and shopper-footfall in retail buildings.

The nonenergy-related benefits associated with daylight are primarily linked to the following:

- The provision of daylight within buildings and/or access to sunlight (enabling tasks to be undertaken, while also enhancing the spatial environment); and
- Establishing a link between the internal and external environment, by providing building occupants with a visual connection to the natural world outside the building.

During the history of mankind the importance of sunlight and daylight has been recognized and then forgotten several times. Ancient civilizations understood the critical importance of daylight associated with human health, happiness, and well-being. Following the fall of the Roman Empire, much of this wisdom was lost during the Dark Ages. It was not until the mid-19th century that the healing properties of light started being appreciated again by healthcare pioneers, such as Florence Nightingale. The importance of the beneficial therapeutic effects of daylight and sunlight reached new levels of understanding with the treatment of tuberculosis

(TB), rickets, and jaundice becoming more widely understood in the early 1900s. This important new branch of medicine was referred to as heliotherapy.

A new architectural language and form of expression centered on exploiting and celebrating the virtues of daylight in buildings was championed by architects such as Le Corbusier in the 1920s and embraced by building developers and designers around the world.

No sooner had solar architecture reached a zenith again, than the benefits were to be forgotten as a result of rapid developments in building technology and medicine. The advent of air conditioning and the introduction in the 1930s of fluorescent lighting enabled architects to design deep buildings, without the need to exploit daylight. This trend was exacerbated by improved public health and in new treatments for TB, coupled with the introduction of antibiotics. As a result, the healing properties of the sun and the benefits of heliotherapy were soon forgotten again.

We now have a legacy of buildings constructed during the past 70 years that rely on artificial light and energy-intensive building services to provide habitable conditions. Many of these buildings have a negative impact on human health, productivity, and well-being. For many occupants, this implies higher levels of stress and in extreme cases the buildings are responsible for debilitating health problems associated with sick building syndrome (SBS).

The issues associated with SBS and/or daylight deprivation, coupled with a renewed interest in the use of daylight in the design of low-energy, sustainable buildings, are leading many architects and engineers to consider innovative ways of exploiting the benefits of daylight (and views) without the negative impacts associated with solar overheating. It is critically important that the positive benefits of daylight do not become confused with the negative impacts associated with excessive solar radiation. (These sometimes conflicting issues are considered further in Sections 5.1 and 6.8.)

There is compelling, objective, independent research evidence regarding human health, happiness, and well-being associated with daylight. Of particular importance are the findings from the healthcare and education sectors, together with emerging evidence regarding the importance of daylight in retail buildings and in providing a link to the natural world in homes.

- In healthcare, research findings demonstrate that access to daylight provides a reduction in the average length of hospital stay, quicker postoperative recovery, reduced requirements for pain relief, quicker recovery from depressive illness, and disinfectant qualities.
- In educational buildings access to daylight has been shown to result in a dramatic and demonstrable improvement in student academic achievement, behavior, calmness, and focus.
- In the workplace numerous studies have identified a preference to work near windows and under conditions that fully utilize natural rather than artificial light.
- In retail establishments, research shows that a substantial improvement in sales can be achieved in daylit shops.

- In buildings of all types, including in the residential sector, many of the studied benefits associated with daylight and connections to the outside world can be equally realized, thus contributing to sensations of well-being.

Color Plate 5 shows an exemplary daylit schoolroom in Singapore with views to the natural world. Also, note the use of low-noise, ultraefficient ceiling fans (to provide adaptive cooling) and the incorporation of a light-shelf to "bounce" daylight deep into the classroom. All artificial lighting is automatically controlled to ensure it is not used whenever daylight provides sufficient illumination.

2.5   The Importance of Good Metrics

William Thomson, 1st Baron Kelvin (1824–1907), said:

> When you can measure what you are speaking about, and express it in numbers, you know something about it, when you cannot express it in numbers, your knowledge is of a meagre and unsatisfactory kind; it may be the beginning of knowledge, but you have scarcely, in your thoughts advanced to the stage of science.

Stated rather more succinctly (and possibly mistakenly attributed to the management guru, Peter Drucker) is the truism that "If you can't measure it, you can't improve it."

Drucker and Kelvin are both stating that you can't know whether or not you are successful unless success is defined and measured. With clearly established metrics for success, you can quantify progress and adjust your process to produce the desired outcome. Without clear objectives, you're stuck in a constant state of guessing.

Currently, building design, construction, and operation are generally devoid of performance metrics and/or quantitative feedback that could be used to enhance building performance. A key component of sustainable building design is the adoption of a number of KPIs associated with critical elements. The KPIs are not only used as the basis for design and design review but also during operation to ensure the building performs and functions as intended.

Many building clients and designers believe that committing to achieve a particular building environmental rating provides a sufficiently robust performance metric. The reasoning goes like this: "If my building is BREEAM Excellent (or LEED Platinum, etc.), then my building by default will be sustainable." Regrettably, this is generally not the case; prerequisite credits requiring minimum performance standards in key performance areas have enhanced the credibility of a certificate (a criticism of earlier scheme iterations); however, the credits are often viewed in isolation, since a project team can "pick-and-choose" the combination of credits to reach the certification level threshold. By nature of the assessment scheme governance, the credit criteria are extremely prescriptive, limiting the opportunity for holistic approaches. Therefore, additional metrics in the form of well-chosen KPIs are required that focus on whole system performance to ensure all critical aspects of the building will operate optimally from an environmental, social and economic perspective. These metrics include:

- Overall building energy use intensity (kWh/m²·yr),
- Building average annual energy requirement per occupant (kW/occupant; for further details, see Figure 2.8),
- Overall building air permeability (m³/h·m² @50 Pa),
- Building overall average U value (W/m²·K), and
- Overall chiller plant performance (kW/ton), including all ancillary pumps, fans, etc.; see Section 5.1.4.4 and Figure 5.7).

The adoption of appropriate metrics can transform the overall energy and environmental performance of a building by ensuring that the design team focuses on the really important issues: Get the basic performance right and the secondary performance issues will generally also be addressed.

Some practitioners are nervous about committing to achieve KPIs at the design stage in the mistaken belief that they will restrict design freedom and/or face possible litigation or liabilities if the building fails to achieve the performance metrics when operational. These concerns are misplaced—clients will increasingly value high-performance buildings, and designers who are prepared to set clear performance targets and then deliver them in practice are likely to thrive commercially.

The performance gap is becoming a major issue. The owners of buildings which fail to perform are already suffering the consequences in terms of lower rental or asset values or quicker rates of depreciation. Conversely, buildings with low owning and operating costs (and/or environmental impact) are delivering enhanced rental returns/asset values.

Access to performance data and the effective use of KPIs at the design and operational stages are becoming essential and invaluable. As the American statistician W. Edwards Deming famously said: "In God we trust, all others must bring data." Deming's plan–do–check–act (PDAC) approach can be usefully applied to building

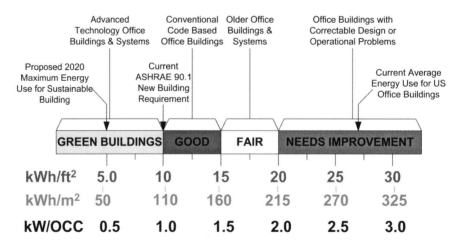

Figure 2.8   Energy use spectrum for commercial office buildings. (Courtesy of the Hartman company).

design, construction, and operation. Critical metrics and KPIs are committed to and agreed on at the outset, with the following steps being followed:

- Plan: Establish KPIs (e.g., metrics, environmental rating) for the building and plan how they will be achieved.
- Do: During the concept and detailed design phases ensure decisions are made that will allow the planned outcomes to be achieved in practice.
- Check: During commissioning and operation measure and check how the building performs in practice. Are KPIs being achieved and, if not, what remedial measures can be taken to enhance performance?
- Act: Learn and disseminate the lessons learned. What worked and what didn't? Closing the feedback loop is critical; unless this happens, those involved will continue to make the same mistakes! Feedback is essential to refine and develop the performance targets and to achieve continuous improvement.

Achieving a High-Energy Performance Commercial Building
Thomas Hartman, Principal, The Hartman Company

"Occupant-centric" building design offers a new approach to building design and operation that will allow not only vastly improved energy performance for most commercial building types, but should also stimulate new thinking regarding how best to quantify actual performance and verify that it is meeting expectations.

Figure 2.8 shows an energy use spectrum for office buildings. Placing the performance of individual or groups of buildings on this spectrum provides a valuable perspective regarding the challenges and issues that must be addressed in improving their performance.

This spectrum shows an energy use intensity (EUI) rating for office buildings in a typical temperate climate. The EUI ratings are in annual kilowatt-hours per square foot (and per square meter). To assess individual office buildings in very warm or cold climates, small adjustments can be made to the values in this spectrum to accommodate such climatic differences. Note, however, that a building properly designed, constructed, and operated for one climate will have only modest annual energy use variations when compared to those operating in other climates.

The current average office building EUI (in kWh/ft^2 and kWh/m^2) for buildings in the United States is more than twice what is mandated by the most recent ANSI/ASHRAE/IES Standard 90.1 requirements. No office building should be considered "green" unless it can demonstrate that it uses less than 110 kWh/m^2 (10 kWh/ft^2) annually year after year. It is surprising how few buildings actually achieve and maintain this level of performance.

The emergence of occupant-centric building design and operation is a process in which the building and its systems are developed from the bottom up—focusing design for conditioning on the occupants instead of the building, and empowering the occupants themselves to set the thermal, lighting, and air flow levels they desire. This new approach to building design and operation, once fully integrated into our industry, will deliver opportunities for further improvement in operating efficiency such that the benchmark for green office building energy use should move to 50 kWh/m² in the near future (see the case studies in Chapter 10 in which a number of exemplar offices demonstrate this level of performance).

The third metric shown in Figure 2.8 is kilowatts per occupant (kW/Occ.), which is recommended as the building performance indicator of the future for many commercial building types. The kW/Occ. metric is the average power usage over a year required to support each building occupant while in the building. It is determined by dividing the total annual building energy (kWh/yr) use by the sum of the total hours spent in the building by all occupants over the year. Focusing on this metric encourages designers to ensure systems are focused on actual occupants. It also encourages designers to be sure systems are shut down when spaces are vacant, even for short periods. As the occupant-centric design approach matures, systems will be able to accurately assess when and where occupants are in buildings, so that the kW/Occ. metric will be easily determined. Effective occupant-centric design will not only empower occupants via their smart devices to set the conditions they desire while in the building, but it will also enlist them as cocustodians of a more sustainable future by encouraging each and every occupant to understand and in turn affect the energy she or he uses.

2.5.1 Measurement and Monitoring

Setting targets and adopting KPIs and metrics is only going to be of value if they can be effectively measured and monitored over time. Careful consideration must be given to the incorporation of appropriate metering, submetering, and instrumentation. It is extraordinary how many major buildings have only the most rudimentary monitoring equipment installed, making meaningful performance assessment of a large energy-consuming plant such as a chiller impossible. All monitoring equipment must be calibrated with the measurement error being small enough to make the data valid for analysis.

Note that effective commissioning is only possible if the performance of key plant and equipment can be accurately monitored (ideally in real time) to enable the opportunities for reducing consumption to be identified and reduced through a process of continuous commissioning (see Section 9.4).

2.6 Sustainable Construction Material Selection and Specification

Jane Anderson, Principal Consultant, thinkstep. Jane also blogs on these issues at constructionlca.wordpress.com.

2.6.1 What Is a Sustainable Construction Material?

To select and specify sustainable materials, it is first useful to ask the question "What is a sustainable construction material?" A common definition is that it is a construction material or product that, when integrated and used in the building, causes minimal impact to the environment; does not harm the people associated with producing, or building with, the material or those using the building in which it is incorporated; and does not incur excessive cost at any point during the life cycle, while providing the required functions of the building.

This definition ensures that the materials are considered at the level of the building. A building can be made of products that are, when considered in isolation, "sustainable" but that do not produce a building that is itself sustainable. For example, a building with single glazed facades may have very low impact in terms of the materials used, but will be very inefficient and uncomfortable in operation.

2.6.2 What Environmental Impacts Are Associated with Construction Products?

All products, not just construction products, have an impact on the environment, whether during raw materials extraction, manufacture, installation, use of the product, or at its end of life. We probably most often consider the impact associated with the use of fossil fuels, which release greenhouse gases when they are burned, leading to climate change. But raw materials extraction can lead to land use, biodiversity, and toxicity impacts and over time may deplete scarce resources; manufacturing can be associated with emissions of pollutants and, at end of life, products may not be recyclable and may require considerable processing to allow them to be disposed of safely. These impacts associated with materials are known as "embodied impacts," to differentiate them from the operational impacts associated with using buildings.

The first study to examine the life cycle impact of manufacturing a product was for Coca-Cola in 1969. The study looked at the resources required and environmental load of different beverage containers. Since then embodied impact studies have evolved from a focus on reducing manufacturing waste and packaging, through to an examination of energy requirements (especially after the 1970s oil crisis), on to recognition of a broad range of impacts throughout the life of a product from its manufacture through use to disposal. This life cycle approach has resulted in the development of life cycle assessment (LCA) methodologies and subsequently the development of international standards to provide consistency in evaluation.

2.6.3 Sustainable Construction Materials Assessment

BREEAM, the United Kingdom's sustainable building assessment scheme, has used the LCA approach as one of the ways it assesses sustainable materials. BREEAM uses the Green Guide to Specification [19], an LCA-based online database, to assess materials in the context of a construction element such as a roof or wall, and compares the overall environmental performance to other elements with similar functionality.

Although U.K. industry has contributed significant data on manufacturing to underpin the Green Guides, much of the data for materials has remained outside the public domain and not many U.K. manufacturers have provided environmental data at the product level, though this is now increasing as BREEAM offers additional credit for use of products with environmental product declarations (EPDs; see Figure 2.9). BREEAM also offers additional credit where a building-level LCA

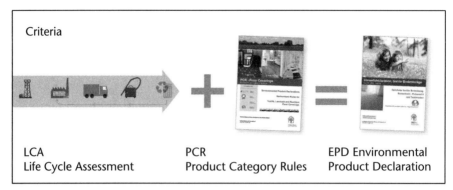

Figure 2.9 The EPD process. (*Source:* InterfaceFLOR.)

has been undertaken, though this credit relates more to the robustness of the LCA tool used than the assessment results.

In Europe, however, the construction products industry has concentrated on consistent reporting, using EPDs. These provide product-level information on a range of environmental impacts associated with the extraction, transport, and manufacture of construction products, and in many cases, their use and disposal too. EPDs use a consistent approach to life cycle assessment, using common rules called product category rules. Since 2012 there has been in place a European standard developed by CEN/TC 350, known as EN 15804, that has been adopted by all the European EPD programs, with over 2,600 construction product EPDs now verified to EN 15804 and published globally.

In both France and Belgium, it is now only possible to make environmental claims about a construction product, such as stating its carbon footprint or that it has a lower impact than others, if an EPD to EN 15804 (and a French Annex in France) has been lodged with the respective government.

In the United States, LEED v4 provides credits for products with an EPD, and this has stimulated the market for EPDs with over 400 now available from UL Environment. LEED v4 also provides credits for undertaking a building LCA and showing improvements. Greenstar (in Australasia) also offers credits for undertaking a building LCA and showing improvements.

2.6.4   Reducing Embodied Impacts at the Building Level

When time and budget are limited, the best approach is to focus on the materials with the largest impact at the building level. If carbon is the main focus, other building-level studies often find that the structures (both structural frame and floor structures) have the largest impact, followed by the external fabric. A hot-spot analysis at the early design stage using areas of different specifications and an indicative carbon footprint for a typical specification from the Green Guide can quickly identify the aspects of the building with the greatest impact. There are also a number of LCA tools linked to BIM, such as Tally, IES VE-ware Impact, and e-tool, that assess a range of environmental impacts using generic LCA data and EPDs and allow the materials and elements that have significant impacts to be identified. Ideally these tools should use the parallel European standard developed by CEN/TC 350, EN 15978, which covers building-level LCA calculations.

At this stage, a number of approaches to reducing impact are possible and can be costed out and evaluated, for example:

- Changes in the building form to reduce the demand for materials;
- Alternative specifications for a building element (e.g., a roof) that use less material;
- Specifying materials that have lower embodied carbon (e.g., the use of cement replacements such as pulverized fuel ash (PFA) and ground granulated blast-furnace slag (GGBS));
- Selection of alternative materials with lower impact, such as timber, reused steel, or construction products with higher recycled content;
- Selection of materials with increased durability and recyclability;
- Designing out of waste and reducing wastage rates; and
- Using alternative sourcing and/or means of transporting products to site.

This approach is recommended by the U.K. Waste and Resources Action Program (WRAP) in their guide to carbon-efficient procurement [20], and highlighted in the model clause that they recommend to be included in project tenders for the design team:

Identify the 5 to 10 most significant cost-effective opportunities to reduce the embodied carbon emissions associated with the project (e.g., through leaner design, designing out waste, reusing materials, and selecting materials with lower embodied carbon over the project life cycle), quantify the savings made through individual design changes, and report actions and outcomes as part of the Carbon Efficiency Plan.

For elements with significant impact, it may also be useful to obtain data from the ICE database to review which materials are causing the greatest impact within the particular specification. For further guidance on measuring and reducing embodied carbon, considerable guidance is available from, for example, WRAP [21], UKGBC [22], and RICS [23].

2.6.5 Sustainable Construction Materials and the Supply Chain

For all materials with significant impact, it is worth starting to discuss with suppliers whether they have specific data such as EPDs or carbon footprints available for their products and if they can advise on how to reduce impact. If the sales team cannot help, it may be worth contacting the company sustainability, technical, or marketing departments because this type of information is not always understood by the sales team.

If an EPD or carbon footprint is produced, it suggests that the company is engaged in environmental issues. First, for EPD, check that it is to EN 15804, has been independently verified, and is registered and listed with a recognized program. EcoPlatform [24] is the European body representing national EPD programs. For carbon footprints, the common standards used are ISO/TS 14067:2013 or PAS

2050:2011, and if the footprint has been certified or independently verified, then this gives the result much more credibility than if it is self-declared.

Once these questions have been addressed, the information can be used to start a conversation. If the EPD covers the product range, then can the manufacturer advise which products in the range have lower impacts and why? What is the biggest cause of the environmental impact, and what is the company doing to reduce it for example? If more than one supplier provides an EPD, then—providing both EPDs are verified to EN 15804 and cover the same declared unit (e.g., per m³ of product) and have the same functionality—how do the results compare? There are always inherent uncertainties in the calculation of environmental data so a difference of less than 10% should not be regarded as particularly significant. More detailed information on what an EPD contains, how it is produced, and how the results can be compared is provided by the Construction Products Association at its website [25].

If companies do not have EPDs or carbon footprints available, then asking if they know what their biggest impacts are and how they are addressing them should provide useful information about the company's approach to environmental issues. You can also ask about recycled content. Increasing the recycled content of a particular material normally reduces its environmental impact; however, when looking at alternative specifications, for example, when comparing masonry with framed construction, specifying materials on the basis of their recycled content may not result in a building with lower environmental impact—some materials with high recycled content can have more impact in manufacture and result in greater amounts of waste at their end of life. If manufacturers promote recyclability of their products, ask about the current recovery rates for product waste arising from construction and from demolition. How much benefit does the recycling create, and is the way you are thinking of using the product going to affect the construction stage or end-of-life recyclability—for example, because of the way it is fixed to other materials?

2.6.6   Other Approaches to Sustainable Material Selection

For products used in interior fitouts, the Ska assessment system [26] provides useful checklists of different aspects to consider for different types of products to identify more sustainable materials. Labels such as the European Ecolabel [27] or Nature-Plus [28] also set product-specific sustainability criteria that products must meet in addition to LCA-based criteria to achieve the label, although very few U.K. products use these schemes.

NaturePlus, for example, has a particular focus on health impacts of products, and their impact on indoor air quality, an aspect that is getting increased focus in recent years with the development of the WELL scheme by USGBC, which assesses the impacts on well-being of a building, for example. Another aspect that is the subject of focus in North America is transparency in terms of product ingredients with increasing numbers of products using health product declarations (HPDs) for example. This has been stimulated by credits in LEED v4, and various "red lists" such as that from the Living Building Challenge and U.S. Environmental Protection Agency. In Europe, REACH legislation ensures that any hazardous aspects of a product's constituents are highlighted.

Good management of the manufacturing process, suppliers, traceability of raw materials, and labor conditions in the supply chain are other aspects of sustainable materials selection that are covered by responsible sourcing certification schemes such as BRE's BES 6001 [29], the U.K. CARES Sustainable Construction Steel scheme [30], the Ethical Trading Initiative [31], and the Forest Stewardship Council [32] certification.

Different schemes cover and focus on different aspects and have different levels of achievement, so it is important to review how relevant any scheme is to the particular product using it. This is particularly relevant if BREEAM or LEED v4 credits are required because they each credit schemes differently. In the absence of any responsible sourcing certification, manufacturers should be asked whether they have ISO 14001, which looks at environmental management; ISO 9001, which addresses quality management; and OHSAS 18001, which looks at occupational health and safety. Publicly available environmental, sustainability or corporate social responsibility reports may also highlight how actively a company is addressing sustainability issues.

References

[1]   Campaign for Architecture and the Built Environment (CABE), Creating Excellent Buildings—A Guide for Clients, 2011, http://webarchive.nationalarchives.gov.uk/20110118095356/http://www.cabe.org.uk/files/client-guides/buildings-client-guide.pdf (July 2016).

[2]   Roadmap for the Integrated Design Process, BC Green Building Roundtable, 2007, prepared by Busby Perkins+Will (now, Perkins+Will) and Stantec Consulting, http://perkinswill.com/publication/roadmap-for-the-integrated-design-process.html (July 2016).

[3]   7 Group and Bill Reed, *The Integrative Design Guide to Green Building—Redefining the Practice of Sustainability,* 2009, ISBN 978-0-470-18110-2.

[4]   Hawken, P., A. B. Lovins, and L. H. Lovins, Natural Capitalism—The Next Industrial Revolution, 1999, http://www.natcap.org (July 2016).

[5]   Yudelson, J., and U. Meyer, The World's Greenest Buildings: Promise Versus Performance in Sustainable Design, 2013, New York and London: Routledge.

[6]   Warwick Wind Trials Final Report Encraft, 2009, http://www.warwickwindtrials.org.uk/resources/Warwick+Wind+Trials+Final+Report+.pdf (July 2016).

[7]   NHBC Foundation, Lessons from Germany's PassivHaus Experience, 2012, ISBN 978-1-84806-287-0.

[8]   Gorse, C. A., et al., "Understanding Building Performance: Implications of Heat Loss and Air Permeability on Building Control," *Journal of Zero Carbon Building*, Vol. 4, 2015, pp. 36–49, http://zcb.hkcic.org/Eng/InformationCentre/Publications.aspx (July 2016).

[9]   Leaman, A., and B. Bordass, "Building Design, Complexity and Manageability," revised July 1994; first published in *Facilities*, September 1993; http://www.usablebuildings.co.uk/Pages/Unprotected/DesCmplxMan.pdf (July 2016).

[10]   Gorgolewski, M., *Do Our Green Buildings Perform as Expected?*, June 2015, http://www.sabmagazine.com/blog/2015/06/01/do-our-green-buildings-perform-as-expected (August 2016).

[11]   Gorgolewski, M., et al., Ryerson University, University of Manitoba, and University of British Columbia working with IISBE Canada, and Stantec, http://iisbecanada.ca/sb-14 (July 2016) and http://iisbecanada.ca/umedia/cms_files/Conference_Paper_1.pdf (July 2016).

[12]   Hopkins Architects website, December 2015, http://www.hopkins.co.uk/s/projects/5/100/ (July 2016).

[13]   Construction of Portcullis House, the New Parliamentary Building, report by the Comptroller and Auditor General HC 750 Session 2001–2002, April 19, 2002, https://www.nao.org.uk/wp-content/uploads/2002/04/0102750.pdf (July 2016).

[14]   World Green Building Council, Health, Wellbeing and Productivity in Offices: The Next Chapter for Green Building, http://www.ukgbc.org/sites/default/files/Health%2520Wellbeing%2520and%2520Productivity%2520in%2520Offices%2520-%2520The%2520next%2520chapter%2520for%2520green%2520building%2520Full%2520Report_0.pdf (July 2016).

[15]   Evans, Haryott, Haste and Jones, The Long Term Cost of Owning and Using Buildings, 1998, Royal Academy of Engineering, p. 5.

[16]   Leaman, A., "Outside the Comfort Zone: Buildings and Basic Human Needs," Human Givens Journal, Vol. 11, No. 2, 2004, http://www.usablebuildings.co.uk/Pages/Protected/OutsideComfortZone.pdf (July 2016).

[17]   Higgins, S., et al., The Impact of School Environments: A Literature Review, 2005, Design Council, http://www.ncl.ac.uk/cflat/news/DCReport.pdf (July 2016).

[18]   Strong, D., "The Distinctive Benefits of Glazing: The Social and Economic Contributions of Glazed Areas to Sustainability in the Built Environment," November 2012, http://www.glassforeurope.com/images/cont/225_12633_file.pdf (July 2016).

[19]   BRE Global, Green Guide to Specification, https://www.bre.co.uk/greenguide/podpage.jsp?id=2126 (July 2016).

[20]   Waste & Resources Action Programme, Carbon Efficiency Procurement Guide, http://www.wrap.org.uk/sites/files/wrap/carbon%20efficiency%20proc%20guide%20action%205B.doc (July 2016).

[21]   http://www.wrap.org.uk/node/20496 (July 2016) and http://www.wrap.org.uk/sites/files/wrap/FINAL%20PRO095-009%20Embodied%20Carbon%20Annex.pdf (July 2016).

[22]   http://www.ukgbc.org/resources/publication/tackling-embodied-carbon-buildings (July 2016).

[23]   http://www.rics.org/Documents/Methodology_embodied_carbon_final.pdf (July 2016).

[24]   http://www.eco-platform.org (July 2016).

[25]   A Guide to Understanding the Embodied Impacts of Construction Materials, http://www.constructionproducts.org.uk/publications/sustainability/a-guide-to-understanding-the-embodied-impacts-of-construction-products (July 2016).

[26]   www.rics.org/uk/knowledge/ska-rating-/ (July 2016)

[27]   http://ec.europa.eu/environment/ecolabel (July 2016).

[28]   http://www.natureplus.org (July 2016).

[29]   http://www.greenbooklive.com/search/scheme.jsp?id=153 (July 2016).

[30]   http://www.ukcares.com/certification/sustainable-reinforcing-steel (July 2016).

[31]   www.ethicaltrade.org (July 2016).

[32]   www.fsc-uk.org (July 2016).

CHAPTER 3

Designing for the Future: Design Quality and Future Proofing, Intelligent Buildings, Whole Life Value, and Closing the Performance Gap

God is in the detail(s).
　　　　—Ludwig Mies van der Rohe

3.1 Knowing Where You Want to Go

3.1.1 Establishing Goals, Targets, and Metrics

The importance of having clearly defined and shared goals, targets, and metrics may seem self-evident, but it is surprising how many major projects fail to specify and articulate the ones that are really important. Most client briefs for a building will specify the headline requirements such as design temperature, humidity ranges, and number of bedrooms for a new hotel, or floor area of office accommodation to be provided and the quality standards to be achieved. Some briefing documents will specify the environmental assessment level to be achieved and strategy to be used to attain that level. Very few specifications will stipulate critically important metrics such as the minimum thermal performance of the envelope, daylight penetration and distribution, or the indoor air quality standards to be achieved (see Section 2.5).

Even fewer client specifications will state the maximum permissible pressure loss in ducts or pipework. There is a presumption that the engineers will competently specify the plant and systems to minimize energy demand, while ensuring construction costs and space requirements are also minimized. Sadly, experience shows that this will generally not be the case, and without clearly defined metrics there is a high probability that major energy-consuming plant and equipment will consume considerably more energy than necessary. This aspect of building services design is considered further in Section 5.5.

3.1.2 How Long Will Your Building Last?

Two decades ago little thought was given by automotive, domestic appliance, or electronic goods manufacturers regarding the end of life and disposal issues associated with their products. Legislative changes and new compliance requirements have resulted in end-of-life considerations having become a major commercial threat (and opportunity).

Generally, few architects or specifiers give much thought to the target life of the building they are designing and/or how it can be either demolished or recycled at the end of its life with minimal environmental impact. Concerns are growing in many countries regarding the environmental impact of buildings at the end of their useful life. Issues such as the embodied carbon inherent in the existing stock, or the hazards of disposing of building demolition waste to landfill, are becoming more increasingly apparent. As a consequence, the design life of our new buildings and how they can be safely dismantled and the materials and components reused is likely to receive greater attention from legislators and regulators.

Rather than demolishing and rebuilding, many countries are encouraging the imaginative transformation and reuse of redundant buildings and structures (see Color Plates 6a and 6b for examples of imaginative reuse of a gasometer and a redundant water tower).

Increasingly, designers will be expected to consider the operational life of buildings and factor into their thinking how the components can be readily recycled, or disposed of, at end of life without serious environmental consequences.

3.2 Design Quality and Future Proofing

Martin Cook, DQM Solutions, http://dqm.org.uk

3.2.1 Overview

The design quality of buildings and their subsequent performance are perennial concerns that stretch back to ancient times. The Vitruvian architectural principles of strength, usefulness, and beauty remain as valid today as they were in Roman times. These principles were successively reinterpreted down the ages by Renaissance architects and engineers through to modern times, and they still persist in definitions of good engineering and architecture. A good design should be robust enough to last for its specified design life and usually beyond it; should function well and be fit for purpose throughout that life; and finally should provide some visual delight and lift the spirits and comfort of the building's occupiers and users.

Strength means more than structural integrity; it implies the robustness of a building's components and systems. Increasingly robust design specifications are demanded to provide resilience to extreme weather events, caused by climate change all over the world. Materials should be resilient enough to withstand the effects of age, so that they weather gracefully with optimal maintenance and repair. Building longevity is a key aspect of sustainable development, invoking the old mantra of "long life; loose fit; low energy." Functionality and fitness for purpose are also implicit aspects of our built environment, aided and refined by post-occupancy evaluation (POE) and management.

3.2.2   Green Vitruvius

Art historian Nikolaus Pevsner's distinction between architecture and mere building is useful to assess beauty or delight. A cathedral is architecture and a bicycle shed is a building. The cathedral has usually survived due to the many structural trials and errors of our ancestors to provide us with a paradigm of successful structural engineering and architecture. However, if the bicycle shed is designed with sustainable materials, it is surely also capable of achieving a higher definition. So, we must add a fourth principle to the ancient triumvirate—sustainability, in its broadest sense.

Good design = strength + usefulness + beauty + sustainability

Good design must achieve all four of the main principles of robustness, functionality, aesthetic appeal, and sustainability to be called good architecture or engineering. Good engineering and architecture do not rely on the artifice of structural decoration or whimsical parametric forms, but transcends these qualities to fuse these four main principles in harmony.

3.2.3   The Fourth Dimension

The subsequent performance of a building over its lifetime is inevitably influenced by, and begins with, its design parameters, program, or brief. The brief is conceived in the systemic context of politics, economics, social systems, technology, legislation, and site environment, inevitably. The complexity of stakeholders and their management provide the inevitable contradictions inherent in the subsystems of this contextual model. The simplistic paradigm of time, cost, and quality is also still useful to define the design parameters and suitable building procurement approaches and contractual arrangements.

American furniture designer Charles Eames defined good design as the appropriate combination of materials to solve problems. Such a pragmatic approach was also advocated by his contemporary Eliot Noyes, who maintained that good design fulfills its function, respects its materials, is suited to the method of production, and combines these in imaginative expression. These definitions seem appropriate to the creation of sustainable architecture. In an era of increasing global population and dwindling finite resources, the fourth dimension of our built environment is critical.

That dimension is *time*—time for design development, subsequent operational efficiency, and consequent longevity. A building's anticipated design life of 60 to 100 years (or much longer) means that the design and construction costs are dwarfed by subsequent maintenance, operating, and business costs. Time for design and construction is crucial to ensure subsequent optimal operational and (planned) maintenance efficiency.

Form Follows Function: London 2012 Olympic Park

Extract from "Sustainable Materials: With Both Eyes Open" by Julian Allwood and Jonathan Cullen, 2011 [1]. Reproduced with permission.

As CO_2 emissions related to the use of buildings are reduced through energy efficiency measures, more attention is focused on the embodied carbon emissions in construction. At the London 2012 Olympic Park more than 90% of embodied carbon is in just three construction materials: concrete, reinforcing steel and structural steel. Each material accounts for approximately 30% of the total. An effective means to reduce embodied carbon in construction projects is to set targets early in the design, preferably in the brief. We found two different stories at the Olympic park.

The architects for the Velodrome had a vision to build a minimum structure building "shrink- wrapped" around the sport and spectators [see Figure 3.1]. As a result the geometry was governed by the track layout and required sightlines; this saddle shape allowed use of a lightweight cable-net roof system where the steel is used in tension to span 130 metres between supports. Despite initial concerns about costs and risks, the contractor could save money and time by using this system and the client approved. The cable-net roof saved 27% of the steel that would have been required in an alternative steel arch option. An advanced dynamic analysis of the seating structure showed that combining the roof, stand and façade support systems gave performance within accepted limits despite being lighter than code recommendations.

The contract for designing the Aquatics Centre was awarded to a signature architect asked to design an iconic building for the London 2012 games [see Figure 3.2]. The roof is a key element—"an undulating roof sweeps up from the ground as a wave." The shape of the roof could be supported only by a conventional truss system. This was optimised during design but is still over five times as heavy as the roof of the Velodrome, which has a similar span and area.

The story of these two stadia at the London Olympics demonstrates that specifying lightweight design early in a contract allows significant material savings: finding a favourable form at the start yields greater savings than highly refining a heavier option later on.

3.2.4 Project Briefing and Communication

The construction industry needs to develop better briefing and design quality evaluation techniques. These should guide clients and their consultants toward informed conversations and key decisions and translate project outcomes into measurable objectives. This starts with the development of a strategic brief and progresses through decision-making checkpoints to culminate in a POE. The Royal Institute of British Architects' RIBA Plan of Work [2] remains a good conceptual framework for this process.

Clients' aspirations in the final project brief need monitoring and evaluation at key stages, so that changes to the original brief and their potential effects on design quality and other outcomes, such as sustainability, are recorded and appreciated. This approach should allow clients to determine evaluation criteria and metrics

Figure 3.1 London 2012 Olympic Velodrome. (*Photo:* Velodrome, Martin Pettitt, CC by 2.0.)

Figure 3.2 London 2012 Olympic Aquatics Centre. (*Photo:* Aquatics Centre, Martin Pettitt, CC by 2.0.)

for the project objectives. It should also allow their consultants to make the often intangible, value-added, aspects of design quality tangible and measurable. Communication is clearly the key, as usual (see Figure 3.3).

3.3 Intelligent Buildings

Prof. Derek Clements-Croome, Professor Emeritus in Architectural Engineering at University of Reading, Editor of Intelligent Buildings International Journal, http://www.derekcroome.com

3.3.1 What Is an Intelligent Building?

An intelligent building is one that is responsive to the occupants' needs, satisfies the aims of an organization, and meets the long-term aspirations of society. It is sustainable in terms of energy and water consumption and maintains a minimal impact to the environment in terms of emissions and waste. They are also healthy in terms of the well-being of the people living and working within them and are functional according to the user needs.

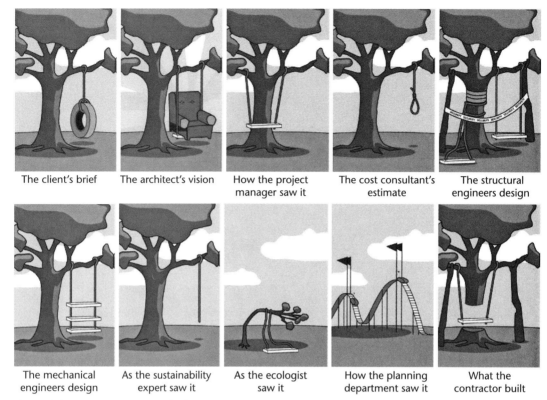

Figure 3.3   Communication is the key. (*Source:* Martin Cook, www.projectcartoon.com CC by 3.0.)

3.3.2   Intelligent Building Guidelines

Intelligent buildings should be sustainable, healthy, and technologically aware; should meet the needs of occupants and business; and should be flexible and adaptable to deal with change. The life cycle process of planning, design, construction, commissioning, and facilities management including a POE are all vitally important when defining an intelligent building. Buildings comprise many systems devised by many people, yet the relationship between buildings and people can only work satisfactorily if the design, construction, and operational processes are integrated and if the integrated team possesses a holistic vision.

Adopting a conscious and subconscious thinking process, buildings affect people in various ways. They can help us to work more effectively, they can present a wide range of stimuli for our senses to react to, and they can provide us with the basics human needs of warmth and security. Intelligent buildings are designed to be aesthetic in sensory terms, to be visually appealing. They are buildings in which occupants experience delight, freshness, and a feeling of space. They should integrate with daylight and should provide a social ambience that contributes to a general sense of pleasure and improvement in mood. If there is to be a common vision, it is essential for architects, engineers, and clients to work closely together throughout the planning, design, construction, and operational stages of a building's total life cycle. This means that planners, consultants, contractors, manufacturers, and clients must share a common vision and set of intrinsic values, and must also develop a single understanding of how patterns of work are best suited to a particular building when served by the most appropriate environmental systems. A host of technologies are emerging that help these processes, but in the end it is how we think about achieving responsive buildings that matters. Intelligent buildings can cope with social and technological change and are also adaptable to short-term and long-term human needs. From the outset, however, this must be delivered through a vision and understanding of the basic function of the building.

Throughout history, clean air, sunlight, sound, and water have been fundamental to the needs of people. Today, sensitive control of these needs may use either traditional or new solutions, or a blend of these, but we have to remember that the built environment is fundamental to mankind's sense of well-being and it is the totality of this idea that we need to understand and value even in this low-carbon-economy age. Intelligent buildings respect these values for the individual, for business organizations, and for society, and we can learn a lot about intelligent buildings by looking at the history of world architecture and seeing how people have adapted buildings to deal with the rigors of climate and the changing face of civilization. There are also lessons from nature, animals, and plants that have evolved to use materials and expend energy optimally in a changing and dynamic environment. Similarly buildings now have to absorb the impact of the technological age, but the implications of climate change and the need for healthy working conditions is now also dominating our thinking as people become more knowledgeable about their environment.

Modern buildings consume a great amount of energy and water in their construction and during their total life cycle operation; they use large quantities of materials and aggregates and generate waste and pollution at every stage of their existence. It is no longer acceptable to consider a building and its systems in isolation from their social impacts; the growth of megacities (over 10 million people) is now part of a rising trend toward urban living and development. Modern livable cities do comprise intelligent and sustainable buildings and infrastructures; however, they are designed to show a respect for the natural environment. Sustainable and intelligent cities are composed of intelligent buildings supported by intelligent infrastructures and are created for the well-being of the residential, commercial, and industrial communities that inhabit them.

In the future, consideration will need to be given to the influences buildings have on society, the local community, and future generations. For this, we will need to consider the environmental, social, and economic impacts of each building throughout all of the processes needed to bring it into being or when refurbishing existing buildings. Whole life value in which quality and whole life costs are assessed is therefore paramount if we are to think long term and meet growing sustainability demands (see Section 3.4). However, this does not mean architecture has to be starved of human considerations—after all, improving the quality of life is an essential ingredient of sustainable development.

For intelligent buildings to be sustainable and to sustain their performance for future generations, they must:

• Remain healthy and technologically up to date,
• Meet regulatory demands,

- Meet the needs of the occupants, and
- Be flexible and adaptable enough to deal with change.

Buildings inherently contain a variety of systems and yet the relationship between buildings and people can only work satisfactorily if integration occurs between the supply and demand side stakeholders as well as between the occupants, the systems, and the building envelope. Systems thinking is an essential approach in planning, design, and management, together with the ability to create and innovate while remaining practical. The ultimate objective should be simplicity rather than complexity, which not only requires technical ability, but also the powers of interpretation, imagination, and even intuition as part of the building process. Building regulations can stifle creativity yet are necessary to set minimum levels of expectation and to satisfy basic health and safety requirements. However, we should aim our work well above these prescriptive requirements—after all, buildings form our architectural landscape, they generate the environment we inhabit, and they should uplift the soul and the spirit of the people within them as well as those who visit.

3.3.3   Key Criteria for Intelligent Buildings

The key criteria for achieving good quality intelligent buildings are:

- Satisfying stakeholder objectives and needs,
- Meeting social and environmental needs including the health and well-being of occupants,
- Recognizing available resources.

An intelligent building starts with a good client brief and should consist of:

- A clearly articulated project vision,
- Recognition of the planning, design, and procurement realities,
- Clarity about whole life value.

The creation of shared visions, effective teams, clear structures, and robust processes ensures that the intelligent building being constructed will demonstrate the purpose for which it was conceived. Times are certainly changing so the project team's outlook needs to be long term, not short term. Sustainability (energy, water, waste, and pollution), the use of information and communication technology, robotics, embedded sensor technology, smart materials including nanotechnology, health and well-being in the workplace, and an understanding of social change all contrive to define an intelligent building. Eventually, by coating and embedding materials with nanoparticles we will be able to specify material properties much more easily. Such materials in façades, for example, will provide sophisticated forms of feedback and high levels of control besides regulating heat losses and gains. Self-healing materials will revolutionize façades in the future. For example, Lotusan paints applied to façades repel water such that rain water can be collected easily. In India the simple use of vetiver grass, which is made from the root of the vetiver plant, is used as a blind dowsed with water in hot weather to enable adia-batic evaporative cooling to occur. Intelligent buildings need a balance of high- and low-tech approaches.

The largest markets for intelligent building control are in the United States, Asia, the Middle East, and Europe but some smaller countries are showing rapid growth. The increasing demand for sustainable, healthy, and low-carbon intelligent buildings seems likely to sustain this dynamic market pull.

Building management systems (BMS) provide control and interoperability be-tween the various systems servicing the building. But now we see an explosion of a much wider range of technology than BMSs such as wearable technologies that allow occupants more personalization. Innovations such as Internet-based commu-nication standards and protocols, wireless sensor technology, robotics, and smart materials embedded with sensors are increasingly making it easier to integrate sys-tems within intelligent buildings and to link the occupant into this control loop.

3.3.4   Guidelines for Planning, Designing, and Managing Intelligent Buildings

We have defined intelligent buildings in terms of responsiveness to occupants, well-being of people, low resource consumption with low pollution and waste, flexibil-ity, and adaptability to change. Above all that, intelligent buildings demonstrate an architecture that reflects the spirit of the age which future generations will enjoy and be proud of. Their development runs along a continuum rooted in vernacular architecture and now moving with innovation toward buildings that are eco-effec-tive, responsive to the occupants' varying needs, healthy, and simple to operate. Old and new buildings can share this evolution. Increasingly we observe how well the plant and animal worlds can show us economies in the optimum use of energy and materials in the most beautiful ways and this is leading to more examples of biomimetic architecture (see Section 4.2).

Intelligent buildings should be eco-intelligent, which means, in terms expressed by Goleman [3], know your impacts, favor improvements, and share what you learn. In this way buildings will be equitable for all in society, have a long-life value, and exist with respect for Nature. Wherever we build, we have to fulfill human needs in an evolving technological world set in particular cultural contexts.

These guidelines will change over time:

- Plan and design with an integrated team so that clients, consultants, contrac-tors, and facilities managers all develop a commitment to the project and want to fulfill the environmental, social, health, and economic aims.

- Systems and holistic thinking are key to ensuring that interoperability works.

- Assess the impacts of the building on occupants and communities nearby.

- Occupant behavior has a large effect on the consumption of energy and wa-ter, so try to increase occupants' awareness about the impact of their actions on resources. Smart metering is a start, but sensor technology is rapidly be-coming applicable in building operation and for use by consumers of equip-ment. Data management systems are important for providing feedback on the performance of different spaces in the building. Use a continual POE process.

- Use a whole life value or whole life performance approach to ensure quality as well as whole life costs are taken into account.

- Aim for simplicity rather than complexity in operation.

- Think about well-being and freshness as well as comfort, and consider all the senses and how air, view, daylight, sound, color, greenery, and space affect us in the workplace.

- Connectivity is important so there is interoperability not only between the systems and the building, but also between the occupant and the building.

- Design for flexibility and adaptability.

- Think of an intelligent building as an organism responding to human and environmental needs but also one that needs to "breathe" through the façade between the external and internal environments. The façade transfers light, solar radiation, air, noise, and moisture, but also links occupants to the outside world. Intelligent or smart façades allow these aspects to be controlled in a way that is functional but also enjoyable to those working and living inside the building.

- Plan the facilities management so not only is the building maintained but the occupants are cared for.

- Balance efficiency with effectiveness. An air supply system, for example, can deliver the amount of air designed for a space and be deemed efficient, but it may not be effective in the space because it has no impact on the breathing zone where the people are.

- Design beyond the expectations defined in regulations.

- Keep abreast of the relevant fields of knowledge.

- Learn from other sectors and disciplines.

Many companies today describe business intelligence in terms of being smart to fulfill enterprise requirements and stimulate new insights; agile by having advanced integration, which allows flexibility and adaptability; and aligned so that pervasive intelligence links strategic, economic, and operational management processes. So software products need to be innovative, agile, and adaptable. This approach to business intelligence allows these aims to be achieved. Intelligent buildings, old and new, need this type of thinking throughout their whole life from concept planning to care in use and beyond [4–6].

3.4 Whole Life Value and Service Life Design: Economic Opportunities and Analysis

Kathryn Bourke, Managing Director, Whole Life Ltd., http://www.wholelifeltd.co.uk

3.4.1 Introduction

Sooner or later in every project the issue of the budget and affordability will arise. Many of us will have experienced the depressing hollowing out of architectural or sustainability objectives at a late stage of design, or even after tenders are returned. This is often termed "value management." The appropriate use of this technique does result in a focus on value, but too often it is actually focused purely on capital cost management.

The problem arises because the design has not progressed alongside the budgetary control, or because unspoken assumptions have been made about the cost implications of the proposed design. Typically, a capital cost budget has been set, at a very early stage of procurement, based on previous projects without adequate consideration of their applicability to the brief and objectives of the client. This is not a simple matter of the cost consultant not doing his/her job properly. Clients may be attracted to specific concept designs without being informed about costs, and designers spend time and effort on developing those designs without having any costing input. Often the long-term implications of the designs have not been considered in any level of detail—so the benefits may not be considered alongside the costs. Integration of the project team is a key part of resolution.

But this section is specifically concerned with long-term costs and opportunities, which are typically measured in construction by various techniques associated with life cycle costing (LCC), all based on discounted cash flow evaluations. These techniques are increasingly used alongside other evaluation methodologies to approach a holistic assessment of sustainability.

3.4.2   Life Cycle Costing as Part of an Integrated Assessment of Sustainability

LCC is governed by principles laid down in ISO 15686-5:2008 [7]. This standard has been widely adopted internationally and national standards have been used to maximize the usefulness locally. The key principle is that costing should include not only initial capital costs, but also the associated ongoing costs through the life cycle of the asset.

It is worth briefly identifying a couple of issues of terminology, which cause ongoing confusion in this area:

- Life cycle analysis (LCA) is a technique to evaluate environmental impacts over time. It is governed by the ISO 14000 [8] series and associated standards. LCC is concerned with economic impacts over time.
- Whole life costing (WLC), which is a broader technique, including land costs, externalities, and incomes, as defined in ISO 15686-5 (see Figure 3.4).

Several other terms are used in various states and regions because they have achieved local adoption through initiatives previous to the ISO 15686-5 definitions. Several of these were examined in a paper by the International Institute for Sustainable Development [9]:

- Total cost of ownership (TCO): Often used to evaluate communication technologies.
- Full cost accounting (FCA): Often used to assess materials management and end-of-life waste streams.
- Life cycle cost analysis (LCCA): Popular strategy that is largely synonymous with LCC. It is sometimes used when nonmonetary benefits or costs are considered [10].

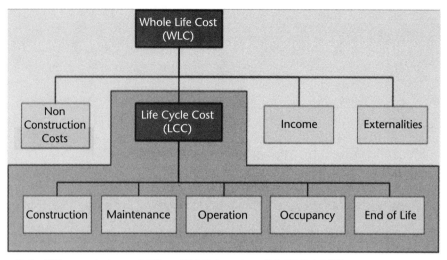

Figure 3.4 Difference between LCC and WLC, based on ISO 15686-5 [7].

- Life cycle engineering (LCE): Often used to assess LCC and LCA jointly in consideration of products.
- Through life cost or management (TLC or TLM): Often used in the United Kingdom in a defense context.
- Whole life value (WLV): Typically used where explicitly broader values are driving the economic assessment; is focused on the optimum balance of stakeholders' aspirations, needs, and requirements.

All of these approaches, and the resultant metrics, can be considered as part of LCC. All include methods of assessing the long-term economic impacts of choices. All of these approaches have in common that future costs are considered, and various metrics exist to allow differing future cash flows (costs) across different options to be brought to a present value. These are based primarily on discounted cash flow, and different metrics may be preferred in specific contexts. The most common metric used, however, is the sum of all these future costs discounted to a net present value (NPV). This is a single sum that represents the future costs and can be used to compare alternatives. A lower NPV represents better performance in economic terms.

Wherever future costs are considered, assumptions about the future are made. LCC as a technique involves assumptions about inflation, service life, maintenance needs, future waste flows, and redundancy. Hence, examination of these assumptions through a sensitivity analysis, which applies different values to variables in the calculations, is often recommended. It is more rarely actually undertaken though, although it is now relatively easy to systematically examine the effects through use of calculation packages of various types.

An important issue when it comes to using economic techniques in association with other evaluation techniques is that an economic evaluation will not necessarily endorse the most environmentally or socially beneficial alternatives. The costs are not necessarily borne by the beneficiaries.

Another important issue is that the life cycle under consideration is not necessarily the whole life cycle of the asset in an economic evaluation. Typically, clients have a limited period during which they expect to hold the asset, and they have limited interest in costs beyond that period. This is a key difference between LCA, which typically considers the cradle-to-grave life cycle, and LCC. However, where comparisons consider both, it is essential that the same life cycle be considered (the period of analysis) and the same scenarios. Hence, integrated assessment standards require that the analysis be on a common basis; see, for example, the CEN standards on integrated assessment of sustainability [10].

3.4.3   The Process of Assessing LCC as Part of Sustainable Procurement and Design

The initial budget, whether in capital (construction) cost terms or LCC terms, is critical. It is remembered by the client, and should fully reflect the objectives of the client and the project constraints. It will invariably be based on previous projects. This means that the scope and relevance of benchmark rates used to generate the initial budget should be very carefully considered.

The focus on the standards and scoping of different techniques early on in the process is necessary because LCC has historically suffered from use of data that were not fully defined and understood. To take a couple of simple examples, if an LCC budget does not include energy costs, it will significantly underestimate future costs for most types of building. Equally, if it has been calculated over a period of, say, 20 years and is multiplied to cover, say, 60 years, it will ignore longer-term replacement requirements. This has led to significant debate about the correct ratio of initial (construction) costs to LCC [11]. The scope and period of analysis and other assumptions will vary this ratio, but it is clear that long-term costs will always exceed initial costs, often by multiples estimated to range from 5 to 10 for construction-related costs and from 20 to 100 for other costs related to occupancy of the building.

The principal stimulus for use of LCC is to achieve better value in the long term through choices made about the design in the initial stages. This does not always lead to higher capital costs though; a key focal point should be what design alternatives minimize initial capital costs while also minimizing ongoing costs.

Cost management involves successively substituting benchmark rates for more specific rates that reflect the evolving design. As specifications, areas, constraints, and workmanship are better understood, the cost estimate becomes less risky, more real. Ideally, this should be reflected in a range of values initially that gradually narrows, but often the preference is for a single value estimate.

The key issue here is that the cost estimates should be adjusted as quickly as possible to reflect the evolving design, not lag months behind the design process. This is where the integration of the project team and the potential of building information modeling (BIM) become critical. Tools are available that allow the cost estimation process to mirror the design process closely—at a minimum allowing actual areas to be calculated readily through automated take-off from drawings.

Typical scenarios of evolving design and how estimation of LCC can inform the design process and keep the client involved and informed on the cost implications of design choices can be produced using tools such as the IES VE suite [12], specifically, use of the IMPACT suite, which is designed for evaluation of LCC and LCA from the earliest stages of design. Other tools are available, and the same process can be undertaken using them. If the data and calculation models have been structured to allow the information to be readily processed, then different tools can report in close to real time on the cost impact of proposed design changes.

A simplified version of the process demonstrates how the key issues are evaluated based on the same information, in accordance with the principles of information management laid out in the BS 1192 series of standards. The architects' design information can be the focus, but the process is equally appropriate to consideration of other specialist design, in particular, with respect to energy modeling where the same assumptions can be used for both the LCC estimate of cost of energy consumption and the services estimate of energy and carbon emissions.

In principle, the process generally involves the following steps [13]:

1. Set up project variables to adjust any benchmark rates to suit the project concerned.
2. Select appropriate specifications.
3. Apply appropriate unit rates (capital, LCC, LCA, etc.).
4. Calculate using actual design project measurements.
5. Check and iterate.
6. Report.

3.4.4 Key Focus Areas for Economic Assessment of Integrated Sustainability

There are several key points at which service life assessment should be considered. These key points are well summarized in Table 2 of ISO 15686-10 [14]. In practice, LCC tends to be used for the following purposes:

- To consider whether new build or refurbishment are more appropriate options.
- To assess budgets for maintenance.
- To assess energy improvement or reduced carbon emission options.
- To consider alternative specifications with lower environmental impacts.

These are often aligned with assessment and certification of environmental performance (e.g., BREEAM, LEED, Green Star). These will often have specific rules associated with them that should be considered in setting up the LCC models. For example, they may specify a default period of analysis or the reporting required for cash flows (e.g., to include both discounted and nondiscounted cash flows or to exclude or include specific cost headings).

A World Green Building Council report [15] identified the following findings as supporting the business case for building green:

- Building green doesn't necessarily cost more.
- Green buildings are easier to let; purchasers will pay more (and expect a discount for nonsustainable buildings).
- Green buildings save money through reduced energy and water use and lower long-term operations and maintenance costs.
- Energy savings normally exceed any premium on design and construction, with reasonably short payback periods.
- A good indoor environment can improve worker productivity and occupant health and well-being, giving bottom line business benefits.
- Sustainability risk factors can affect rental income, asset value, and return on investment, increasing risk of obsolescence.
- Reduced maintenance requirements provide less disruption to normal operation.

Each of these is an economic argument that can be used alongside environmental or social arguments and may have more force with some accountants, investors, and clients. But it is necessary to make the case economically as well if they are expected to pay for the benefits.

3.5   Adopting "Soft Landings" to Ensure Buildings Perform Better in Use

Bill Bordass, Usable Buildings Trust, http://www.usablebuildings.co.uk

To meet the challenges of the 21st century, buildings need to perform much better: as sustainable assets, for their occupiers, and for the environment. For example, EU policy is for new buildings to be "nearly zero energy" by 2020; and for the energy and carbon efficiency of the existing stock to improve dramatically.

To respond, the construction industry will need to provide a very different service. At the moment, designers design (and sometimes inspect), constructors build, and everybody usually melts away after a building is handed over. This makes no sense now that buildings contain increasingly complicated mechanical and electrical systems intended to meet exacting performance criteria, but which seldom benefit from tune-up in operation. How can one have responsible innovation without follow-through and feedback?

Soft Landings (SLs) [16] can help clients, designers, builders, and managers to improve the processes of design, construction, and commissioning so they converge to provide better performance in use, rather than diverge from client and design intent, as so often happens today (see Figure 3.5).

Some people think SLs is only about the handover process. This is indeed where it started, but its initiators soon discovered the importance of effective preparation and follow-through. The Soft Landings framework [17] reinforces five main areas:

1. Inception and briefing,
2. Managing expectations during design and delivery,

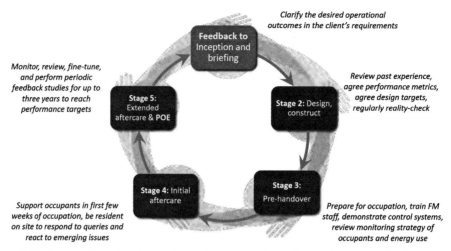

Figure 3.5 Soft Landings key stages. (Copyright BSRIA. Reproduced with permission.)

3. Preparing for handover,
4. Initial aftercare in the first few weeks after handover, and
5. Extended aftercare, monitoring, and feedback over the first 3 years of occupancy.

SLs can save money: They help clients and their teams to work more efficiently, avoid unnecessary capital expenditure by improving the focus on what really adds value, and include activities to help tune up the building, its systems, and its management after handover.

SLs is not prescriptive. The framework is designed to work with whatever procurement system you choose, in a sharing approach in which the client, the design and building team, and the building's users and managers can work together to improve outcomes. The process helps to:

- Avoid common problems that crop up after handover.
- Reduce credibility gaps between design intent and performance in use.
- Pass on knowledge from design and building teams to occupiers and managers.
- Learn from the experience, to improve future projects.

You can think of SLs as a golden thread that runs alongside your chosen processes, sharpens the focus on outcomes, and is a vehicle for feedback and continuous improvement. Figure 3.6 is based on findings from building performance studies by the author in the 1990s. It illustrates the blindness of all stakeholders to the difference between claimed and in-use energy performance. In hindsight, a policymaker should also have been included, perhaps observing the proceedings through a telescope with the lens cap on! Unfortunately, it is only in the past 5 years, or less that the existence of these performance gaps has become widely accepted—and yet they persist. The following sections summarize how Soft Landings can help clients, designers, builders, occupiers, and managers.

Figure 3.6 Flying blind. (*Source:* By Louis Hellman for cover of W. Bordass, Flying Blind, Association for the Conservation of Energy, London, 2001. Reprinted with permission.)

3.5.1 Helping Clients

Clients often want to specify building work by the performance required. However, since the construction industry does not monitor the performance of its buildings routinely, it has little experience of delivering to specified in-use performance levels. Not so long ago, government and major clients had technical services departments that did research and obtained feedback from practical experience, but in recent years many have been disbanded or outsourced, with a loss of both formal and informal feedback loops.

Client leadership using SLs will help to establish appropriate systems at the outset to improve communication and monitoring and promote learning from feedback. Positive outcomes will include better performing buildings, a more aware construction industry, and improvements in building management.

3.5.1.1 Getting Started

- Clients should state their commitment to SLs as early as possible, and make it part of their requirements.
- All team members should sign up to undertake a Soft Landings project.
- Make sure the team has a Soft Landings process and budget.
- When selecting firms, review candidates' attitudes to, experience of, and plans for follow-through and feedback. Many now say they do SLs, but don't really understand it.

SLs needs planning and budgeting for, but some clients are discovering that the process is affordable within normal budgets:

- During design and construction, SLs can help integrate and streamline current procedures, hence covering its costs, though there are costs associated with the learning curve.

- Aftercare activities do need budgets, but these can be justified by the lower operating costs of a well-tuned building, not to mention increased occupant satisfaction.
- For clients with building programs, capital costs may also be reduced on subsequent projects, as teams learn from the experience and feedback they obtain that it is possible to get better results by doing fewer things, but more thoroughly.

3.5.1.2   Things Clients Should Watch Out For

The use of SLs implies a change in attitude. This needs dedication from all team members. Clients must therefore provide leadership and ensure the following:

- The SL is taken seriously by all parties (including the client) throughout a project.
- Consider having a SL champion on the client side—a team member who is given the additional role of maintaining the focus on outcomes.
- Make sure sufficient time is allowed to review proposals with the design and building team and with other stakeholders where relevant.
- Occupiers and facilities managers are actively involved in discussions with the design and building team.
- Staff to operate the building are engaged early, so they can influence the design and work with the SLs team.
- Suitable maintenance arrangements are put in place.
- Budgets are preserved for handover and aftercare work, in particular fine-tuning of the engineering systems and controls to improve performance and avoid waste.

3.5.2   Helping Design Teams

A SL helps design teams to obtain firsthand understanding of how your buildings actually perform. This will:

- Increase your job satisfaction, as you help the occupier to get the most out of what you put into the building.
- Consolidate relationships with clients and colleagues.
- Provide opportunities for future work.
- Give you insights that you can carry forward to your future projects and to benefit professional practice.
- Build your reputation as a firm that understands how its buildings perform and what needs to be improved.
- Allow you to respond effectively and realistically to client requirements based on building performance.

3.5.2.1 Getting Started

The SL framework is not a box-ticking exercise, but a way of changing the culture of the construction industry to engage properly with outcomes. The whole team needs to be committed to working in this new way, so:

- Make sure the whole team is on board. A workshop early on, at which people share lessons learned from previous projects, can be a good place to introduce SLs and to gain commitment.
- Review your design, construction, and aftercare program in relation to the SL framework, agree on what needs to be done, and program it accordingly.
- Select a team member or members to be SL champions—advocates who can help to ensure that the management of the project takes into account outcomes and agreed-on SLs requirements.

3.5.2.2 Things Design Teams Should Watch Out For

A SL involves collaboration between client, designer, builder, operator, and user. Designers must alert clients to situations where links are missing, such as these:

- Delayed decisions about how the building will be managed result in mismatches between the expectations of the designers and the skills actually available.
- Specialists, for example, in ICT and catering, are not involved early or deeply enough, causing problems later (e.g., clashes, poor internal conditions, and high energy use).
- Building and facilities managers are not sufficiently engaged or active during preparation and aftercare periods to put the input of the Soft Landings team to effective use.
- Cost-cutting exercises (sometimes in the name of value engineering) that threaten the functionality of the building or SL activities themselves.

3.5.3 Helping Contractors

Sharing an interest in performance and closing the feedback loop are now necessities, not options. Increasingly, specifications include requirements for levels of performance, particularly environmental performance, that nobody is sure they can meet. The bar is constantly being raised, and the industry is being called on to innovate. However, innovation is not novelty for its own sake, but a shared responsibility for purposeful improvement, with good feedback to monitor the consequences of innovations, show what really needs doing, and make changes where required.

SLs can help contractors to:

- Respond to the situation by adapting existing procedures.
- Spend money in the right places, often by making things simpler, but doing them better and more carefully.

- Stimulate development of better products and processes.
- Help to improve certainty and reduce operating costs, which may be of particular interest in third-party, finance, design, build, and operate contracts.
- Save time and money by getting things done better.

3.5.3.1   Getting Started

Learn about SLs and consider how you can apply it to your processes, improve your service, and retain clients:

- In conventional procurement, your understanding and experience of SLs will help to put you on tender lists and improve the success of your bids.
- In turnkey contracts and PFIs, SLs could give your bid a cutting edge, especially if you have a track record in implementing SLs and obtaining genuinely better outcomes.

3.5.3.2   Things Contractors Should Watch Out For

Contract management needs to support SLs effectively and explain what it means to subcontractors. Case studies have revealed particular problems in the aftercare period; examples include:

- Slow response to items that contractors may regard as trivial from the viewpoint of construction defects. For example, attending to faulty submeters or poor BMS interfaces may not be regarded as urgent, but can be critical to understanding performance and improving outcomes, and benefit from rapid and effective attention.
- Specialist contractors failing to attend site meetings to investigate difficulties (e.g., with air-handling units or motorized windows) or sending inappropriate people (e.g., callout staff where a problem is actually strategic).

Contractors may also wish to develop troubleshooting services that are better equipped to deal with such emerging issues.

3.5.4   Helping Building Occupiers and Managers

SLs can help occupiers and managers obtain a better building, by:

- Getting management and users more involved in the development and review of design proposals, leading to a more usable building that is easier to operate;
- Making better informed predictions of in-use performance, for example, by helping to eliminate the notorious energy performance gap;
- Building in greater clarity of design intent in the design of the building, its systems, controls, and user interfaces, and in the written guidance provided;

- Getting help from the design and building team with information, training, troubleshooting, and fine-tuning, especially in the weeks before and after handover;
- Encouraging a cycle of continuous improvement through longer-term monitoring, evaluation, and dissemination; and
- Reducing running costs, by getting the building and its management better tuned-up.

3.5.4.1 Getting Started

- Don't take no for an answer. If yours is not a SLs project, ask why not. Even if the project is already under way, many things can still be done.
- Participate actively if your project is a SLs one. Make sure that people who will run the building are sufficiently involved in discussions. If they are not available, get advice.
- Don't be afraid to ask questions. You are the one who is going to have to use the building in the end.
- If you are uncertain about anything, ask to see similar buildings or installations or ask for samples and mock-ups.

3.5.4.2 Things Occupiers Should Watch Out For

Soft Landings is a team effort between the client, the design/build team, and the occupier. To reap the benefits, you need to play an active part and not sit back. In particular:

- Make sure you understand the design intent, what this means for you, how you will use and manage the building, and the likely operating costs.
- Make sure you have a strong enough facilities management team to operate and look after the building, with attitudes and training that allow them to benefit from the SLs service.
- If the design looks as if it may be too hard and costly to operate, make sure the design team appreciates your constraints and tries to simplify its solutions.
- Think carefully about complicated technology: Will its benefits justify the inevitable support costs?

For more information regarding Soft Landings see BSRIA [18] and/or the Usable Buildings Trust [19].

References

[1] Allwood, J., and J. Cullen, "Sustainable Materials: With Both Eyes Open," 2011, http://www.withbotheyesopen.com/index.html (July 2016).

[2]   Royal Institute of British Architects, *RIBA Plan of Work*, 2013, https://www.ribaplanof-work.com (July 2016).

[3]   Goleman, D., *Ecological Intelligence*, 2009, London: Allen Lane.

[4]   Clements-Croome, D. J., *Creating the Productive Workplace*, 3rd ed., 2016, London: Taylor and Francis.

[5]   Clements-Croome, D. J., *Intelligent Buildings: An Introduction*, 2013, London: Taylor and Francis.

[6]   Clements-Croome, D. J., *Intelligent Buildings: Design, Management and Operation*, 2013, London: ICE Publishing.

[7]   ISO 15686-5:2008, Buildings and Constructed Assets—Service Life Design—Part 5 Life Cycle Costing.

[8]   ISO 14040:2006, Environmental Management—Life Cycle Assessment- Principles and Framework; ISO 14044:2006, Requirements and Guidelines.

[9]   International Institute for Sustainable Development, *Life Cycle Costing in Sustainable Public Procurement—A Question of Value*, 2009, http://www.iisd.org/library/life-cycle-costing-sustainable-public-procurement-question-value (July 2016).

[10]   EN 15643-4:2012, Sustainability of Construction Works—Assessment of Buildings. Part 4: Framework for the Assessment of Economic Performance and Associated Standards.

[11]   Hughes, W., et al., Exposing the Myth of the 1:5:200 Ratio Relating Initial Cost, Maintenance and Staffing Costs of Office Buildings, paper presented at 20th Annual ARCOM Conference, 2004, http://centaur.reading.ac.uk/12142/1/File12142.pdf (July 2016).

[12]   *Impact Compliant Suite*, https://www.iesve.com/software/ve-for-engineers/module/IMPACT-Compliant-Suite/3273 (July 2016); *IMPACT: Integrated Material Profile and Costing Tool*, http://www.impactwba.com (July 2016).

[13]   http://shop.bsigroup.com/Browse-by-Sector/Building--Construction/BIM- (July 2016).

[14]   ISO 15686-10:2010, Buildings and Constructed Assets—Service Life Design. Part 10: When to Assess Functional Performance.

[15]   World Green Building Council, The Business Case for Green Building.—A Review of the Costs and Benefits for Developers, Investors and Occupants, 2013.

[16]   Soft Landings, http://www.softlandings.org.uk (July 2016).

[17]   BSRIA and the Usable Buildings Trust, BSRIA BG 54/2014, 2nd ed., 2014.

[18]   BSRIA, https://www.bsria.co.uk/services/design/soft-landings (July 2016).

[19]   Usable Buildings Trust, http://www.usablebuildings.co.uk (July 2016).

CHAPTER 4

Working with Nature and Natural Systems

Our culture designs the same building for Reykjavik and Rangoon; we heat one and cool the other; why do we do it that way? I call this the Black Sun.
—William McDonough

4.1 Introduction to Bioclimatic Design

The advent of concrete, steel, plate-glass, air conditioning, mechanical ventilation, and fluorescent lighting in the 1920s and 1930s has allowed us to design and construct thousands of "climate-excluding" buildings that can function in almost any climate and in any country (see Color Plates 7a and 7b). It has also led to an unfortunate cookie-cutter approach to architecture, with fully air-conditioned buildings being built in countries where the climatic conditions would allow much less energy intensive buildings to be constructed. The freedom that modern materials, air conditioning, and construction methods provide to build in this way comes at a considerable cost, not only in terms of the energy implications (embodied and in-use), but also often resulting in "sick" buildings with low levels of occupant satisfaction, health, productivity, and poor comfort conditions.

4.1.1 Climate-Excluding Versus Climate-Adaptive Buildings

Climate-excluding buildings rely on the building envelope to provide a physical boundary between the temperature-controlled internal space and the external environment.

In contrast, climate-adaptive buildings enable seasonal and/or diurnal temperature changes and passive ventilation and daylight to be fully utilized to reduce energy demands and provide a comfortable and productive internal environment.

The energy implications associated with ventilating, heating, cooling, and illuminating the occupied space in a climate-excluding building are often very significant. Clearly, in some regions climatic conditions dictate and necessitate the

73

specification of a climate-excluding building (e.g., an Arctic research center and some tropical locations), but in many countries a climate-adaptive building can deliver major savings in operational energy usage and cost.

A well-designed climate-adaptive building fully exploits the opportunities provided by natural systems to provide (for free) for a significant proportion of occupied hours:

- Ventilation,
- Cooling,
- Heating, and
- Daylighting.

A climate-adaptive building based on best practice bioclimatic design principles can deliver significant benefits not only to the owner/operator in terms of reduced operational cost, but also in occupant satisfaction.

However, considerable care is required and it should be recognized that bioclimatic design is considerably more challenging and requires a higher level of architectural and engineering intelligence to deliver a successful outcome than an energy-intensive climate-excluding building. Also, greater care is required in construction, operation, and maintenance to achieve optimum performance from a climate-responsive building—again, keeping the building design simple helps to reduce these risks (see Figure 4.1).

4.1.2 Bioclimatic Design: Learning from Vernacular Architecture

For millennia, comfortable internal conditions were achieved (often in places with very hostile/extreme climatic conditions) without the use of complex energy-intensive systems. Architectural styles and construction types emerged based on a vernacular that not only provided comfort, but also used locally supplied indigenous materials (see Color Plate 8).

(a)   (b)

Figure 4.1   Climate responsive buildings in the Netherlands. (*Photos:* David Strong.)

There is much the modern architect and engineer can learn from examining and sometimes adopting, or adapting, the local vernacular as a starting point for a well-designed sustainable building (see Figure 4.2).

The following sections explore further what we can learn from nature and natural systems and how they can be used to deliver significantly more sustainable buildings. The chapter also examines how restoring ecosystem services and promoting biodiversity are essential to sustainable development.

4.2 Biomimicry: Learning from Nature

Michael Pawyln, Exploration Architecture, http://www.exploration-architecture.com

4.2.1 What Is Biomimicry?

Biomimicry is a rapidly developing discipline that finds inspiration in the startling solutions that natural organisms have evolved over the course of the past 3.6 billion years. Proponents of biomimicry contend that many of the solutions that we will need during the sustainability revolution are to be found in nature: superefficient structures, high-strength biodegradable composites, self-cleaning surfaces, zero waste systems, low energy ways of creating fresh water, and many others. *Biomimicry* (also referred to as *biomimetics*) is distinct from biomorphic design (copying or alluding to natural forms and shapes for symbolic effect) in that it is a functional discipline—it involves studying how functions are delivered in biology and then translating that understanding into design solutions that suit human needs.

Typically, human-made systems and products involve using resources in linear ways. Often the resources are derived in highly energy intensive ways, then used inefficiently and ultimately end up as waste. Although some benefits can be derived by looking at each of these stages separately, it is worth remembering Einstein's maxim that problems are not solved by thinking within the same level of

(a)   (b)

Figure 4.2 Vernacular architecture has much to teach us. (*Photos:* Morocco and Skopelos, Greece, D. Strong.)

consciousness that created them. Biomimicry offers completely new ways of approaching design such that the whole system can be optimized and radical increases in resource efficiency can be achieved.

If future generations are to enjoy a reasonable quality of life, then we urgently need to redesign our buildings, our products, and our systems to be completely closed loop and running off available solar income. While no one would suggest that these transformations are going to be easy, biomimicry offers a vast and largely untapped resource of solutions to such problems. There are countless examples of plants and animals that have evolved in response to resource-constrained environments, and a lot can be gained by treating nature as a mentor when addressing our own challenges. Biomimicry can be conveniently divided into three strands, deriving inspiration from natural forms, natural systems, and natural processes. This section studies each of these in turn and outlines some of the potential that this approach presents.

4.2.2 Inspiration from Natural Forms

The challenge when designing the Eden Project (by Grimshaw Architects) was to radically reinterpret an established building type, producing a botanical enclosure that was fit for the 21st century. The design team also had to contend with the client's demand for "the eighth wonder of the world," which added a certain amount of pressure to the design process! To make matters more difficult, the site was still being quarried so the team had no way of knowing what the final ground levels were going to be. The approach adopted was to conceive of the building as something that would inhabit the site rather than the site being shaped to suit the architecture. Taking inspiration from various natural forms including soap bubbles, Buckminster fullerene molecules, and pollen grains, the scheme that resulted was a highly original piece of architecture that achieved a factor of 100 savings in its envelope design at a third of the cost of a conventional approach. Toward the end of the project, it was calculated that the steel, aluminium, and ETFE superstructure of the Humid Tropics Biome was lighter than the air that it contains. With a slightly bigger budget it could have been made even lighter.

Janine Benyus [1] has described eloquently how natural forms are being used by scientists and designers to develop forms of adhesion based on gecko's feet or a mussel byssus, color effects without dyes using the principles of structural color found in butterflies and bird feathers, self-cleaning paint finishes inspired by lotus flowers, and many other revolutionary new designs.

To date architects have only mimicked nature to a fairly limited extent and often the results would be more accurately described as biomorphism rather than biomimicry. The distinction is between an approach that copies natural forms and one that learns from the principles that lie behind those forms. The opportunity therefore exists for architects to learn from a vast resource of design solutions, many of which will have evolved in response to resource-constrained environments. Within nature one can find examples of incredible efficiency that can point the way to more sustainable solutions: examples of using shape and tension membranes rather than mass to achieve strength, using passive ways to control internal temperatures, and making use of what is locally abundant rather than transporting materials over vast distances.

4.2.3   Inspiration from Natural Systems

A number of organizations have looked at natural systems for ways in which man-made systems and products can be rethought to yield much greater efficiencies.

The Cardboard to Caviar project [2], developed by the Green Business Network in Kirklees and Calderdale, managed to transform a low-value material into a high-value product and earn money at each stage in the process. Others such as Gunther Pauli of Zeri.org have achieved similar alchemical transformations, creating man-made systems that mimic ecosystems. In one example Zeri reworked a brewery from being a linear wasteful system into a highly interconnected network that produces not just beer but fish, mushrooms, bread, pigs, and gas. There are also an increasing number of eco-industrial parks (EIPs), such as Kalundborg in Denmark, that colocate industries in order to facilitate interconnections of resource flows such that the output from one process can become an input for something else in the system and, overall, it can move toward being highly productive and zero waste—exactly like real ecosystems.

Ecosystems are a wonderfully rich interaction of different species that thrive in exactly the ways that human civilization will need to develop: closed loop and living off current solar income. Although traditional economists have consistently denied that there are limits to growth, we are becoming increasingly aware of the finite nature of our resources and there is an urgent need to adopt solutions based on the densely interconnected and cyclical efficiencies found in nature.

4.2.4   Inspiration from Natural Processes

The Namibian fog-basking beetle (see Figure 4.3b) lives in a desert and has evolved a way to harvest fresh water in this arid environment. This example of a natural process has inspired innovations in a number of fields of design including architecture. Grimshaw Architects' Las Palmas Water Theatre is a carbon-neutral desalination plant that takes the form of a stunning outdoor amphitheatre. The Sahara Forest Project is a proposal for restoring large areas of desert to agricultural land while producing large quantities of fresh water and clean energy.

One area in which the construction industry could potentially learn a huge amount from nature is the world of manufacturing. Aside from the energy required to operate a building, this is one of the most significant environmental impacts that the construction industry has on the environment. Nature generally makes materials with a minimum of resource input, at ambient pressure, close to ambient temperature and does so in a way that enhances the environment rather than polluting it.

Abalone shells (see Color Plate 9a) are a great example of natural manufacturing that produces a material twice as tough as high-tech ceramics and highly resistant to crack propagation. The shells are a composite made from very tough disks of calcium carbonate glued together with a flexible polymer mortar. The

(a)   (b)

Figure 4.3   (a) Eden Project roof. (*Photo:* Hexagons Eden, Liz Jones, CC by 2.0.) (b) Namibian fog-basking beetle. (*Photo:* James Anderson, reprinted with permission.)

combination of hard and elastic layers stops cracks from propagating and the shell behaves like a metal deforming elastically under load. Research into abalone shells may well lead to stronger car bodies, building components, or anything that needs to be lightweight but fracture resistant.

Technology that would allow manufacturing at a molecular level is clearly some way off but 3D printing, or additive manufacturing (AM), represents a very promising direction. AM approximates molecular manufacturing in that it allows the material to be placed exactly where it is required. If we look at the way we build things at the moment, the technology is relatively crude. Steel tubes, for instance, are uniform along their length even though the bending moment varies enormously. AM offers the potential to create far more efficient structures with a fraction of the weight.

4.2.5   Conclusions

Janine Benyus has made the valid point that the typical involvement of an ecologist in the construction industry is as a consultant that joins the team only after the scheme has been designed. Clearly, a much more constructive relationship is possible, and we are likely to see an increasing number of ecologists working with industry and designers to introduce biological thinking into the earliest stages as part of a whole system approach.

Biomimicry offers enormous potential to transform our buildings, products, and systems. For every problem that we currently face—whether it is generating energy, finding clean water, designing out waste, or manufacturing benign materials—there will be precedents within nature that we can study. All of those examples will be running on current solar income, and they will be closed loop in all their use of resources. As with any period of dramatic change, the early adopters of new ideas and new technologies are likely to be those that achieve the greatest success.

Further information regarding the opportunities presented by biomimicry can be found in Michael Pawlyn's book, *Biomimicry in Architecture* [3].

4.3   Green Roofs and Living Walls

Gary Grant, CEnv FCIEEM, Green Infrastructure Consultancy Ltd.

4.3.1   Building-Integrated Vegetation

The use of building-integrated vegetation—established deliberately on buildings in the form of green roofs or living walls—is not new. Buildings have featured trellises, roof gardens, or sod roofs for millennia; however, it is really only since the second half of the 20th century, following advances in waterproofing materials and techniques, that architects, engineers, and builders began to seriously consider these features. The German landscape construction industry body (FLL) [4] first published guidelines for roof greening in 1984 and these guidelines have formed the basis of other national guidelines as the green roof industry has spread across the globe.

Green roofs are usually classified as either intensive or extensive (see Color Plate 10), with intermediate types (semi-intensive or occasionally semi-extensive). Intensive green roofs are roof gardens, which are irrigated and receive frequent maintenance. The purpose-made growing medium (usually known as substrate) is usually relatively deep on an intensive green roof (typically 450 mm but sometimes deeper), which can support the establishment of a full range of vegetation, including trees, shrubs, and lawns. In contrast, extensive green roofs are not irrigated and receive little maintenance, typically one or two visits a year. These green roofs tend to be relatively lightweight, with a shallow layer of substrate (typically less than 100 mm in depth), although there are also systems where vegetation carpets are established on water-absorbent mats, with no inclusion of substrate [5].

The extensive green roof industry that developed in Germany in the latter part of the 20th century popularized the use of stonecrop (a species of the *Sedum* genus), low-growing, drought-tolerant plants that form easily maintained carpets of vegetation.

Ecologists have also sought to maximize the ecological value of green roofs. It has been demonstrated that the biodiversity of extensive green roofs has been increased by varying the depth of substrate (between 80 and 150 mm), seeding and planting with a range of wild flowers, and placing untreated logs and stones on roofs to provide habitat for invertebrates [6]. The term *brown roof* refers to the practice of placing demolition rubble on roofs and then allowing natural colonization to take place as a way of mitigating the loss of habitat provided by neglected brownfield sites (see Figure 4.4). Semi-intensive green roofs are usually irrigated and have more than 100 mm of substrate. They are planted with a wide range of species designed to provide year-round visual interest. Maintenance is less intensive than that required for a roof garden but more intensive than that of an extensive green roof.

Creating vegetating walls is relatively straightforward when climbing plants or vines are rooted into soil at ground level or in planters (see Figure 4.5). Some climbing plants (ivy, for example) cling directly to masonry or brickwork, while others require trellises. Trellises can be constructed from timber, wires, or mesh and can be removed with relative ease to access the façade behind for maintenance. Trellises also create a useful protective air gap, which reduces heat loss and gain and

(a)

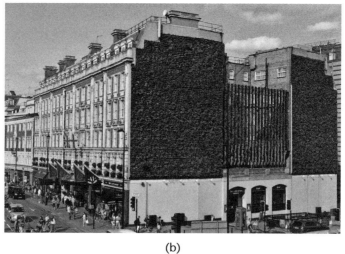

(b)

Figure 4.4 (a) The original biodiverse rubble roof on the Laban Dance Centre, Deptford, London. (*Copyright:* Dusty Gedge.) (b) Modular, irrigated living wall on the Rubens at the Palace Hotel, Victoria, London. (*Copyright:* Red Carnation Hotels.)

(a)   (b)

Figure 4.5   (a) Living wall created by planting climbing plants against wire trellis, shopping center, Basel, Switzerland. (*Copyright:* Gary Grant.) (b) Biodiverse extensive green roof retrofitted to TfL HQ St. James, London. (*Copyright:* Dusty Gedge.)

provides space for nesting birds and roosting bats. French botanist Patrick Blanc [7], inspired by the way epiphytes grow on trees with no soil, pioneered the use of irrigated fabrics to cover walls with a wide variety of plants. Other hydroponic systems involve the use of irrigated modules filled with horticultural rockwool, into which vegetation can be preplanted. Another approach is to fill purpose-made metal or plastic modules, pots, or fabric pockets or wire cages with growing media. These systems can be preplanted, planted on site, or even seeded or allowed to colonize.

4.3.2   The Benefits of Building-Integrated Vegetation

The reasons for covering buildings in soil and vegetation are varied. The grassland green roofs on the Wollishofen water treatment works in Zurich, for example, were installed in 1914 after hot weather during the facility's first summer had caused overheating of the water within the building [8]. More recently, detailed work by Marco Schmidt of the Technical University of Berlin has shown that compared with conventional roofs, green roofs reflect almost twice the incoming radiation of the sun and provide almost 10 times the evaporative cooling [9]. Recent research at several institutes has now confirmed that both green roofs and living walls slow the loss of heat from buildings in winter and also provide valuable evaporative cooling in summer [10]. Green infrastructure, of which green roofs can form the dominant element in densely developed urban areas, reduces the urban heat island effect [11].

Other important roles for green roofs have also been identified. When sufficient water-absorbent substrate is placed on a roof, that roof can become a source control element within a sustainable drainage system (SuDS; see Section 7.2.8). Green roofs are particularly effective at reducing the impact of sudden downpours by slowing the rate of runoff. A typical extensive green roof absorbs, and loses through evapotranspiration, about 50% of the rain that falls on it over the course of a year [12]. There are now living walls with integral storage tanks that receive rainfall that has been redirected from downpipes. For more on the environmental benefits of green roofs, see Berardi et al. [13]. Finally, the presence of vegetation has been shown to promote better mental health and well-being [14].

4.3.3 Design Stage Opportunities and Risks

This potential for multiple benefits has been recognized by city planners in many jurisdictions, who encourage or require roof greening by subsidy or regulation. For example, in Basel, Switzerland, all new flat-roofed buildings must have green roofs; in London, where the mayor has encouraged roof greening since 2008, several boroughs including the City of Westminster and City of London issue planning conditions that require green roofs [15]. Even where green roofs are not required by regulation, developers may need to rely on them to provide the ecological mitigation recommended by ecological impact assessments. In some cases, functionally equivalent habitat to that lost at ground level can be created at roof level. Invertebrates in particular may benefits from this, but also some species of birds [16].

The roof structure must be of sufficient strength to support a green roof. Even a relatively lightweight green roof with a protective fleece, drainage board, filter sheet, and substrate with an overall depth of 100 mm may have a saturated weight of 120 kg/m^2. Problems can arise when a decision to green a roof is made after the roof structure has already been designed. Therefore, it is important for the option of including a green roof to be considered at an early stage. The temptation for design teams to specify the most lightweight green roofs available will affect water storage capacity to prevent the vegetation from drying out completely and severely curtailing the cooling effects. Ultra-lightweight green roofs are also unlikely to support the diversity of vegetation that may be required. For these reasons, green roofs with sufficient substrate depth should be installed. In order to store water, extensive green roofs should be created with a sufficiently deep layer of substrate—aim for a depth of at least 120 mm.

Pregrown sedum mats or blankets, laid onto substrate or moisture-retentive materials, do not support the range of plants or invertebrates that may be found on substrate roofs that have been seeded and planted with drought-tolerant wild flowers. If one of the intentions of greening a roof is to increase biodiversity, this intention needs to be made explicit in the design brief and tender documentation. There are many examples of green roof projects that have not met stakeholder requirements because of misunderstandings about the limited ecological value of sedum mats.

Conventional topsoils, including those developed for horticultural purposes, are not suited to green roofs; they tend to be heavy and contain too much organic material, which can decompose, blow away, or clog drains. Green roof substrates should be free draining and water absorbent and, ideally, manufactured locally. Excessive irrigation can lead to excessive growth of unwanted species, including wind-blown weeds, and should be avoided. Where irrigation is applied on green roofs, it should be used in a carefully controlled way that prevents vegetation loss during periods of drought or extreme heat.

The establishment of living walls presents opportunities to vegetate parts of the built environment that would normally remain bland or hostile. The appearance of buildings and neighborhoods can be dramatically improved and the overall area of vegetated surface can be significantly increased through the use of living walls. This can have very beneficial effects in terms of reducing heat gain in summer and increasing biodiversity by increasing the area of habitat available.

The cost of creating and maintaining modular living walls is relatively high, area for area—usually at least five times as much as green roofs. More materials and equipment are needed to hold the plants and growing media and irrigation systems in place than green roofs, and access for maintenance usually involves the use of suspended cradles or mobile elevated working platforms. If cost is an issue, however, it may be possible to make a living wall affordable by using climbing plants rooted into the ground. When planning a living wall, the designer must ensure safe access for maintenance.

4.3.4   Operational Issues

Extensive green roofs require relatively little maintenance, usually one or two visits per year, for removal of unwanted vegetation, replacement of eroded substrate, repair of vegetation mats, reseeding, application of fertilizer, and the unblocking and clearing of drains and pebble margins. It is possible for maintenance of extensive green roofs to be neglected for several years without any serious consequences. Intensive green roofs require frequent maintenance; roof gardens will become overgrown if neglected.

Living walls normally require at least four maintenance visits a year and some suppliers recommend monthly visits. Living walls are usually highly visible and any flaws in their appearance are soon noticed. Persistent problems with living walls have led to dissatisfaction and questioning of their worth; often due to a lack of understanding of important design and maintenance requirements such as appropriate plant specification, local environment, and proper irrigation [17]. Maintenance contracts for living walls should be sufficiently flexible to allow repairs to be made quickly. Remote monitoring of irrigation and moisture levels, using sensors that can send alerts to maintenance staff, is now routine and can reduce the need for manual inspections.

In conclusion, there are so many benefits associated with building-integrated vegetation that it makes sense to consider the possibilities for creating it, for both new build and refurbishment projects. The temptation to use off-the-shelf systems without consideration of purpose and performance should be resisted—not all green roof and living walls are alike. Aims and objectives need to be identified, and integration and coordination with other design work streams needs to be explored, including water management, energy, biodiversity, the needs of the building owners and occupants, and wider environmental issues, such as climate change adaptation.

Exemplary use of building-integrated green spaces includes these projects:

- *Namba Parks, Osaka, Japan (2003):* The dynamic roof top gardens of the office and shopping complex over eight levels incorporate tree groves, rock gardens, waterfalls, ponds, and outdoor terraces (see Color Plate 11).
- *The Park Royal at Pickering, Singapore:* WOHA Architects' hotel-in-a-garden achieved a Green Mark green plot ratio (which encourages restoration

of the existing site within the new development as green spaces) of 12—far exceeding the Green Mark criteria top threshold of 6.0. The greenery spans 15,000 m² of sky gardens, waterfalls, planter terraces and green walls (see Color Plate 12).

4.4 Preserving and Enhancing Biodiversity in the Built Environment

John Newton, Founder and Managing Director, The Ecology Consultancy

4.4.1 What Is Biodiversity?

Biodiversity is a contraction of two words—biological diversity—and in the simplest of terms means the diversity of life. Overall the biodiversity of the planet has been in decline for many years. In 1992 it was one of the major issues of concern at the United Nations Conference on Environment and Development. At that conference a number of nations signed the Convention on Biodiversity, which for the first time in international law recognized that the conservation of biological diversity is "a common concern of humankind" and is an integral part of the development process.

Unfortunately, the Convention has not been as successful as hoped and the rate of loss of biodiversity is still worryingly high. Some experts assess the rate at which species are becoming extinct at 1,000 to 10,000 times higher than the natural rate would be. Inappropriate development is one of the principal causes of this loss [18].

Why worry about biodiversity? Broadly biodiversity provides humans with food, medicines, and raw materials. It has been estimated that between 10,000 and 20,000 plant species are used in medicines worldwide. It also delivers many other goods and services that we need. For example, forests provide us with wood, oxygenate the air, purify water, prevent erosion and flooding, moderate the climate, and turn waste into nutrients or raw materials such as oil and gas. It has been estimated that the value of the goods and services provided by ecosystems (an interconnected system of organisms and their physical environment) is approximately 26 trillion a year—twice the value of what humans produce each year. Estimates suggest that biodiversity could be worth billions of dollars in providing ecosystem services. The health benefits alone of living close to green space are worth up to $500 per person per year [19].

4.4.2 Biodiversity and Sustainable Buildings

Humans have always lived in proximity to biodiversity, but in earlier times our day-to-day dependence on biodiversity was more immediate and indeed more obvious. Not that long ago our cities and towns were punctuated by a variety of green spaces in the form of orchards, market gardens, spas and wells, and common land that not only fed and watered their human population but also maintained a rich variety of wildlife. In the 19th century species that are now much rarer were abundant, even in our largest cities.

But it wasn't just the green and blue spaces that wildlife occupied—it was in the buildings themselves. Organic materials of wood, plaster, horsehair, and so on inevitably created niches and habitats for a variety of species, some less desirable than others. Even in the Victorian era, with its improved construction techniques, demand for higher density development and the use of less organic materials, wildlife still managed to take a hold.

However, the population pressures and forever changing materials and techniques have continued to reduce the innate friendliness of buildings to wildlife. While some animals (mice, rats, pigeons) may not be missed—and will possibly never be completely absent—other more desirable and acceptable, and indeed often rarer, species have continued to decline.

4.4.3   Green and Blue Spaces

All towns and cities need green space if only for the human population to relax and play sport in. Most also have some blue space usually because they were formed at an important crossing point of a river or because of some other commercial importance associated with a river, channel, estuary, or coastal position.

As cities grew, however, many of these green and blue spaces were lost to development or their wild character tamed with a resultant loss in biodiversity interest (see Figure 4.6). Some of our most urban green spaces are often reduced to a green desert with lollipop trees or, worse, green space replaced with hard landscapes in order supposedly to minimize the maintenance budget.

In many cities the wilds of their riverside marshes have been tamed to provide much loved and appreciated parks and green space but with a huge reduction in their biodiversity interest—birds, plants, mammals, reptiles, and amphibians are all much depleted. In many instances this "progress" is inevitable as the sheer weight of the human population and its demands mean that wild places struggle to exist in urban areas.

4.4.4   Biodiversity: Key Issues

So what are the key issues to address when designing a new development whether it be a village, town, city, or mega-city? The principle of island (or more correctly insular) biogeography helps inform our planning here. This principle maintains that

(a)   (b)

Figure 4.6   Habitats are required within the built environment for amphibians. (*Photos:* (a) Newt, Doron Ben Avraham, CC by 2.0; (b) frog, Christine und Hagen Graf, CC by 2.0.)

the bigger a wildlife area is, the proportionately more species it will hold—the converse thus being true, the smaller an island the proportionately fewer species it will hold. Bigger is generally assumed to be better. However, the ultimate issue is what does the green (or blue) space comprise? There are some basic principles here too: diversity in species, habitats and structure, and connectivity. Generally the more species of plants, the more likely you are to attract a wider variety of invertebrates and consequently birds, mammals, reptiles, amphibians, and so forth. Similarly, where there is diversity in structure (e.g., meadows, scrub, and trees) and a water body of some kind, then again the greatest diversity will be achieved. This is perhaps best exemplified in our gardens, which, where they are floristically and structurally rich, have an amazing biodiversity that rivals that of rural nature reserves.

Another aspect of insular biogeography is connectivity and the related aspects of immigration and extinction of species. Connectivity in habitats provides highways for species to move around our urban areas in safety—to immigrate to new areas and to avoid local extinction. Some species are clearly more mobile than others; for example, some species of birds can hop around green spaces, whereas hedgehogs require continuous green space to move around in safety (see Figure 4.7). Thus, always look at ways in which any green space being created as part of your development can connect with existing (or soon to be created) green space and if possible match the habitats that connect up, for example, woodland with woodland, scrub with scrub.

Of course, the same applies to blue infrastructure. With watercourses the connectivity is obvious but the quality of the habitats may not be. Sadly many of our urban watercourses have disappeared altogether or are in a much degraded state, being little more than a conduit for water rather than a valuable ecosystem. Thankfully, there is a more enlightened attitude to river management these days than in the past, and the more natural alignment of watercourses is the preferred option where space allows. In some cases watercourses are being broken out of their concrete strait jackets and restored to a more natural alignment. However, in addition to the quality of the water that flows along the watercourse, the quality of the habitat both within the channel, at its sides, and on its bank makes a huge difference to

Figure 4.7 Mammals such as hedgehogs are at particular risk within the built environment (*Photo:* hedgehog, Justin Beckley, CC by-ND 2.0.)

its value for biodiversity (and its value as an ecosystem service provider). Wherever possible ensure that any watercourses provide connections along their length in terms of the habitat they support, whether that is, for example, emergent plants at the margins such as common reed or willow scrub along its banks. If possible envelop watercourses within a linear park and realize the additional benefits of a combined blue/green strategy.

Ponds, rain gardens, and other SuDS features that comprise water bodies—again, provided they include a variety of healthy habitats—are excellent features to include in developments. They represent totally different ecosystems than terrestrial ones and even watercourses. If designed and managed effectively, they host a range of wild plants, invertebrates including dragonflies, and amphibians such as frogs, toads, and newts and also provide important water and food supplies for birds.

4.4.5   Building Biodiversity

As discussed earlier, biodiversity has always coexisted with its human neighbors both in green and blue space in towns and cities, but also on and within the buildings themselves. Some of those species, such as rats, mice, squirrels, and various invertebrates (e.g., woodworm), may be less desirable than others particularly when, in providing for themselves, they damage the very fabric of the building that supports them. There are other species that we may just not be very keen on sharing our living space with: spiders, cockroaches, wasps, and so forth. But there are some species that do not cause any damage and may actually bring joy to our lives in seeing them or may have significant conservation value. Swallows, house martins, and swifts are, in particular, bird species that have adapted very much to the built environment (see Figure 4.8a) as indeed have certain species of bats such as pipistrelles and long-eared bats.

Invertebrate boxes are also available (see Figure 4.8b). These are intended to provide appropriate habitat especially for beneficial species such as bees (see Figure 4.9), lacewings, and ladybirds. Such invertebrates are critical for pollination and/or for controlling pest insects and bugs. Again, ideally they need to be located among vegetation where the appropriate mix of food plants is available. Also food plants for larvae and adults are usually different, so if the intent is to attract a certain species, all life stages should be catered for in any planting proposals.

4.4.6   Legislative Drivers

In many parts of the world, wildlife species are protected by legislation. For example, in the United Kingdom all birds are protected by the law when nesting and some species (e.g., peregrine falcon) are protected even from disturbance while nesting. Across Europe other species such as bats and great crested newts are protected by even more stringent legislation that protects them from pretty well anything that may affect individual animals or populations.

Before undertaking any form of development, details regarding the levels of protection for wildlife should be understood because their impact on a project

(a)   (b)

Figure 4.8   (a) Nesting boxes for birds and (b) invertebrates (*Photos:* Nesting boxes, Tony Hisgett, CC by 2.0; bug hive, Chalons-en-Champagne, France, David Strong.)

Figure 4.9   Bees provide essential ecosystem services. (*Photo:* Bee hives, Glen Bowman, CC by 2.0.)

program can be significant. Also ensure that you have received advice from an ecologist to ensure that all the necessary ecological surveys have been completed in order to inform and maximize the wildlife potential of any development.

References

[1]   Benyus, J., *Biomimicry Innovation Inspired by Nature,* 1997, New York: HarperCollins, https://biomimicry.org (July 2016).

[2]   *Cardboard to Caviar,* February 2009, http://www.tyf.com/cardboard-to-caviar (August 2016).

[3]   Pawlyn, M., *Biomimicry in Architecture,* 2011, RIBA Publishing, ISBN 978-1-85946-375-8.

[4]   Forschungsgesellschaft Landschaftsentwicklung Landschaftsbau e.V., http://www.fll.de (July 2016).

[5]   *Bauder Sedum Blanket Extensive Green Roof System,* http://www.bauder.co.uk/green-roofs/non-accessed-green-roofs/lightweight-low-maintenance/sedum-blanket-system/xf301-sedum-blanket (July 2016).

[6]   "Creating Green Roofs for Invertebrates: A Best Practice Guide," 2012, Buglife, https://www.buglife.org.uk/sites/default/files/Creating%20Green%20Roofs%20for%20Invertebrates_Best%20practice%20guidance.pdf (July 2016).

[7]   Patrick Blanc, http://www.murvegetalpatrickblanc.com (July 2016).

[8]   *Moos Water Filtration Plant (Seewasserwerk Moos),* http://www.greenroofs.com/projects/pview.php?id=680 (July 2016).

[9]   Schmidt, M., "Energy Saving Strategies Through the Greening of Buildings" paper presented at RIO 3: World Climate & Energy Event, December 1–5, 2003, Rio de Janeiro, Brazil, http://www.rio12.com/rio3/proceedings/RIO3_481_M_Schmidt.pdf (July 2016).

[10]   Scharf, B., U. Pitha, and S. Oberarzbacher, *Living Walls—More Than Scenic Beauties,* 2012, https://www.academia.edu/6649534/Living_Walls_more_than_scenic_beauties (July 2016).

[11]   U.S. Environmental Protection Agency, *Reducing Urban Heat Island: Compendium of Strategies,* 2008, https://www.epa.gov/heat-islands/heat-island-compendium (July 2016).

[12]   Stovin, V., G. Vesuviano, and H. Kasmin, "The Hydrological Performance of a Green Roof Test Bed Under UK Climatic Conditions," *Journal of Hydrology,* Vols. 414–415, January 2012, pp. 148–161, http://www.sciencedirect.com/science/article/pii/S0022169411007347 (July 2016).

[13]   Berardi, U., A. H. Ghaffarian Hoseini, and A. Ghaffarian Hoseini, "State-of-the-Art Analysis of the Environmental Benefits of Green Roofs," *Applied Energy,* Vol. 115, February 2014, pp. 411–428, http://www.sciencedirect.com/science/article/pii/S0306261913008775 (July 2016).

[14]   Natural Capital Initiative, *Urban Green Infrastructure and Human Wellbeing,* 2014, http://www.naturalcapitalinitiative.org.uk/urban-green-infrastructure-and-human-wellbeing (July 2016).

[15]   Mayor of London, *Living Roofs and Walls, Technical Report: Supporting London Plan Policy,* 2008, https://www.london.gov.uk/sites/default/files/living-roofs.pdf.

[16]   Green Roofs and Biodiversity, special issue, *Urban Habitats,* Vol. 4, December 2006, http://www.urbanhabitats.org/v04n01 (July 2016).

[17]   Irwin, G., "Living Wall Breakdown—Material and Flora Relationship," *Green Walls,* 2015, http://www.greenroofs.com/content/articles/145-Living-Wall-Breakdown-Material-and-Flora-Relationship.htm#.V6cv_iN96fU (July 2016).

[18]   De Vos, J. M., et al., "Estimating the Normal Background Rate of Species Extinction," *Conservation Biology,* Vol. 29, No. 2, April 2015, pp. 452–462, http://www.ncbi.nlm.nih.gov/pubmed/25159086 (July 2016).

[19]   "Hidden Value of Nature Revealed in Groundbreaking Study," https://www.gov.uk/government/news/hidden-value-of-nature-revealed-in-groundbreaking-study (July 2016).

CHAPTER 5

Energy-Optimizing Architectural Design and Engineering

無駄

Muda (無駄) is a Japanese word that has no direct English translation. However, an essential element of Japanese culture and thinking, it can be loosely interpreted as futility, uselessness, idleness, waste, wastage, wastefulness. Perfected by Taiichi Ohno, the philosophy of continuous improvement and the removal of *muda* is at the core of the Toyota production system (TPS). The TPS has been so successful its principles have been adopted by automotive manufacturing companies worldwide. Sadly there is currently no analogue for the TPS associated with buildings.

It is self-evident that there is much *muda* associated with buildings and building services. Figure 5.1 shows how 100 units of fuel input is reduced to only 9.5 units of useful energy output as a consequence of inefficiencies and losses. Much of this *muda* can be removed (or very substantially reduced), particularly by reducing the demand for energy and radically improving and transforming the way energy systems within buildings operate. However, a forensic and almost obsessive attention to engineering detail is required to identify the savings and to eliminate waste. The rewards can be huge with a factor of 4 or even 10 savings frequently being achieved (i.e., a total building energy demand of ¼ to 1/10 of a "normal" building).

This chapter describes how significant savings can be achieved during the design stage by eliminating *muda*.

5.1 Whole System/Whole Building Optimization

Critical choices are implied by the comfort specification associated with any building design brief. The suppliers and manufacturers of air-conditioning equipment will predictably argue the case in support of tight temperature control and the benefits of having a sealed building. Air conditioning may be the only viable option in some locations, or where internal heat gains are very high, but in many locations research has shown that an adaptive approach to thermal comfort can deliver significant benefits [1].

Utilizing an adaptive approach to thermal comfort where the occupants have a greater connection to the outdoors and much greater control over the internal

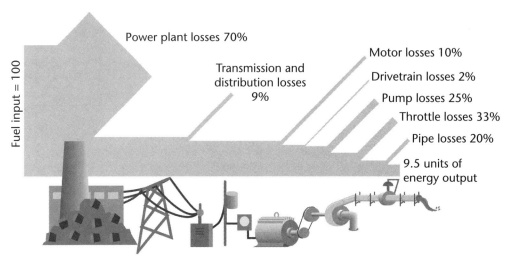

Figure 5.1 Typical losses associated with water pumping. (Copyright E Source. Reprinted with permission.)

environmental conditions provides significant opportunities for a reduction in operational energy. The strategy allows the occupants to "adapt" to a wider range of internal temperatures, but still maintain the perception of being comfortable. This approach enables a much wider range of internal temperatures to be specified in naturally ventilated (or mixed-mode) buildings.

Mixed-mode, naturally ventilated buildings typically adopt the following internal temperature requirement:

- Winter: 20°C ± 2°C.
- Summer: Not to exceed 25°C for more than 5% of occupied hours. Not to exceed 28°C for more than 1% of occupied hours.

It is important to note that air-conditioned buildings generally have much more demanding temperature control requirements, typically:

- Winter: 20°C ± 1°C.
- Summer: 21°C ± 2°C.

If an adaptive approach to comfort is adopted, very significant savings in CAPEX and OPEX are achievable along with considerable environmental benefits by utilizing bioclimatic design strategies that incorporate free cooling, coupled with natural or mixed-mode ventilation and optimum use of daylight (see Figure 5.2). Adaptive comfort in the summer is highly dependent on the following:

- Providing increased air movement throughout the building (including the use of high-efficiency/low-noise ceiling fans).
- Allowing occupants to have control over their environment. This includes opening and closing windows, adjusting temperatures, switching lighting

(a)   (b)

Figure 5.2   (a) Ceiling fans are an excellent way of achieving adaptive comfort. (Photo: Ceiling fan, russellstreet, CC by-SA 2.0.) (b) Adaptive comfort measures: openable/lockable ventilation shutters, light shelf, external shading, and manually operated internal blind. (*Photo:* David Strong.)

on or off, and closing and opening blinds or manually adjusting internal shading.

- Incorporating external shading/shutters.

- Allowing occupants to wear seasonally appropriate clothing; this enables higher internal temperatures to be tolerated in the summer and lower temperatures in the winter.

The following sections consider the key steps required to minimize energy consumption and to meet some or all of the energy demands using renewable energy generation.

5.1.1   Step 0: Location, Location, Location

The process of optimization normally starts with the site, building orientation (Step 0), and consideration of the envelope/façade. These are key architectural and aesthetic considerations and are based on a response to the client brief and building function.

Selection of the site, initial designs, and servicing strategies must take into account the opportunities and constraints of the building location to take advantage of the low-energy options available.

Prevailing wind direction, elevation above sea level, climate, and sun paths must inform building orientation and passive ventilation and daylighting strategies, as well as solar and rain income for harvesting energy and water. Optimizing of external views, infrastructure, and local network and supply chain links will all influence the building's design and immediately identify systems to discount or explore further.

5.1.2   Step 1: Fabric First!

At the outset of any project there are a bewildering array of design options. There is an old adage that "paper is cheap, bricks and mortar expensive," which implies that the predesign and schematic design phases provide major opportunities for radical improvement at low cost (see Section 2.1).

The advent of easy-to-use building modeling and simulation software provides major opportunities for further refinement during the schematic design phase (see Section 6.2). Of particular importance is early-stage analysis to determine the comparative performance offered by optimizing the following parameters:

- Envelope thermal performance:
  - U values,
  - Thermal bridging,
  - Incorporation of shading (see Figure 5.3), and
  - Façade orientation.
- Air tightness/overall building air permeability.
- Façade and roof albedo/surface reflectivity.
- Daylight.
- External shading.

Figure 5.3   Simple measures such as the incorporation of shutters (or external shading/brise-soleil) can have a dramatic impact on reducing internal temperatures and allow natural ventilation in temperate/hot climates, without recourse to air conditioning. (*Photo:* David Strong.)

5.1.3   Step 2: Explore the Potential Offered by Passive Solutions

Passive/natural systems have been used for millennia to keep buildings comfortable, ventilated, and illuminated without recourse to complex, costly, and energy-consuming building services. Of particular importance are the opportunities to reduce energy demand provided by the systems discussed next.

5.1.3.1   Thermal Mass

This refers to the use of the thermal mass of a building to attenuate internal temperatures (to reduce overheating and/or underheating) by exploiting the diurnal temperature differences between day and night. (Note that this approach is only applicable where weather conditions provide a sufficient diurnal temperature range.) The opportunities provided by thermal mass can be enhanced by incorporation of innovative strategies such as underground labyrinth storage systems and/or the incorporation of earth ducts to pre cool or preheat the ventilation supply air (see Color Plate 13).

5.1.3.2   Passive Ventilation

Passive ventilation strategies use wind-driven forces and/or the natural buoyancy of warm air to move ventilation air through the building without the use of fans (see Color Plate 14). Hot/humid air is vented at high level, with fresh air being induced from outside. (Note that this strategy may not be useful in inner city areas where noise and/or air contamination might require filtration.)

Passive ventilation can be enhanced by using ventilation stacks/wind towers, an approach that has been used in vernacular architecture in hot and dry Middle Eastern countries (see Color Plate 8).

In certain locations and with some building types, a mixed-mode approach to providing ventilation and space conditioning may be appropriate. This is a hybrid solution that utilizes a combination of natural ventilation (from openable windows, either manually or automatically controlled) together with mechanical systems.

5.1.3.3   Free Cooling

Provided there is a diurnal temperature swing (i.e., the difference between the daytime and nighttime temperature) of greater than 5°C, significant free cooling can be achieved by exploiting a combination of exposed thermal mass and passive ventilation strategies.

Nighttime cooling is sometimes referred to as *night-purging*; it can be a passive (relying on natural ventilation), active (requiring fans to move the air within the building and over the thermal mass), or hybrid approach (relying on natural ventilation, but with fan assistance at certain times). Note that careful analysis is required and both computational fluid dynamics (CFD) and/or physical modeling can be helpful in addressing the risks associated with poor air quality or stagnant zones within the building (see Figure 5.4). Also, high levels of exposed thermal mass can result in acoustic issues and care is required to reduce and effectively mitigate the risk.

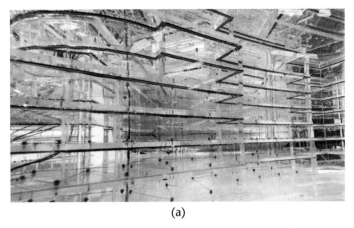

(a)

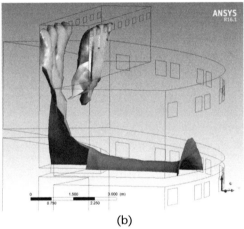

(b)

Figure 5.4 (a) Water bath natural ventilation model. (Photo: Courtesy of Breathing Buildings and Foster + Partners.) (b) CFD natural ventilation model. (*Photo:* Breathing Buildings.)

5.1.3.4   Using Trees and Vegetative Screening

To reduce solar gains, enhance biodiversity, and provide the occupants with a link to the natural world, consider the use of deciduous tree planting and/or the use of vegetative screens to provide window shading. Color Plate 15 shows the use of box-head (pleached) hornbeam trees around the sun-facing perimeter of a refurbished office building. On facades exposed to sunlight the trees provide window shading in summer, and in the winter (having shed their leaves) enable useful passive solar gains to enter the building (to offset space heating requirements). Note that careful modeling is required to ensure the trees are positioned/planted so that the shadows cast by mature trees fully shade the windows in summer.

5.1.3.5   Optimize Daylight

Optimize the use of daylight to limit the use of artificial lighting. Note, however, that daylight factor (DF) analysis is unhelpful and a very crude way of evaluating daylight. The specification and use of DF often results in very poor design outcomes, such as glare and overheating, as a consequence of excessive solar gains.

It seems perverse that credits are still awarded for DF by a number of the major building environmental assessment methods. At its best DF is useful for comparative purposes, but only in locations with typically overcast sky conditions. However, it is important to note that DF takes no account of the building location or façade orientation and is not useful in optimizing the use of daylight (see Section 6.7 for further details). LEED now provides additional credits if the U.S. Illuminating Engineering Society LM-83 metrics/dynamic daylight modeling is used.

Two alternative approaches to daylight modeling are shown in Figures 5.5 and 5.6. This figure is a false color image of daylight autonomy (DA) across a typical bay of a narrow 1920s San Francisco office building. DA images allow a designer to understand interior layouts and design options to fully exploit daylight.

Figure 5.6 shows useful daylight illuminance (UDI). UDI is a modification of DA to provide an indication of when daylight falls in certain ranges: below 100 lux, 100 to 2,000 lux, above 2,000 lux, with artificial lighting being required below 100 lux and with solar gains possibly being problematic above 2,000 lux. Graphical representations are used to illustrate when UDI criteria are met for a specified percentage of time. DA and UDI offer a much greater level of useful information than DF since they both take into account the building location and façade orientation.

5.1.3.6   Avoid Passive Design Pitfalls

There are many examples of first-generation green buildings that have attempted to utilize passive solutions, but which have failed to deliver good indoor air quality (IAQ) and/or comfort. The energy savings offered by passive systems are considerable, but the risks must be recognized and addressed.

Considerable care is required to avoid unmanageable complexity and the incorporation of conflicting or competing systems. Effective control is essential, to-

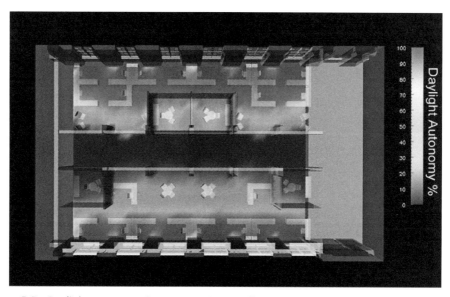

Figure 5.5   Daylight autonomy in a narrow 1920s office. (*Source:* LOISOS + UBBELOHDE. Reproduced with permission.)

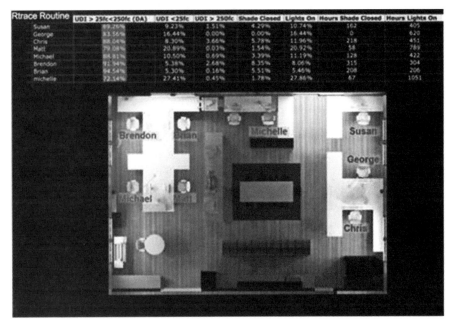

Figure 5.6 Useful daylight illuminance in an office. (*Source:* LOISOS + UBBELOHDE. Reproduced with permission.)

gether with an understanding of how the various passive and active systems will function in practice.

Highly insulated/low-air permeability buildings can be prone to overheating, both in the winter and in the summer, as a consequence of solar gains and/or poor control. Dynamic computer modeling/simulation can be very effective in identifying and addressing these issues and establishing how the passive design risks can be addressed and mitigated (see Chapter 6).

5.1.4   Step 3: Ensure All Active Energy Systems Are Highly Efficient

Substantial operational energy savings can be achieved by ensuring that the active energy systems are specified to operate at the highest levels of efficiency.

5.1.4.1   Ductwork and Pipework Design and Specification

Simple changes in ductwork and pipework sizing together with the specification of efficient best-in-class motors, fans, pumps, and low-pressure loss filters and attenuators can deliver very substantial reductions in electrical demand and additional benefits.

Any additional cost resulting from increasing duct/pipe sizing to reduce pressure losses will be recouped through savings in operational energy demand (see Section 5.5 for further details).

5.1.4.2 Motors and Drives

Motors consume a considerable amount of energy in building. In many instances very substantial savings can be achieved by incorporating high-efficiency motors together with a variable speed drive (VSD) control. The cost of VSD has fallen dramatically and major reductions in operational energy use, improved control and reduced maintenance cost can be achieved by designing out the use of dampers and throttling devices, which are extremely wasteful of energy, and utilizing a VSD instead.

It is important to recongize that if variable frequency drives are used to regulate pump speed in variable flow distribution systems, the pump laws dictate that the pump can supply 50% of the flow at 50% of the speed and require only 12.5% of the full flow power (for further information, see Ref. [2]).

5.1.4.3 Lighting

As the energy requirements associated with cooling and heating of green buildings are reduced through good design, the energy requirements associated with artificial lighting can be the largest single energy load in many building types. In air-conditioned buildings it is important to recognize that internal loads/heat sources such as lighting contribute in two ways to the building energy requirements and operational costs: (1) the electricity consumption associated with the lamp and (2) the energy requirement associated with the chiller (and associated pumps, fans, cooling towers, etc.) to remove the heat generated by the lamp.

The latest generation of modeling and simulation tools has a key role to play in optimizing lighting design and layout. The *Whole Building Design Guide to Lighting Design* [3] summarizes the following best practice approach:

- *Daylighting*—the design should supplement the available daylight.
- *Task/Ambient/Accent systems*—a lighting system that layers these components provides flexibility in its use and comfort.
- *Control of systems*—with daylight, occupancy, vacancy, schedule, time, and user preference.
- *Efficient and effective luminaires*—making the best use and distribution of the light source.
- *Efficacious light sources*—designer should choose the most efficacious (lumens of light per watt of power) that still accomplishes the design goal for that source and luminaire.
- *Exterior Lighting*—while enough light needs to be provided for nighttime visibility, too much can cause glare, adaptation problems, and light trespass."

The cost and sophistication of lighting control systems has fallen dramatically in the past decade. Modeling is required to ensure that the risks associated with glare and/or overheating (as a consequence of solar gains) are fully addressed (see Section 6.8).

5.1.4.4 Optimizing Chilled Water Plant

One of the most useful metrics for setting and assessing the overall performance of large centralized chiller plants is kW/ton (see Figure 5.7). This value is based not only on the electricity consumption of the chiller, but also on all of the ancillary power requirements for chilled water pumps, cooling tower fans, and so forth. Accurate assessment of kW/ton performance requires calibrated instrumentation, correctly installed (see Refs. [4] and [5] for further guidance).

In tropical/equatorial countries a centralized chilled water plant typically accounts for 60% of building energy consumption, with the plant generally operating year-round. Substantial improvements (i.e., reductions) in the kW/ton energy requirements of large centralized chilled water systems have been achieved in countries such as Singapore, as a consequence of concerted action. This has encouraged forensic attention by the government, forensic attention to detail by system designers to reduce the frictional losses associated with pipework layout and sizing (see Section 5.5), maximization of motor efficiency, use of VSDs, and use of efficient pumps and fans. It is also essential to optimize cooling tower sizing and positioning (to ensure free air flow without recirculation) and to utilize efficient/ close approach temperature heat exchangers.

Web-based continuous monitoring and checking of diagnostics of large central chillers enables plant performance to be optimized and faults to be quickly detected and rectified.

5.1.4.5 Minimizing Other Loads

Strategies for reducing the energy demand of other loads (e.g., information technology equipment, elevators, escalators, catering equipment, etc.) must be carefully considered to reduce the overall building energy load and kWh/m^2 p.a.

Good practice is to locate equipment such as printers and photocopiers in separate conditioned spaces. Most IT equipment can be set to an energy-saving mode, enabling the equipment to shut down or switch into a standby mode automatically. This provides savings in energy demand and internal heat generation. (*Note:* A typical desktop computer has a power consumption of 100W, a laptop about 1W.)

Again, in air-conditioned buildings the internal heat gains associated with these loads add to the operational energy requirements of chillers and ancillary plant/ equipment.

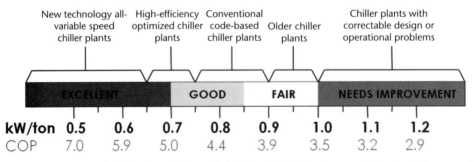

Figure 5.7 Average annual chiller plant efficiency in kW/ton (COP). Input energy includes chillers, condenser pumps, cooling tower fans, and chilled water pumping. (*Source:* Courtesy of the Hartman Company [2].)

5.1.4.6   Avoiding the Active Energy System Pitfalls

There are huge commercial interests promoting the specification and inclusion of sophisticated technologies. Many of the first generation of green buildings incorporated complex and costly energy systems such as heat pumps , combined heat and power systems (cogeneration), trigeneration systems (power, heating, and cooling), interseasonal underground heat/cool storage, and so forth.

Complex active energy systems have a role to play, but it is essential that the demand for energy is addressed and reduced as the first priority, before consideration is given to the incorporation of complex/costly active systems. In many cases the need for complex systems can be designed out or the size/capacity of the proposed system very significantly reduced. For example, reducing the energy demand might make the economic case for cogeneration (or trigeneration) unviable, by substantially reducing the requirement for heating and/or cooling.

Given the cost, additional risks, and maintenance costs, complex energy systems should only be specified as a last resort. They should never be incorporated simply to bolster the building's green credentials, or to gain credits in an environmental rating scheme.

5.1.4.7   Adopt Effective Control Systems

The introduction of low-cost sensors enables active energy systems to be controlled to minimize energy consumption. Systems such as demand-controlled ventilation enable the ventilation rate to be varied depending on the CO_2 concentration within the occupied space. This ensures that spaces are adequately ventilated when occupied, but with reduced ventilation being provided at times of low or no occupancy (see Section 5.4).

5.1.4.8   Adopt Energy Efficient Cooling and Ventilation Systems

If active building cooling/air conditioning is unavoidable, consider chilled ceiling/chilled beams coupled with displacement ventilation. This approach can deliver major energy savings and should be considered in buildings that require air conditioning where cooling requirements have been reduced to low values as a consequence of good design (see Section 6.1). This approach is generally not appropriate in tropical climates or where cooling loads and humidity are high.

Mechanical ventilation with heat recovery (MVHR) can be a useful technology in countries where space heating is required. The successful incorporation of MVHR is highly dependent on the envelope being airtight (a minimum of less than 3 $m^3/h \cdot m^2$ at a test pressure of 50 Pa and ideally less than 1 $m^3/h \cdot m^2$ at a test pressure of 50 Pa). Filters must also be oversized and easily accessible for replacement (preferably in separate filter boxes, allowing for the specification of oversized, low-cost, low-pressure-drop filters rather than the use of small, high-pressure-drop, expensive filters incorporated by manufacturers in mass-produced MVHR units). Ductwork must be designed and specified to minimize pressure loss and noise (see Section 5.5).

In many locations, there can be real merit in linking the MVHR fresh air inlet to a low-cost earth duct (e.g., see Color Plate 13 where the earth duct utilizes standard drainage pipes). This can alleviate the need for an expensive MVHR frost protection heat exchanger, while providing air preheating in the winter and free cooling of the supply air in summer.

5.1.4.9 Count All the Savings and Assess Impact on Supply Infrastructure

When appropriate passive measures have been adopted and when low-friction/low-pressure-loss systems and efficient components have been specified, significant savings can be realized in the size/capacity of the incoming electrical supply, transformers, switchgear, plantroom size, and so forth.

It is essential for all savings attributable to the inclusion of passive measures *and* efficient plant and equipment specification to be identified. Too often, cost consultants (and some architects/engineers) will suggest, for example, removing external shading, or reducing ductwork sizing to save CAPEX. However, they fail to fully understand (or assess) the consequences on OPEX, or the potential missed CAPEX savings associated with reduced infrastructure cost (such as the potential for reducing the capacity of the incoming electrical supply cabling, switchgear, transformers, etc.).

5.1.5 Step 4: Consider the On-Site Renewable Energy Generation Options

Integrating renewable energy generation into buildings should only be considered once all the options for reducing/minimizing energy demand have been fully considered and incorporated. The main forms of building integrated renewable energy systems are discussed next.

5.1.5.1 Solar Energy

The cost of photovoltaic (PV) electricity generation has fallen dramatically since 2010 with manufacturing capacity increasing every year. Roof-mounted panels have dominated the incorporation of PV into the built environment. Building-integrated PV (BIPV), which double as shingles, walls, roof, or other building materials, represents less than 1% of solar PV capacity being installed worldwide. New BIPV opportunities are emerging that use thin-film nanotechnology printed onto glass, which could enable a glazed façade or roof lights to also generate electricity. PV also offers the potential to be utilized to not only generate electricity, but also as a shading device, enabling a reduction in cooling demand. It is important that all the benefits are captured in a cost benefit analysis

Opportunities for PV are particularly attractive in sun-belt countries and where local electricity supply costs are high [6]. In some counties the cost of PV has already achieved grid parity; that is, the cost to supply electricity from PV is the same or cheaper than buying-in electricity from the local supplier. Many countries have introduced tax incentives or feed-in tariffs to encourage PV installation.

PVs should be oriented to face the sun, with shadowing being avoided because shade from trees, buildings, etc., will substantially reduce output and economic viability.

Solar energy is also used for solar water heating. Solar thermal is a cost-effective technology that can be used in many geographic locations. Solar thermal is not as sensitive to shading as PV, but excessive shadowing should be avoided to ensure optimum performance. Although this technology is relatively simple, care is required in design, installation, and control to ensure that a solar thermal system will perform well.

5.1.5.2 Biomass

Biomass is derived from wood or plant material and takes a number forms, including logs and pellets (see Figure 5.8a). If biomass is to be used, consideration must be given to fuel storage, delivery, and maintenance implications. In urban environments concern has been expressed regarding the potentially harmful nitrogen oxide (NO_x), smoke, and particulates arising from biomass combustion. These issues require careful consideration to ensure that no unintended consequences are associated with the use of biomass heating systems.

5.1.5.3 Heat Pumps

Heat pumps can be used to heat and cool buildings, sometimes simultaneously (see Figure 5.8b). Heat pump heat sources include air, water (typically rivers, lakes, aquifers, sea), and the ground. The heat sink is either air or water.

The efficiency of a heat pump is referred to as the coefficient of performance (COP). For space heating, the COP is the ratio of the heat output and the total energy input. For cooling, it is the ratio of effective cooling delivered to the total energy input. COPs can be defined in different ways (peak, seasonal, standardized laboratory test conditions, etc.) and considerable care is required to ensure that the basis of the COP being claimed is clearly stated so that a realistic estimate of operational performance and operational cost can be made.

To maximize the performance of a heat pump, it is important to minimize the temperature lift (i.e., the difference between the heat source and heat sink

(a)   (b)

Figure 5.8 (a) Biomass pellet room heater. (b) Ground source heat pump (*Photos:* David Strong.)

temperatures) and ensure that seasonal performance factors and the energy requirements of pumps, fans, evaporator defrosting, and other ancillary equipment are fully accounted for. Although heat pumps are often described as a renewable energy system, it is important to note that they require an energy input to function (electricity, gas, etc.).

5.1.5.4   Geothermal

The use of geothermal electricity generation is highly dependent on location, making it cost effective in some regions. Incorporating geothermal energy into a building's energy system can provide free space heating and cooling (when used to provide the heat source for an absorption chiller). Care is required for these types of systems because of the potential for corrosion and heat exchanger contamination from salts and other deposits associated with geothermal energy.

Ground source heat pumps are often referred to as using geothermal energy, but this is somewhat misleading because in most locations geothermal energy has little or no impact on the performance of a ground source heat pump.

5.1.5.5   Hydropower

Like geothermal energy, hydropower is very location specific. Small- and medium-scale hydropower systems can provide a viable and cost-effective energy supply for a building provided (1) the river and stream have sufficient flow all year and (2) the fall/drop is sufficient to enable a turbine to function effectively.

Utilizing hydropower often requires a licence and/or permission from an environmental agency to ensure precautions are taken to avoid damaging fish stocks and wildlife.

5.1.5.6   Small- and Microscale Wind Power

The incorporation of small/micro wind turbines onto buildings is seldom cost effective or viable:

- In most locations, surrounding buildings and trees cause ground turbulence of the wind, which results in very poor turbine power output.
- In some cases the parasitic losses associated with connecting a small building-mounted wind turbine to the electricity network can result in the wind turbine being a net consumer of electricity.
- Building-mounted wind turbines can cause noise, vibration, and structural issues.

The correct location of a wind turbine is critical. The proposed wind resource should be monitored for a year or more. Exposed (e.g., coastal) sites can be attractive.

Small wind generators (greater than 2 kW) should ideally be mounted 10 to 15m (30 to 50 ft) above the highest structure or tree in a 150-m (500-ft) radius.

It is unfortunate that some first-generation green buildings incorporated small micro wind turbines as a visual symbol of the buildings' eco-credentials, but in many cases this was nothing more than tokenism (see Figure 5.9).

For further information regarding renewable sources of energy see *Whole Building Design Guide—Alternative Energy* [7].

5.2   Sustainability of the Building Envelope

Rob Bolin, PE, Syska Hennessy Group (edited by D. T. G. Strong). Copyright National Institute of Building Sciences, *Whole Building Design Guide* [7]. Reproduced with permission.

5.2.1   Introduction

For the design, construction, and operation of a facility, the interface between the indoor and outdoor environments—the building envelope—is particularly important. The building envelope is comprised of the outer elements of a building: foundations, walls, roof, windows, doors, and floors. The prime functions of the building envelope are to provide shelter, security, solar and thermal control, moisture control, indoor air quality control, access to daylight, views to the outside, fire resistance, acoustics, cost effectiveness, and aesthetics. Because of the varied and sometimes competing functions associated with the building envelope, an integrated, synergistic approach considering all phases of the facility life cycle is warranted. This sustainable approach supports an increased commitment to environmental stewardship and conservation and results in an optimal balance of

(a)

(b)

Figure 5.9 Incorporating small/micro wind generators is generally little more than tokenism. (*Photos:* David Strong.)

cost, environmental, societal, and human benefits while meeting the mission and function of the intended facility.

The main objectives of sustainable design are to avoid resource depletion of energy, water, and raw materials; to prevent environmental degradation caused by facilities and their infrastructure throughout their life cycle; and to create built environments that are accessible, secure, healthy, and productive (see Section 5.3).

5.2.2 Building Envelope Fundamentals

This section discusses sustainability recommendations pertaining to the design and construction of the building envelope.

5.2.2.1 Optimize Site Potential

- *Consider climatic conditions.* Consideration of the local climatic conditions (temperature, moisture, wind) can influence the materials of construction of the building envelope, the amount of and performance of glazing used specific to each orientation, and the overall energy performance of the building.
- *Reduce urban heat islands.* The design of the horizontal elements (roof) of the building envelope should consider the impact on the site's urban heat island. Finish the facility's roof with light-colored finish materials or vegetated components to reduce energy loads and extend the life of the roof, especially in warmer climates. Consider incorporating vegetated roof materials. Use a roofing product that meets or exceeds Energy Star standards (see Figure 5.10a).

5.2.2.2 Optimizing the Envelope to Minimize Energy Use

- *Optimize thermal insulation.* Optimize the insulation performance of the envelope's opaque elements for both heating and cooling seasons.
- *Incorporate high-performance, spectrally selective glazing.* The orientation, amount, and performance of vertical and horizontal glazing should be appropriate for the climate of the building. Carefully analyze the thermal (U factor), solar (solar heat gain factor [SHGF]) and daylighting (visible transmittance [VT]) performance of glazing on each elevation of the building. The performance criteria will vary depending on orientation and dominant strategy (e.g., solar performance or daylighting performance).
- *Employ effective solar shading devices.* Use exterior shading devices such as overhangs, vertical fins, and light shelves as energy efficiency measures (with consideration of maintenance and security/safety issues).
- *Consider using lighting sensors.* Lighting sensors are used to control perimeter lighting levels when adequate daylight is available. This results in reduced power and HVAC loads, particularly at peak demand periods, which often coincide with times for high daylight availability.
- *Integrate photovoltaic panels.* Incorporate BIPV panels as part of the building envelope system or solar shading system as a way of generating on-site,

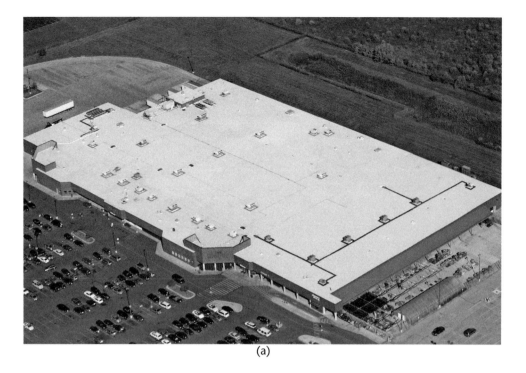

(a)

(b)

Figure 5.10 (a) Energy Star compliant roof; high-reflectance, and high-emissivity roofing can lower roof surface temperature by up to 55 C° (100°F), decreasing the amount of heat transferred into a building (photo courtesy of Duro-Last, Inc., reproduced with permission). (b) A 203% Swiss PlusEnergy building incorporating a 750 kWp full-roof BIW array. (*Photo:* Roland Zumbuehl, Umwelt Arena, Switzerland, cc by sa 3.0).

renewable energy (see Figure 5.10b). Rapidly emerging BIPV technology includes thin-film solar cells that can be printed directly onto silicon, or glass. This could enable a paradigm shift in the aesthetics, performance, and cost of both current solar panels and façade-integrated PV systems by enabling some or all of a glazed façade to be utilized for on-site energy generation.

- *Analyze envelope performance with energy simulation.* Use energy simulation and life cycle analysis tools to optimize the performance of all components of the building envelope. Make informed decisions about the components of the building envelope based on life cycle performance (see Section 3.4 and Chapter 6).

- *Commission envelope elements.* The building commissioning process should include commissioning of the building envelope to ensure that all performance requirements are being met. Commissioning of the building envelope can identify areas of concern related to air infiltration and leakage, moisture diffusion, surface condensation, and rainwater entry—all issues that can negatively impact the building's energy performance and indoor environmental quality. Of particular importance is to begin commissioning of the building envelope during the design phase when design modifications can be easily incorporated, rather than waiting until construction when remediation can cost significantly more.

While the LEED Green Building Rating System requires buildings to undergo fundamental building commissioning of systems to achieve certification, it merely recommends that some form of building envelope commissioning be incorporated. Lemieux and Totten [9] have proposed a building envelope commissioning process that could supplement the fundamental building commissioning required for LEED certification. For further information regarding envelope design see the *Whole Building Design Guide—Building Envelope* [10].

5.3 Optimizing Indoor Environmental Quality

Prof. Rajat Gupta and Adorkor Bruce-Konuah, Oxford Brookes University

5.3.1 Introduction

Human beings spend over 90% of their time in indoor spaces, at home, at work/school, in recreational spaces, and in vehicles. Buildings offer a place primarily for shelter and security from the outside where conditions can be harsh and harmful, but because of the amount of time spent indoors, they are also required to provide comfortable and healthy environments for occupants. Indoor environmental quality is defined as the quality of the building's environment with respect to comfort, health, well-being and productivity and in order to achieve these, energy is often expended for operations such as heating, cooling and lighting. A sustainable building should not only have reduced energy demand and emissions and low running cost but should be able to provide high quality indoor environments that will protect and enhance occupant comfort, health, well-being, and productivity.

Indoor environmental quality (IEQ) comprises the thermal and moisture conditions; indoor air quality, which focuses on ventilation, airborne pollutants, and odor; acoustics; lighting; and visual impacts. All of these parameters are interrelated and are influenced by factors such as the building's design, external weather conditions, and the presence and activities of occupants. IEQ parameters have been shown to have significant impacts on occupants, affecting our health and comfort in both domestic and nondomestic environments and productivity in both working and learning environments. In commercial buildings, this can have a significant cost implication due to increased rates of absenteeism and sick leave, and in educational spaces it can have an impact on student's academic attainment. Symptoms of poor indoor environmental quality may be short lived because they tend to improve when the occupant leaves the room. However, the cost/benefit of improving IEQ can exceed the cost/benefit of implementing sustainable initiatives that are aimed at reducing the building's energy demands. The success or failure of a sustainable building project may lie in its indoor environmental quality because occupants who are satisfied with their indoor environments are more likely to be more comfortable and productive and rate the building highly.

Enhancing the indoor environmental quality is one of the fundamental principles underpinning sustainable building design, construction, and operation (see Table 5.1). The challenge of designing buildings to more stringent energy standards will be the greater dependency on optimizing IEQ to provide adequate thermal

Table 5.1   Recommended Limits for Indoor Environmental Quality Parameters

IEQ Parameters	Recommended Limits
Thermal comfort	
Indoor temperature in mechanically ventilated spaces	Summer: 22–25°C
	Winter: 19–21°C
Indoor temperature in naturally ventilated spaces	Depends on outdoor temperature: 5°C comfort band for 90% acceptability and 7°C comfort band for 80% acceptability
Indoor relative humidity	40–70%
Air speed	0.15 m/s; temperature should be increased to maintain thermal comfort (cooling effect)
Indoor air quality and ventilation	
Total outdoor air supply rate (no smoking and no significant pollutant sources)	10 L/s per person
CO_2 concentration	1500 ppm
Other pollutants (VOCs, formaldehyde)	TVOC: <0.2mg/m²h for low polluting buildings and <0.1 mg/m²h for very low polluting buildings
	Formaldehyde: <0.05mg/m²h for low polluting buildings and <0.02mg/m²h for very low polluting buildings
	Odor from materials: Dissatisfaction below 15% for low polluting buildings and dissatisfaction below 10% for very low polluting buildings
Noise (ambience levels)	Nonresidential: 35–50 dBA
	Residential: 30–45 dBA
Lighting (maintained illuminance)	Nonresidential: 300–500 lux
	Residential: 50–300 lux

Source: CIBSE Guide A, EN 15215.

comfort; lighting and aesthetic comfort; ventilation and good indoor air quality, reducing the buildup of indoor air pollutants; and acoustic comfort and privacy.

5.3.2 Thermal Comfort

Thermal comfort is associated with the need to maintain a stable core body temperature and it is crucial for our health and well-being. It is affected by environmental parameters (temperature, air velocity, and relative humidity) and by personal parameters (clothing levels and activity levels). There are several mechanisms for thermal regulation that can be grouped into physiological mechanisms and behavioral mechanisms (see Color Plate 16a). Physiological mechanisms include the body producing, transferring, and using heat to maintain a core body temperature within safe limits for organs in the body to function. Behavioral mechanisms include consciously interacting with the environment (e.g., changing clothing levels and opening windows) to achieve and maintain comfortable thermal conditions. The role of designers, architects, and building engineers, therefore, is to design buildings that meet occupants' thermal comfort needs through enabling them to effectively use the available mechanisms for maintaining thermal comfort (see Color Plate 16b).

The following are factors to consider when setting thermal comfort criteria in a sustainable building:

- The use of the building and the different indoor spaces must be clearly defined because thermal comfort requirements will be dependent on the activities carried out in the building.

- The external environmental conditions should be taken into considerations when specifying thermal comfort standards.

- Appropriate design standards and regulations such as ASHRAE Standard 55 and EN 15251 should be used as the basis for thermal comfort

- Understand the heating, cooling, and ventilation mechanisms in the building because this will have an impact on the thermal comfort requirements in the building.

- Consider the impact of seasonal variations in environmental conditions on thermal comfort criteria, particularly in naturally ventilated and mixed-mode buildings (e.g., changes in use of space or flexibility in use of spaces).

- Building/facilities managers and occupants should be engaged and educated about the thermal expectation of the building and the role of different adaptive mechanisms, that is, on the operation of building controls to adjust their thermal environment and the role of personal control to adapt themselves (e.g., adjust clothing, cold/hot drinks).

- Consider the provision of appropriate levels of personal control for occupants. This must be dependent on the type of building/space (e.g., classrooms or offices) and the activities carried out in the building.

- Designers, architects, and engineers of sustainable buildings should be keen to undertake thermal comfort surveys with the majority of occupants in order to review the performance of their buildings. This can be done through occupant surveys using the well-known ASHRAE or Bedford seven-point scales.

For further information regarding the important issues associated with thermal comfort see the *Guide to Setting Thermal Comfort Criteria and Minimizing Energy Use in Delivering Thermal Comfort* [11].

5.3.3   Visual Comfort

Visual comfort generally refers to the provision of a suitable amount and quality of light for various activities combined with pleasant views. Visual comfort plays a vital role in the quality of any indoor environment in terms of maintaining physical as well as mental well-being of the occupants. Visually appealing views of the outdoors, particularly those of nature, provide relief to the eyes, reduce fatigue, and prevent headaches and eye strain. At a mental level, they allow occupants to look away from computer screens or written documents, which positively affects cognitive skills and enhances the individual's ability to deal with challenging situations.

Along with external views, adequate daylighting and indoor sunspots are key factors that contribute to a visually pleasant indoor environment. Additionally, a combination of appropriately chosen colors, textures, materials, and spatial layouts provides a certain level of sensory variability within the indoor environment and subsequently enhances the visual comfort levels of the occupants. However, it is crucial that design decisions pertaining to visual comfort are made with the long term in mind.

The following are some factors to consider while designing for visual comfort in a sustainable building:

- Use daylighting and ambient lighting wherever feasible to save on energy.
- Use energy-efficient/low-energy light fittings where artificial lighting is required.
- Artificial lighting should have occupancy sensors to save on energy.
- Ambient lighting should be supplemented with task lighting with dimming features that can be controlled by the occupant.
- Passive infrared sensor (PIR) lights should be installed in communal and transitional spaces.
- Measures must be taken to reduce glare from both natural and artificial light, particularly in classrooms and offices where visual display equipment is used.
- Biophilic indoor spaces should be provided where possible to facilitate relief from visual strain.
- Materials that are cost effective, easy to maintain, low in VOCs, and suitable for the space function are recommended in order to prevent frequent changing, loss of embodied energy, and waste generation.

5.3.4 Indoor Air Quality

Acceptable indoor air quality (IAQ) is defined as air in which there are no known contaminants at harmful concentrations as determined by cognizant authorities and with which 80% or more of people exposed do not express dissatisfaction. The criteria for adequate IAQ are based mainly on comfort and also on health. The principal role of ventilation is to provide an appropriate level of IAQ by diluting and removing airborne contaminants from the indoor space, and it is dependent on occupant density, activities, and pollutant emissions in the space. Indoor air may contain over 900 chemicals, particles, and biological materials with irritating and sensitizing potential. Because of the limited size of indoor spaces, concentrations of pollutants can increase and quickly exceed concentrations in outdoor air and these can cause a variety of effects on occupants. The intensity of symptoms will tend to increase with the time spent in the building and improve or disappear when the building is evacuated.

Heat loss is associated with ventilation and infiltration; hence, to realize the potential of reducing building energy use it makes sense to increase building airtightness in order to reduce infiltration. If infiltration provides significant additional dilution of indoor air pollutants, measures to improve airtightness should lead to appropriate ventilation design to maintain adequate indoor air quality.

There is evidence that ventilation rates more than double the current recommended limits are associated with reduced sick building syndrome symptoms and respiratory illness in children. It is therefore important to ensure that the designed ventilation systems meet or exceed the standards.

Carbon dioxide (CO_2), which is a by-product of respiration, is often used as a proxy for ventilation rate and IAQ, and limits are set for acceptable levels of CO_2 in indoor spaces. It is easy to measure and so should be monitored to provide diagnostic feedback on ventilation rates.

In mechanically ventilated buildings, HVAC systems must be installed appropriately and commissioned to validate and document the design intent and the maintenance plans. Seasonal commissioning plans can be used to ensure maintenance plans are carried out accordingly.

Pollutant-emitting sources such as paints and furnishings must be kept at a minimum, and in spaces such as bathrooms, kitchens, and workshops, exhaust vents must be installed to extract moisture, odors, and air pollutants.

In naturally ventilated buildings, windows are widely used for adaptive actions to control both temperature and air quality. The air supply intake should not be obstructed from the outside (e.g., by noisy environments or pollution) or the inside (e.g., by furniture). Windows must therefore be accessible and easy to use.

5.3.5 Acoustic Environment

An indoor environment needs to have an acceptable level and quality of noise in order to remain comfortable for its occupants. Internal and external sources of noise can not only cause considerable distractions in performing daily tasks but can also adversely affect the occupants' health by increasing stress levels and impacting the overall experience of a space. Good acoustics, free from reverberation and intrusive noise levels, facilitate effortless verbal communication and comfortable learning, working, and living environments.

The building envelope, along with its key elements such as windows and glazing, is an important component to control sound within a building. The size and location of windows combined with an appropriate type of glazing need to be chosen at an early stage of any project, making it necessary to take acoustic comfort into consideration during the conception of any project.

The following are some factors to consider in order to achieve an acceptable acoustic environment in a sustainable building:

- Design room shape, size, and degree of enclosure to reduce echoes and reverberation by creating sound barriers at appropriate locations.
- When choosing the glazing type, keep in mind the orientation of the building and its proximity to distracting noise sources.
- Minimize transmission of noise from external sources by introducing high sound transmission class (STC) walls.
- Reduce the reverberation period by installing sound-absorbing materials to dampen the sound.
- Consider introducing white background noise through sound masking systems.
- Minimize the noise from HVAC systems by avoiding small-diameter ducts for high- velocity air flow and through-the-wall package terminal air conditioners (PTACs).
- Consider furniture with sound-absorbing surfaces, particularly in nonresidential environments.

5.4   Effective Building Control and Monitoring

Alan Johnson, BSC CEng MEI, Honeywell, Energy & Environmental Solutions

5.4.1   Introduction

To effectively control and monitor intelligent buildings, building systems must be designed holistically, not only to meet the needs of the occupants, but also to provide optimum performance and flexibility for the building owners and predictable and reliable outcomes for the building operators.

In nondomestic buildings these needs are met by the building management system (BMS), which is designed to ensure that a building remains sustainable, compliant, and resilient through its life. A BMS makes buildings more sustainable by maintaining optimum comfort conditions at minimum operational cost by effectively controlling the HVAC systems, optimizing energy consumption, and extending the operational life of the building services plant.

Energy-efficient control strategies ensure that the plant runs effectively for better user comfort and that alarm events are transmitted to field staff who can then provide a proactive maintenance response. Monitored data can be interpreted remotely by smart analytics designed to report by exception, meaning that issues are only flagged when a potential problem is identified.

The fundamental need of all building operators is that of complying with legislation. Compliance is often taken for granted in favor of energy efficiency, but it is essential in all building design. Compliance metrics, usually in the form of contractual KPIs, should be designed into the BMS at the outset so that actual performance can be demonstrated in real time.

5.4.2 Maximizing BMS Effectiveness

To maximize the effectiveness of buildings, better sensing and intelligent metering should be included with the BMS to provide a level of data granularity that matches the building's intended use. Early consideration of a data strategy needs to be included in the design process and should be protected against the erosion of design intent during procurement and value engineering.

As a result of the convergence of open standards and IP technology, the BMS is now central to the connected building, providing interoperability with other building systems and enabling enterprise management of performance data from distributed systems that can be collated and analyzed centrally. This requires a break from the traditional engineering views of the HVAC plant and the adoption of dashboard-style data visualization to simplify the interpretation of high volumes of data.

Enterprise management will continue to grow as cloud services become more commonplace and data get easier to collect through wireless Internet-of-Things (IoT) technologies. The availability of data means that powerful management information (MI) will inform decision making based on actual building use and performance.

With the increasing complexity of building systems and big data, it is more important than ever to consider how building users interact with their environment. The development of smart phone and web technology means that the user experience will become more personalized and building designers will need to consider this human factor. Engagement with the user is essential because it highlights how the user and building affect each other and improves the perception of comfort. BSRIA [11] estimates that this can improve productivity by up to 15% by increasing thermal satisfaction, which is a mix of how comfortable the building occupant feels and how effectively the building operator communicates and responds to issues.

A properly implemented BMS can allow building systems to perform seamlessly and thus free up businesses to focus on operational issues. This can have a significant impact on operational cost, which is often underestimated in design, and any system that can help to reduce the operational element of the cost base is extremely valuable. Table 5.2 provides a checklist for designers and specifiers.

Table 5.2   BMS Checklist for Designers and Specifiers

Design	Evaluate the building system design based on whole life cost.
	Engage with system specialists early to develop/validate technical solutions.
	Define KPIs for statutory compliance and post-occupancy performance.
	Specify the use of proven control strategies that are energy efficient.
	Specify demand-based control to ensure the main plant only runs when required.
	Comply in full with the manufacturer's cybersecurity recommendations.
	Include the provision of a clear data strategy.
	Integrate to deliver better operability, not simply to reduce capital cost.
	Use open protocols to add value, but avoid unnecessary complexity of hybrid systems.
	Design clean systems with clear maintenance demarkation and choice or provider.
	Design with the building users in mind. Consider how they will interact with the building.
Construction	Procure the BMS as a separate package to ensure design compliance.
	Allow sufficient time to commission and protect this against program slippage.
	Allow for soft landings and seasonal commissioning.
	Ensure all users are appropriately trained and revisit after a bedding-in period of 3 to 6 months.
Post-Occupancy	Specify maintenance regimes that are measured on outcomes rather than output or ppm.
	Utilize specialists with access to optimization tools and software for complex systems.
	Include BMS reporting in the soft landings POEs.
	Use the BMS to demonstrate actual environmental performance (e.g., BREEAM).
	Allow for an element of continuous commissioning in maintenance regimes.
	Incorporate ongoing optimization into maintenance regimes.

5.5   Low-Friction, Low-Pressure-Loss Engineering

Prof. Tim Dwyer, Visiting Professor of Building Services Systems, UCL Institute for Environmental Design and Engineering (IEDE), The Bartlett, UCL Faculty of the Built Environment

5.5.1   Reducing the Environmental Impact of Moving Air and Water Around Buildings

Moving air and water account for a significant proportion of the energy used in buildings. The actual amount will vary from building to building; however, Figure 5.11 provides a snapshot based on data collected across Europe (used in the development of the EU's ecodesign directive). It indicates that approximately 40% of the energy consumed in the servicing buildings is related to fans and pumps. When considering the energy (and environmental) building footprint, "small is beautiful" may well be the clarion call. However, when designing the fluid flow systems (typically ducts for air movement and pipes for water-based systems), a relatively small increase in their normal size can yield disproportionately high savings in the energy used to power the fans and pumps. Possibly a case of "bigger is better"?

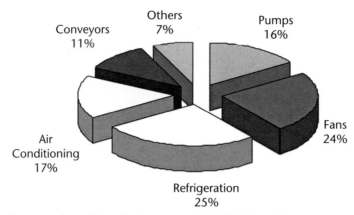

Figure 5.11   The proportions of electrical energy consumed in the services sector across Europe [13].

5.5.2   Why Design for Low Friction and Low Pressure Loss?

The design pressure drop in ducted air and piped water systems affects not only the sizing calculations, system noise, and potential controllability, but also the installation costs and lifetime carbon footprint of a system.

The physical relationships and the defining equations that determine the energy required to move fluids (water and air) through conduits (pipes and ducts) are well understood and relatively simple and will be touched on later in this section. However, the underlying principles are something that humans intuitively understand and apply daily without even knowing anything of the formalized physics and mathematical relationships. For example, consider the person in Figure 5.12a who is able to slip down the rails because they are smooth, offering little frictional resistance as he is moved down from the top by the pull of gravity. If the handrails were made of, for example, rough wood not only would his speed be reduced but he might also feel the effect of the heat as the rough surface slides against his trousers. There would still be the same driving force (that of gravity attracting his body's mass), and he may well get to the bottom of the flight of steps, but he would get there at a somewhat slower pace. If the rails were particularly rough, he may reach a point where his speed combined with his body mass and gravity are too much to allow him to continue sliding and he might end up tumbling off the rail. He effectively detaches from the rail's surface as the forward momentum of his body makes him tumble and what was a pleasant linear flow down the rail becomes a turbulent rolling fall. Not a desirable result!

For a further example of how humans naturally understand the concept of flow and resistance, someone purchasing an extra-thick milkshake (see Figure 5.12b) will instinctively reach for the fat (larger-diameter) straw to ensure that she/he can enjoy the full pleasure of consuming the dense, viscous fluid without employing too much suction energy. If the individuals were to seek a challenge, or wish to eke out the pleasure, then a slimmer straw might be chosen. This would impose a greater resistance to the flow and so would reduce the flow rate of sticky fluid while still requiring as much, or perhaps even greater, suction. The roughness of the internal surface of the straw together with its diameter will affect the resistance to flow. Larger circular conduits (straws) have a smaller proportion of surface area (which causes the friction and is typically known as *wetted area*) compared to the

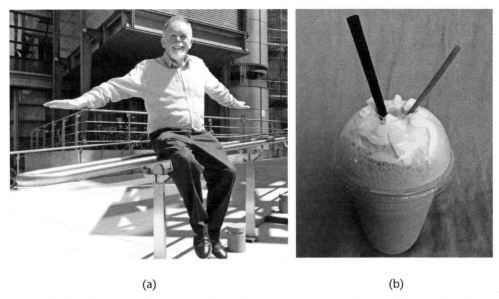

(a)   (b)

Figure 5.12   (a) The smooth handrail allows for swift passage with little heat (from friction)—all powered by gravity! (b) A fat straw enables the dense milkshake to be consumed with low suction power—imagine trying that with the slim straw! (*Photos:* David Strong.)

cross-sectional area. As the diameter doubles, the surface area will double but the cross-sectional area will quadruple, making it easier for fluids to pass through. The fluid will stick to the surface, so it will go slower nearer the wall of the straw compared to the milkshake in the middle of the flow. There are shearing (tearing) forces holding it back as the faster-flowing fluid in the center attempts to drag away.

It is actually the atmospheric air pressure that is driving the milkshake into the mouth (as well as collapsing the cheeks). The tongue is acting like a small reciprocating suction pump by briefly reducing the pressure in the mouth so that it is lower than the air pressure surrounding the milkshake, thus making the drink flow from the high-pressure area of the cup into the (relatively) low-pressure mouth. It manages this despite the gravitational pull on the milkshake. (In between sucks the mouth will return to atmospheric pressure and the milkshake will continue its journey to the stomach powered by a combination of gravitational pull and the human body's amazingly complex autonomic swallowing action.)

These same physical considerations affect the flow of air and water in ducts and pipes used in building services systems. So generally:

- The larger the conduit, the lower the resistance to flow and so less energy is required to move the fluid within the pipe or duct.
- Smooth internal conduit surfaces will cause less frictional resistance (or drag) to the passing fluid and so the power that is supplied to the prime mover (the pump or fan) will be reduced.

5.5.3   Duct and Pipe Sizing: The Importance of Forensic Attention to Detail

When considering flow through buildings services systems, the frictional resistance is converted to a pressure drop at particular flow conditions. Tables, spreadsheets, charts, software tools, and apps are readily available, including those published by CIBSE and ASHRAE, that provide the pressure and flow characteristics of conduits. Whether it is air in a duct or water in a pipe, the same basic principles apply. For example, if an open plan office had an air flow requirement of 1.5 m³/s of air at 15°C to keep it cool (by providing 15 kW of cooling), then the size of a 40 m length of main duct running from the ventilation plantroom toward the office could be determined. Using a standard industry spreadsheet calculator [13], a circular steel duct of 500 mm would convey this air with a pressure drop of 1.135 Pa per meter run of ductwork. So for 40 m this would provide a pressure drop of $40 \times 1.135 =$ 45.4 Pa. A rectangular duct, which is often easier to accommodate than a circular duct, could be used and selected to provide exactly the same pressure drop. From the CIBSE Guide C4 tables this could, for example, be a 600 mm × 350 mm rectangular duct or a 900 mm × 250 mm duct. The rectangular duct will not have the same cross-sectional area as its circular equivalent since its pressure drop is determined by a combination of its aspect ratio and its perimeter. This equivalent-sized rectangular duct requires proper selection using tables or basic equations; otherwise, unwanted results can follow if a duct with simply the same cross-sectional area is used. The best performance will be from circular ducts. The most effective rectangular ducts are square; as the aspect ratio increases, the geometric area of the duct will need to increase to maintain lower pressure drops.

This pressure drop through the duct can simply be converted to power by multiplying the pressure drop by the air volume flow rate, so in this case the basic power requirement to move this air would be 1.5 m³/s × 45.4 Pa = 68.1 W. There would be an advantage, however, to considering an increase in the duct size. If, for example, the duct diameter was just 50 mm greater, the losses in this straight duct would be reduced by about 40% for just a little extra material (and its associated embodied carbon) and a small increase in capital cost.

The duct material will affect the pressure drop. If the duct were to be made of plastic (which has a smooth surface), it would have just 85% of the pressure drop, or if fair-faced brick ducting were used, it could be 50% more. Also as the duct ages and gets dirty, its surface roughness will alter, which would increase the pressure drop.

But the straight duct is likely to be only a small part of the total pressure drop in the ducted system; there will be bends and restrictions (e.g., around downstand beams or through open fire dampers). The effect of bends will be related to how sharp they are and also whether they use turning vanes to guide the air around the change in direction.

If the bend in Figure 5.13(a) were used with a rectangular steel duct of 600 mm × 350 mm, the radius r of the bend would significantly alter the pressure drop. If this were a very sharp (practically right-angled) bend with $r = 260$ mm, the pressure drop would be twice as much as it would be if the bend were slightly less severe, say, $r = 350$ mm. In this particular example, it reduces the pressure loss from 13 to 6.5 Pa.

For tight bends significant advantage is gained by adding *turning vanes*, curved plates designed to make the air pass through the bend in a more streamlined fashion. For example, adding one turning vane to the improved *(r = 350 mm)* bend in Figure 5.13(a) would further reduce its pressure loss by 80%, down to 1.3 Pa. In any case the use of this curved radius bend provides improved performance over

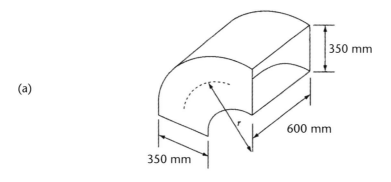

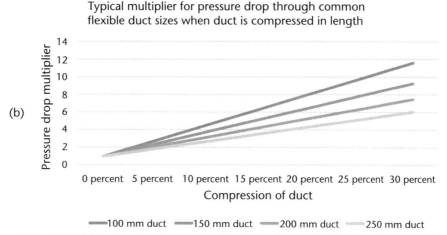

Figure 5.13   (a) Variables affecting the pressure drop in a radius bend with no turning vanes. (*Source:* CIBSE Guide C4, 2007, Table 4.60.) (b) Effect of compressing flexible ductwork. (After ASHRAE Fundamentals, Chapter 21, Eq. 22, 2013.)

a sharp, box-shaped, right-angle bend because the air will pass more smoothly around the curve (see Figure 5.14). To reduce the impact of changes in duct direction, they should be placed at least two to three duct diameters' distance downstream of any piece of equipment (such as a damper or heating coil). This allows any disturbances in the air stream to settle before reaching the bend; such disturbances are likely cause the air to strike the bend more awkwardly.

All duct fittings, such as the flexible connections, will add to the energy consumption of the system. However, if not installed correctly, their standard, published pressure loss factors will bear little resemblance to the actual installed pressure drop (Figure 5.13b). The pressure drop through the flexible duct when it is compressed by 30% might be anything from 6 to 11 times that when it is fully extended, depending on the diameter. As might be expected smaller ducts are affected worst since they already have a higher proportion of wetted area.

5.5.4   Ductwork Layout

The best practice is to design the ductwork layout in conjunction with the architectural design to minimize changes in direction and size. This reduces the need

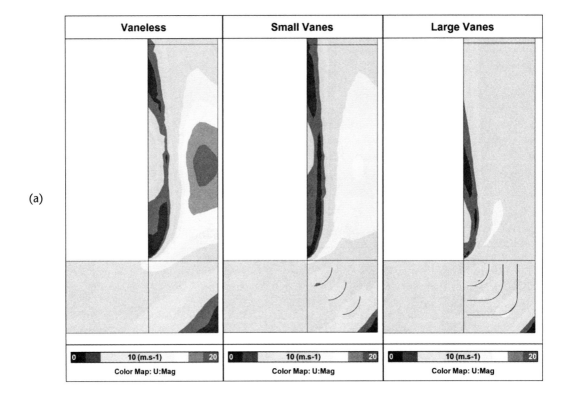

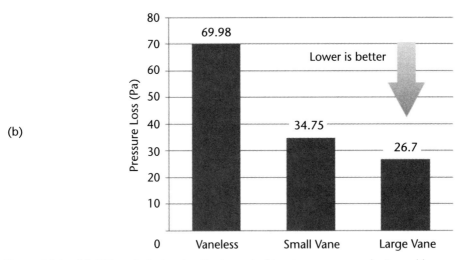

Figure 5.14   (a) CFD analysis showing the impact of turning vanes on velocity and hence pressure loss in a square duct corner. (b) Turning vane pressure loss comparison. (Image and analysis courtesy Symscape, http://www.symscape.com.)

for bends and other fittings. If changes in direction are required, they should be as gradual as the possible (within the constraints of the building fabric and other services and equipment). For example, using one (or two) 45 deg bends to replace a 90-deg bend or a Y-junction in place of a T-junction can reduce the pressure drop significantly and in some situations also reduce the length of ducting required.

In a ductwork system operating 10 hours a day and supplying 1.5 m³/s of air (as in the earlier example), every savings of 10 Pa will reduce annual running costs by about $10 and will reduce carbon emissions by over 27 kg CO_2 per year (this assumes that the combined fan, motor, and control is about 65% efficient in converting electricity to air power). In larger systems such changes will have magnified benefits and many will operate 24/7, increasing these numbers to about $25 and 65 kg CO_2 per year for each additional 10-Pa pressure loss. (See case study "How Modifying Typical Ductwork Layout and Specification Can Reduce Fan Power Requirement (and Operational Cost) by Over 80%".)

5.5.5 Pipework Layout and Design

For pipework the pressure drops can be substantial (typically 150 to 300 Pa for every meter run), but the volume flow rates are somewhat lower than air because water can move large amounts of energy. Hence, the overall energy consumed to move heat around is significantly less than that consumed when using air. If, for example, the open plan office discussed earlier had a perimeter heating system that required around 15 kW of heating (requiring 0.179 kg/s heating water), then the flow and return pipework from the boiler plantroom can be obtained from tables [6] as being a nominal 20-mm-diameter steel pipe with a pressure drop of 162 Pa/m. Increasing the size to the next standard size of 25 mm reduces the pressure drop by two-thirds with marginal additional total installation costs. As the pipe size increases, the embodied energy will also increase (for further details see Section 5.5.6).

A larger pipe size will also reduce the velocity of the water. The energy losses in pipe fittings (open valves, bends, and tees) will vary with the square of the velocity, so if the velocity is halved the pressure drop will be quartered. (For commercial applications a minimum velocity of 0.5 m/s is recommended to reduce the opportunity for air locks and the accumulation of sludge.) The surface roughness and shape of the inside of the bends make a substantial difference to the pressure loss, and as pipes age they are likely to become rougher. CIBSE [16] warns that the particular design and finish of the elbow can significantly alter its flow performance, so manufacturers' specific data should be used if available. Jointing techniques for pipework will affect the energy consumed in operation; for example, steel pipes that are screwed together will consume more energy when in use than those that are flanged due to the unevenness of the pipe surfaces across the connection. So in the case of the 20-mm-diameter steel pipe referred to earlier, a smooth-surfaced but sharp elbow will have about half the pressure drop of a rougher, screw-jointed one. That loss of energy could be further cut in half by using a swept bend rather than a sharp elbow.

5.5.6 Embodied Carbon Considerations

There is always a concern that enlarging a conduit will increase the life cycle carbon footprint of a system due to the additional embodied carbon. This can be examined by considering the carbon emissions due to the operational energy (from the generation of electricity) in addition to those of the embodied energy of manufacture and installation. The final model depends on the location of the installation, the carbon intensity of the electricity, the actual materials used, and the distance that they have traveled. As an example, the simulation that created the graph in Figure 5.15a can only be taken as indicative of a particular small pipework system; however, the technique is equally appropriate for all system sizes, whether ducted air or piped water. In this case it shows a swiftly diminishing benefit as the pipe size is increased beyond the standard 32 m pipe size. Realistically there would also be a need to analyze the comparative costs of the systems.

Simply using lower pressure drop components and designs can provide remarkable benefits. A CIBSE publication [16] covers this area in greater detail and shows that an office using good practices in design and operation can practically halve the fan and pump energy use compared to a traditional design. For example, Figure

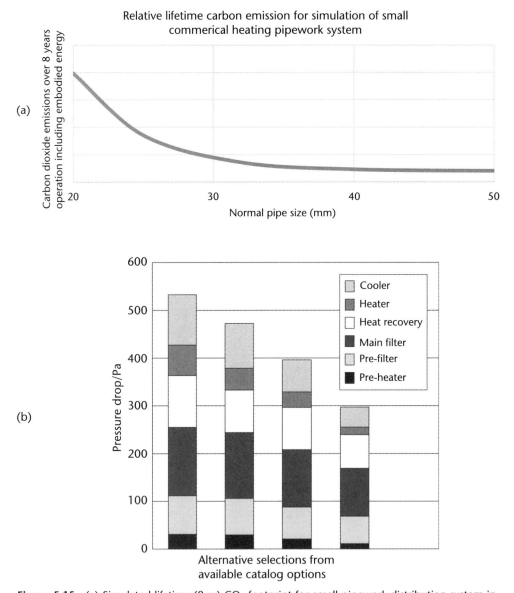

Figure 5.15 (a) Simulated lifetime (8-yr) CO_2 footprint for small pipework distribution system including the emissions due to both embodied and operational energy. (b) Reducing air handling pressure drop through careful component selection.

5.15b (taken from [16]) shows how the pressure drop of the air handling unit may be reduced through thoughtful selection.

5.5.6.1   Ten Key Do's and Don'ts in Pipework Design to Minimize Pump Power Requirements (After Lee Eng Lock and Rocky Mountain Institute [18, 19]).

1. Minimize fluid velocity by oversizing pipes to minimize friction and hence pressure loss (see Section 5.5.3 for further details).
2. Keep pipework as short and straight as possible—the greater the pipe length, the greater the friction.
3. Every unnecessary bend or fitting increases pressure loss and hence pump power requirement—eliminate them where you can.
4. Avoid right-angle bends. Use two 45 deg bends or, better still, one 45 deg bend with the pipe running diagonally to reduce its length.
5. If 90-deg bends are unavoidable, use swept elbows and use Y-junctions rather than T-junctions.
6. Use variable-speed drives on pump motors to regulate fluid flow, rather than energy-wasting valves and throttles.
7. Design the system to be hydraulically balanced, rather than relying on wasteful balancing valves.
8. Use forensic attention to detail to eliminate unnecessary fittings—each one wastes energy.
9. Pay particular attention to reducing fluid turbulence at the pump inlet and outlet by using straight transition sections to smoothly reduce (or enlarge) the pipe diameter.
10. Mount pumps on concrete plinths so they are directly in-line with the heat exchanger outlet/inlet. This will reduce fittings, bends, and turbulence at the pump inlet. A plinth is a much cheaper and more efficient option than using multiple bends and fittings (see Figures 5.16a and 5.16b).

Case Study: How Modifying Typical Ductwork Layout and Specification Can Reduce Fan Power Requirement (and Operational Cost) by Over 80%

Color Plates 17 and 18 and Figures 5.17a and 5.17b show two design options for a simple toilet mechanical ventilation system. System A is based on a typical conventional design. This system will require a continuous fan electrical power input to function of 365 W (costing about $320/year if operating 24 hours per day, at 10 c/kWh). *Note:* System A is based on typical building services design criteria and normal rules of thumb.

System B demonstrates how reductions in fan power can be achieved by making the following straightforward changes to the design and component specification:

Step 1.   The system delivers the same air flow rate as system A, but the ductwork route has been simplified, duct diameters have been increased by 40% to 50%, and low loss fittings/duct transition sections incorporated. These

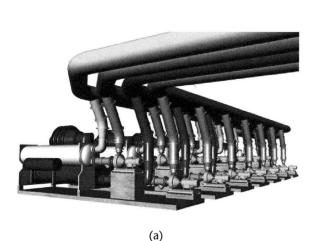

(a)   (b)

Figure 5.16 (a) Chillers and pumps configured to minimize pumping power requirement and enhance overall kW/ton performance. (*Source:* Lee Eng Lock. Reproduced with permission.) (b) Pump mounted on concrete plinth to reduce number of fittings and hence pressure loss. Note the use of smooth Y transitions and 45 deg bends to reduce pressure loss. (*Photo:* David Strong.)

simple changes reduce the fan power requirement by 45% at a lower CAPEX.

Step 2. This step incorporates step 1 but in addition the high-pressure-loss standard panel filter is replaced with a low-loss bag filter, resulting in the fan power being nearly 60% lower than system A.

Step 3. This step incorporates steps 1 and 2 and adds the specification of an air handling unit (AHU) that is optimized for operating at the lower system pressure loss, with a high-efficiency fan and motor combination. This change reduces the fan power by almost 75% over system A—nearly a Factor 4 savings!

Step 4. This step demonstrates how the incorporation of demand-controlled ventilation (DCV) can provide further savings. Many mechanical ventilation systems operate at their design air flow rate 24 hours per day. A simple CO_2 sensor monitors air quality and the DCV regulates the fan speed to reduce/increase the volume flow rate based on the CO_2 level. (Alternatively, a simple low-cost time switch could be used to reduce the flow rate at times of low occupancy.) Step 4 shows that when operating at 50% of the design flow rate (including steps 1 to 3), the fan power can be reduced by 85%, a Factor 6 savings over the base case of system A. If the system delivers 50% of the design flow rate for 12 hours per day and the design flow rate for 12 hour per day, the annual fan operational energy cost will be reduced from $365/yr to $67/yr, a reduction of 80%. Further refinement and system changes (e.g., the incorporation of a low loss silencer, low loss diffusers etc.) could enable Factor 10 savings to be achieved.

The results from these simple changes are remarkable and demonstrate the importance of forensic attention to detail in ductwork design and component specification. The results are summarized in Table 5.3.

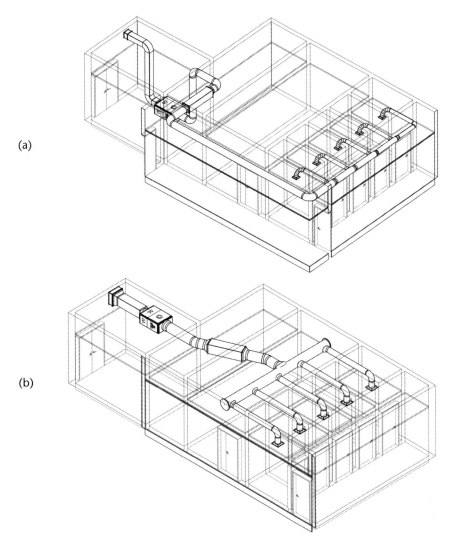

(a)

(b)

Figure 5.17   (a) System A has a typical/conventional ductwork specification. (b) System B has a low-loss, efficient ductwork specification. (*Source:* Drawings and analysis courtesy of e3 Consulting Engineers, http://www.e3ce.com.)

Table 5.3   Ductwork Design Changes and Impact on Fan Power Requirement

Step	Design Specification Change	Flow Rate (L/s)	System Pressure Drop (Pa)	Pressure Drop % Reduction from System A	Fan Power (W)	% Reduction in Fan Power
0	System A (base case)	250	272.5	—	365	—
1	System B (improved duct-work design)	250	113.1	58.50%	200	45%
2	Step 1 + lower filter pressure loss	250	88.1	67.67%	150	59%
3	Step 1 + step 2 + improved fan and motor efficiency	250	88.1	67.67%	95	74%
4	Step 1 + step 2 + step 3 + demand-controlled ventilation @ 50% flow rate	125	39.5	85.50%	60	84%

Analysis undertaken by e3 Consulting Engineers. Reproduced with permission.

References

[1]   Nicol, F., M. Humphreys, and S. Roaf, *Adaptive Thermal Comfort: Principles and Practice*, 2012, London: Routledge, http://www.worldcat.org/title/adaptive-thermal-comfort-principles-and-practice/oclc/730403966 (July 2016).

[2]   Hartman Company, *Low Power Pumping,* http://www.hartmanco.com/innovate/lowpwr/1tech.htm (August 2016).

[3]   Givler, T., *Whole Building Design Guide—Lighting Design,* 2013, https://www.wbdg.org/design/dd_lightingdsgn.php (August 2016).

[4]   BCA Green Mark, *FAQs on Instrumentation for Permanent Measurement and Verification for Water-Cooled Chilled Water Plan System,* https://www.bca.gov.sg/greenmark/others/fqamv.pdf (August 2016).

[5]   Singapore Standards eShop, *Code of Practice for Long-Term Measurement of Central Chilled Water System Energy Efficiency,* 2013, https://www.singaporestandardseshop.sg/Product/Product.aspx?id=1a9a2a41-5f9d-4e0b-a17f-f8b7810d272a (August 2016).

[6]   Sunbelt Potential of Photovoltaics, Third Edition, March European Photovoltaic Industry Association. http://www.mesia.com/up-content/uploads/2012/08/EPIA-Unlocking-the_sunbelt_potential-of-PU.pdf

[7]   Aldrich, R., *Whole Building Design Guide—Alternative Energy,* https://www.wbdg.org/resources/alternativeenergy.php (July 2016).

[8]   Bolin, R., *Whole Building Design Guide—Sustainability of the Building Envelope,* https://www.wbdg.org/resources/env_sustainability.php (July 2016).

[9]   Lemieux, D. J., and P. E. Totten, *The Importance of Building Envelope Commissioning for Sustainable Structures,* 2004, http://www.techstreet.com/standards/the-importance-of-building-envelope-commissioning-for-sustainable-structures?product_id=1724689.

[10] *Whole Building Design Guide—Building Envelope,* http://wbdg.org/design/envelope.php (July 2016)

[11] Regnier, C., *Guide to Setting Thermal Comfort Criteria and Minimizing Energy Use in Delivering Thermal Comfort,* 2012, Lawrence Berkley Laboratory, http://eetd.lbl.gov/sites/all/files/lbnl-6131e.pdf (July 2016).

[12] BSRIA, *BMS Maintenance Guide—2003,* BG4/2003.

[13] de Almeida, A. T., et al., "Energy-Efficient Motor Systems in the Industrial and in the Services Sectors in the European Union: Characterization, Potentials, Barriers and Policies," *Energy,* Vol. 28, 2003, pp. 673–690.

[14] Chartered Institution of Building Services Engineers (CIBSE), *Flow of Fluids in Pipes and Ducts,* CIBSE Guide C4, accompanying spreadsheet, 2007.

[15] Chartered Institution of Building Services Engineers (CIBSE), *Flow of Fluids in Pipes and Ducts,* CIBSE Guide C4, Table 4.11, 2001.

[16] Chartered Institution of Building Services Engineers (CIBSE), *Flow of Fluids in Pipes and Ducts,* CIBSE Guide C4, Section 4.9.2, 2001.

[17] Chartered Institution of Building Services Engineers (CIBSE), *Improve Life Cycle Performance of Mechanical Ventilation Systems,* CIBSE TM30, 2003.

[18] Lock, L. E., *Negawatts for Buildings: Observations from 25 years,* January 2009, Lawrence Berkeley National Laboratory, EETD Distinguished Lecture, http://eetd.lbl.gov/dls/pdf/dls-lock-01-20-09.pdf (August 2016).

[19] Chan-Lizardo, K., D. Lindsey, and A. Pradhan, *Big Pipes, Small Pumps: Interface, Inc. Factor Ten Engineering Case Study,* February 2011, Rocky Mountain Institute, http://www.rmi.org/Knowledge-Center/Library/2011-04_BigPipesSmallPumps (August 2016).

CHAPTER 6

Modeling and Simulation as a Design Tool

All the really important mistakes are made on the first day.
—Old design adage

Every architect and building engineer has access on their desktop to a powerful array of software tools that allow design choices and options to be assessed and evaluated quickly and effectively. Dynamic modeling can be used to visually demonstrate in real time the direct impacts of design decisions on the design (and on CAPEX and OPEX) of servicing systems, providing a valuable tool during the design process for all stakeholders, including the client, and facilitating integrated working practices. The following sections explore how computer modeling and simulation can be used to avoid the "really important mistakes" and deliver a paradigm shift in the energy performance, comfort, and productivity of the next generation of sustainable buildings.

6.1 How Modeling Can Help Design Better Buildings

Andrew Corney, PE, M.CIBSE, M.ASHRAE, Product Director, Sefaira, http://sefaira.com

Building a computer simulation for any aspect of a building is an exercise that takes time. For this reason, whenever you attempt a simulation, it is important to have a clear idea of what you are trying to achieve from the exercise before you start.

There are three broadly recognized reasons for doing simulation on buildings. Any exercise is likely to fall into one of these categories:

1. Comparing alternate strategies with the goal of being better informed when choosing among design options;
2. Demonstrating compliance with a code or standard relating to building performance (some codes just want you to show what you've done, but most are looking for more detailed information); or
3. Predicting the future—doing analysis to obtain precise information about how the building will work. These types of studies are difficult and usually take up a lot of time.

Comparing alternatives is the best way to use modeling to help design better buildings. Even if you are comparing on the basis of some predictive metric like energy cost or performance against a code, keep in mind that during the early stages of design it is *relative* performance that you should be using to help you make a decision.

Work with the team to establish the options to be considered and the basis of how they should be compared before analysis starts (even if you are the person doing the analysis). Analysis often stimulates new ideas but this should not be depended on to drive the creation of options. It is not a bad idea to think about what you expect the answer to be and how much you or the client values the metrics being tested before you see the results as well.

Various types of studies can be done during the design phases of a project. We discuss a few in the following sections and how they can help inform good decisions.

6.2   Determining Peak Loads

Peak loads are an extremely important concept for any building project with heating or cooling. The peak load tells you how much heat needs to be added or removed from a space in a design condition to maintain the desired temperature setpoint (comfort condition) in the space.

Specifically, the *peak cooling load* is how much heat needs to be removed from each space to keep it at a maximum temperature when the building is full of people and equipment on a design day (almost always the hottest day of the year). The *peak heating load* is how much heat needs to be added to each space to keep it at a minimum temperature when there is nobody in the building on a design day (almost always the coldest day of the year).

6.2.1   How Are Peak Loads Useful?

By telling you how much heat needs to be added or removed in design conditions, peak loads are great proxies for two key aspects of any heating or cooling system:

1.   Whether certain types of heating and cooling design solutions are likely to be feasible for the project (many low-energy systems have limits in terms of how much heat they can add or remove), and
2.   The capacity requirements of the system in each zone (which, of course, translates to capital cost and space)

6.2.2   Applying the Peak Load Values in Practice

Peak loads are generally most useful when considered as area-weighted values. In other words, what is the peak cooling or heating load in watts per square meter (or foot) of floor area? By considering the peak load in W/m^2, it is then possible to test how effective different strategies will be at removing or adding heat and, ultimately, the relative size of the systems that need to be installed. Table 6.1 provides an ex-

Table 6.1   Cooling and Heating Loads—Peak Thresholds

Cooling Load Objective Example	Threshold Example
Keep suspended ceiling depth below 500 mm	130 W/m^2
Enable passive chilled beams	90W/m^2
Use higher efficiency chilled water (e.g., via higher temperature)	70 W/m^2
Enable natural ventilation only	50 W/m^2
Enable displacement ventilation	30 W/m^2 solar load
Heating Load Objective Example	
Enable heated floor	50 W/m^2
Enable heating to be done electrically without imposing excessive energy cost	25 W/m^2

ample of how you would use the area-weighted peak cooling load to see if a heating and cooling design is likely to be viable.

To be calculated properly, peak loads should also be considered in the context of orientation-specific perimeter and core (or center) zones. Figure 6.1 provides an example of a zone map that shows the peak load for each zone. It is generated by one analysis tool from Sefaira Systems [1]. In this example the peak loads can be seen relative to each of the zones in the floor plate. This enables you to easily see which parts of the building's façade need modification if some of the zones are not meeting your requirements. A response curve shows how increasing the horizontal shading ratio in different steps reduces the worst zone peak cooling load.

Software should also be able to tell you what the main contributors to the peak loads are. In Figure 6.1 you can see that the northwest façade has a high solar load. Immediately you can begin to work on solutions that reduce the peak cooling load on that façade in order to support the sort of system you would like to incorporate.

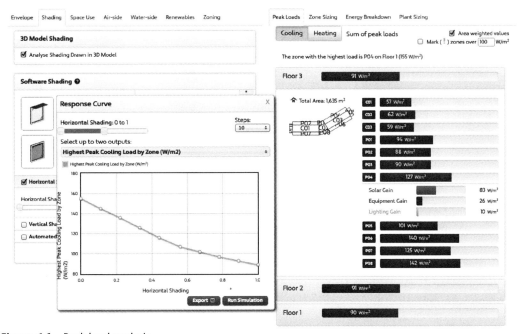

Figure 6.1   Peak load analysis.

Peak cooling loads do not just contribute to whether or not a system is viable—they directly add to the cost of all components supporting whatever heating and cooling system you choose. If you do not have time to look at HVAC sizing and have a narrow building, they can be a reasonable proxy for system size.

The effort required to reduce peak load is not always linear. For example, it might be much easier to reduce the peak load from 120 to 100 W/m² than from 60 to 40 W/m². Make sure you know what your internal loads are because they will drive a peak cooling load no matter what you do.

Note that if you are distributing hot and cold water or air centrally as part of the heating and cooling design, then your system will have what are known as *coincidental peaks* rather than independent peaks summed together. It is good to know this and use the software to determine the coincident peaks rather than the sum of peaks when looking at the overall impact on load of design alternatives.

6.3 HVAC Sizing: Doing Better Than Rules of Thumb

The HVAC system will typically represent 5% to 25% of the total cost of a project and take up most of the area set aside for building services equipment. HVAC sizing is the calculation of how big that equipment needs to be to do its job of heating and cooling the building.

6.3.1 Why Is HVAC Sizing Useful?

The concept and schematic design stages are the stages at which the biggest changes are made to a façade's design. Architects often have to consider how much glass to have in a building, whether any shading will be included, and perhaps the materiality of the building form. Often the shape and form of the building are also being changed and considered.

Many HVAC engineers during this design process will stick to conservative rules of thumb to size the HVAC systems in a building. Many of these rules of thumb are based on industry standards or experience in practice, but they do not serve to inform whether some design solutions are good or not. It is virtually impossible to compare the impact that different envelope or façade options will have on the size of the HVAC system without doing a model.

6.3.2 Studying HVAC Sizing in Practice

Fortunately, an HVAC model does not need to be complicated to get good direction on the impact of design changes. A fairly simple box model with perimeter-core zoning will provide excellent feedback on the impact of window ratios and properties, shading, and building form options.

The model shown in Figure 6.2 is an example from Sefaira Systems. The three-story building is a long, thin bar with a predominantly south- and north-facing aspect. For this type of exercise, the glazing and shading could be added in the software, so the only detail that needs to be drawn into the 3D SketchUp model is the floor plate shape, extruded up to the height of the ceiling for each floor.

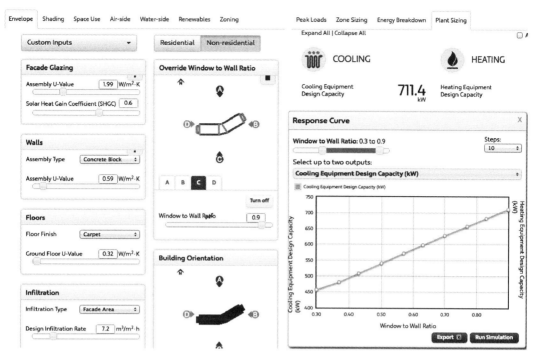

Figure 6.2   Window-to-wall ratio analysis.

Ultimately, if an architect is looking for a narrative to support building features such as shading, then HVAC size reduction could drive a more compelling story than energy savings. Similarly, if the architect is looking to use extensive amounts of glazing, then it might be worth seeing what the cost is in terms of equipment size and ultimately cost, location, space requirements, and layout of plantrooms.

This first example (see Figure 6.2) shows the impact of a south façade window-to-wall ratio that varies from 0.3 to 0.9 on a building in London using a Sefaira Systems model. The cooling system could be reduced by over 40% depending on glazing proportion.

The second analysis (see Figure 6.3) shows the impact on the north façade of shading applied to a variable air volume (VAV) system in Sydney using the Sefaira Systems model. The user is able to optimize the shading depth to find a point of diminishing returns in reducing the size of the air systems.

Note that when looking at large-scale HVAC sizing, it is good to know what will affect space the most. Generally air distribution has the biggest relative impact on space, then cooling, then heating. This means that options that reduce air volumes or cooling by decent amounts will probably have the biggest impact on cost and floor area [2].

6.4   Natural Ventilation Design with Analysis

Many buildings, especially in milder climates such as Europe, southeast Australia, and the west coast of North America, aspire to employ natural ventilation in lieu

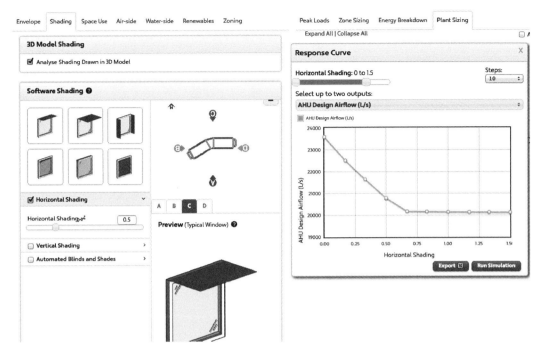

Figure 6.3   Impact of shading on air handling units (AHU) design air flow rate. (*Source:* Sefaira, Trimble.)

of full air conditioning. This is especially true for buildings such as schools and residential apartments and houses.

Contrary to what some may believe, thermal modeling can be used to tremendous effect in designing these sorts of projects. However, the process of using modeling to design these sorts of buildings is counterintuitive to engineers who are used to designing conditioned buildings, because the analysis process is, by definition, more iterative (see Figure 6.4a and b).

Two types of software are used for designing natural ventilation. The first is bulk air flow analysis. Examples include: EnergyPlus, TAS, and IES. This is an hourly simulation that divides the building up into bulky elements (i.e., zones) that are usually just rooms or typical thermal zones. It outputs comfort by the hour and is the most common method for designing natural ventilation.

The second type is computational fluid dynamics (CFD) software. This is a simulation of a single time step that simulates much smaller elements (say, the size of a square inch). CFD provides a graphic interpretation of performance for a design condition or series of design conditions.

The first of these types of software is much more accessible to most practitioners and although it is often useful to support it with the second type, bulk air flow analyses should be considered primarily. Replacing cooling with natural ventilation is the most commonly studied workflow. (PassivHaus projects are now trying to eliminate heating as well, but even then it is generally more straightforward.)

6.4.1   Getting to a Natural Ventilation Design That Works

As shown in the workflow diagram of Figure 6.4b, natural ventilation is an iterative design process. To be able to design a natural ventilation system, the ideal

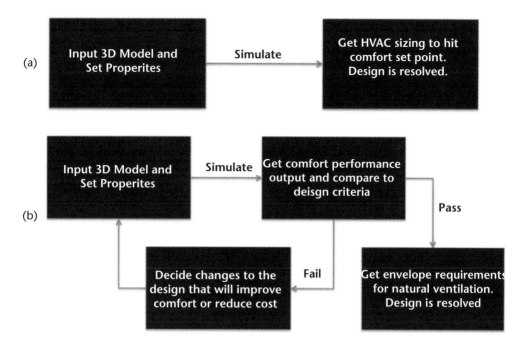

Figure 6.4   Workflow for using software to design (a) mechanically cooled buildings—linear design process and (b) naturally ventilated building—iterative design process.

starting point is to know the design criteria for comfort. These could be expressed in many ways. Table 6.2 lists some common methods and standards for determining whether a design "passes."

Once you have a design target, it is usually a good idea to see how your current design is working and then make decisions about specific zones and whether added design features are needed. You will need a thermal model with each room zoned separately. The best types of projects to start with when doing natural ventilation are single-sided apartments, classrooms, and cellular offices, which are uncomplicated to study.

Table 6.2   Common Decisions That Are Usually Made with an Energy Model

Common Design Decision Enhanced Through Energy Analysis	When the Decision Is Typically Made
Selection of building form	Concept design
HVAC system selection	Schematic design
Window ratio and shading design	Schematic design
Space plan layout	Schematic design
HVAC energy conservation measures	Detailed design
Renewable system options	Detailed design
Glazing, insulation, and assembly requirements	Detailed design
Lighting design	Detailed design
HVAC controls	Detailed design / construction documents
Tenant or owner equipment	Construction documents

6.4.2 Testing the Natural Ventilation Opening Size Requirements for Windows

The first step is to work out the free area opening size of the windows that will be openable in the space. The free area is the unimpeded area through which air can flow. It varies based on the window type and whether there are obstructions, such as insect screens. Most software will let you vary the free area of the opening as a proportion of the floor area. A good initial study is then to study steps in free area from 1% to 8% of the floor area and plot the comfort target against each step. Generally, you should expect to see a point of diminishing return or a point where the opening beats the design target. That's an ideal opening requirement for your window free area.

6.5 Adding Shading and Improving Glazing and Thermal Mass

Generally speaking, if you have a well-designed façade with good solar control, you should expect to see a fairly clear point of diminishing return on window free area. However, if too much solar gain is getting into the space or if the space is not able to retain coolth during the day, you are more likely to see a straighter line on the free area curve and you may even see that your space is failing to meet the design target.

In this instance, it is probably a good idea to look at adding shading or thermal mass. Both can be investigated using a similar method to free area percentage as follows:

- *Shading:* Consider gradual increases in overhang depth and/or fin depth or angle as a percentage of window height and plot them against the design target. You should expect to see a point of diminishing return for an effective shading design.
- *Thermal comfort:* Increase the thickness of the wall, floor, and ceiling materials in your model that have good thermal mass properties. Make sure you add anything you would expect to have in real life that would diminish the effect of thermal mass, such as carpet or plasterboard. In climates where mass is effective, you should expect to see improvement to a point, then a diminishing return.

These techniques with bulk air flow analysis can help quickly iterate toward a design solution—one that meets the comfort benchmark set for the project (see Figure 6.5). In most cases it will need to be iterative, either adding features to enable the project to achieve comfort levels, or optimizing features to reduce the design cost of the natural ventilation system (see Figure 6.6).

6.6 Energy Analysis

Substantial books have been written on the singular topic of energy analysis in buildings—it is an extensive topic. However, if you are going to dive into the

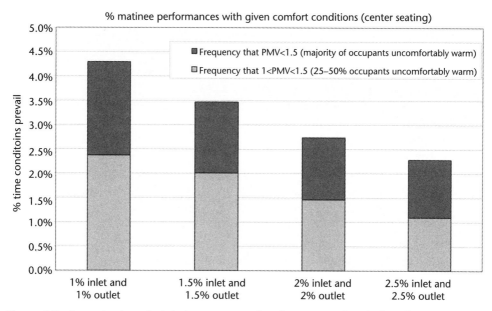

Figure 6.5   Example of comfort design target predicted mean vote (PMV) plotted against free area (*Source:* WSP | Parsons Brinkerhoff.)

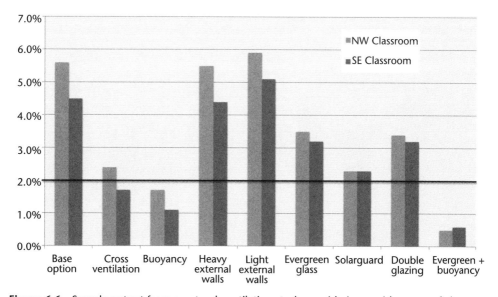

Figure 6.6   Sample output from a natural ventilation study considering a wide range of classroom options, benchmarked against the percentage of time the zone exceeds the comfort criteria. (*Source:* WSP | Parsons Brinkerhoff.)

world of using energy analysis to help inform your design, you should know some fundamentals that will help prevent you from wasting your time.

6.6.1   Energy Analysis: Know Your Task

The most important objective with energy analysis is to know what you are trying to achieve through the exercise. This may sound obvious, but many energy models are built without knowing the question they seek to answer.

Generally speaking, analysis that is used as a design tool should be tailored to answer the questions at the current stage of design and recognize the limitations of the information available. For example, it is acceptable to want to compare options at the schematic design stage against an energy standard such as ASHRAE 90.1 as long as you are realistic about all of the information that is not yet available. If you have started to worry about the minutiae of things like internal condition schedules at the schematic design stage, rather than a model that is the minimum needed to compare A versus B, then you are probably on the wrong track.

It is not uncommon to build a model to solve just one of the decisions shown in Table 6.2 although ideally you will be able to use the model to test multiple issues during a single project phase.

User operating schedules and internal loads for energy models are important, but are not a design decision until later in the design. Until the point is reached of knowing exactly what the tenant operation and loads are likely to be, design decisions can be made with good assumptions based on accepted codes and standards. These items are typically those that are likely to have the biggest impact on energy. Generally speaking, you will want to have a feel for sensible inputs for the subsequent phase while you are making a decision about the current phase. For example, if you are making a decision about building form, your model should have some reasonable assumptions built in that relate to window ratio, HVAC system, and space use (see Figure 6.7).

6.6.2   Energy Analysis: Workflow

Two common workflows are employed when using energy analysis to make design decisions:

1. Cost/benefit analysis, where energy analysis is used to generate an annual operating cost for two or more options being compared, which can then be considered against differences in capital cost (see Figure 6.8).
2. Steps to an energy target, where energy analysis is used to show progress toward an energy goal, such as net-zero energy or a reduction against a code target. This process is useful in showing the value of different steps, although it needs to be considered carefully because the sequence of strategies can overvalue some strategies against others.

6.6.3   Renewable Energy Generation

Modeling and simulation tools can also be used early in the design process to quickly and accurately assess the renewable energy generation potential offered by the incorporation of PV panels. The software can also determine the area and optimum location of PV to offset a building's energy demand and/or carbon emissions (see Figure 6.9). Sefaira's EnergyPlus web application enables users to optimize the size of a solar PV array by running different area sizes in parallel and then plotting the subsequent net energy use of the project against the array size.

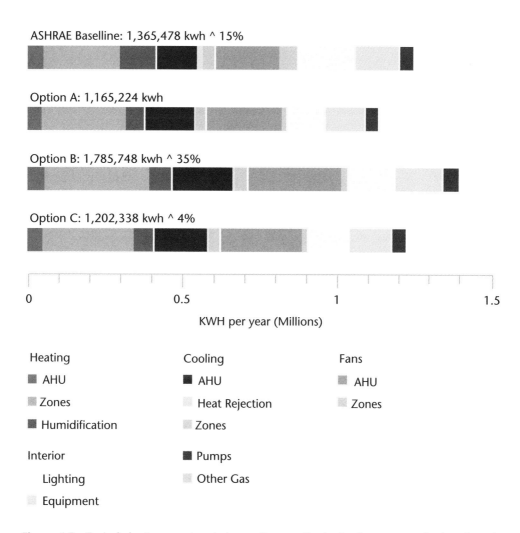

Figure 6.7   Typical chart comparing design options on the basis of energy use, broken down by type to help identify where the major uses are. (*Source:* Sefaira Systems.)

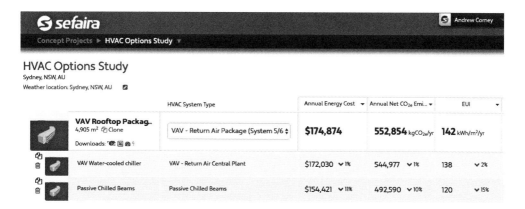

Figure 6.8   An example output generated in Sefaira to quickly compare annual running costs for three systems.

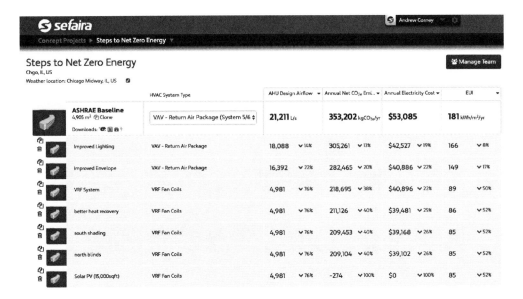

Figure 6.9 Steps to net-zero energy. (*Source:* Sefaira, Trimble.)

6.7 Daylight Analysis: How to Interpret the Pretty Pictures

Of all the design analysis that engineers and architects would like to be able to do, daylight analysis is probably at the top of the list. The graphics are almost always alluring and make great content for reports and presentations. However, it is precisely the alluring nature of the imagery that can be generated that distracts designers from making the most of daylight analysis.

6.7.1 Daylight Analysis: What Is the Goal of the Design Exercise?

If you are designing a building, daylight design really comes down to the optimization of two elements: (1) vertical glazing (windows, effectively) and (2) roof lights. In both instances the goal is usually to maximize the amount of daylight provided while minimizing the nasty side effects of lots of glass: glare, excessive heat gain, and discomfort.

6.7.2 Daylight Analysis: Annual Versus Instant Analysis

Daylight analysis was historically made very complicated by the time taken to set up and run simulations and the fact that each simulation only represented a single moment in time. Historically, metrics like daylight factor were used to get around this.

6.7.2.1 Daylight Factor

The daylight factor is the fraction of horizontal illuminance from the sky that lands on a surface. When calculating the daylight factor, an overcast sky is used, usually one that is a representative sky, typically 10,000 lux, which is somewhere around the 85th percentile in terms of brightness during working hours for most locations. This means that a daylight factor of 2% would result in 200 lux on a surface for 85% of the time—technically a good outcome. It is important to note that daylight factor does not take into account the actual building location or façade orientation. Figure 6.10 shows a daylight factor simulation.

6.7.2.2   Annual Daylight Simulations

The general consensus now is that daylight factor is a poor means of measuring daylight because it encourages excessive use of glazing and does not account for any of the visual drawbacks of having too much glass (let alone the thermal impacts). Fortunately, annual simulations can be done using software engines such as Daysim. These simulations analyze a point array hourly and then plot a representative contour of the performance of annual metrics on the planes (see Table 6.3 for examples of daylight simulation metrics).

These values provide the designer with a good feel for how often the daylight conditions would be bright enough to provide a minimum threshold of light on a surface. Theoretically this can then be translated into energy savings; whenever the minimum threshold of daylight is met on a surface, electric lights could be switched off (see Color Plate 19).

By averaging the annual metric across a zone, say, design alternatives such as the location and properties of glazing can be assessed in terms of how often good light conditions would be achieved, on average, in the zone.

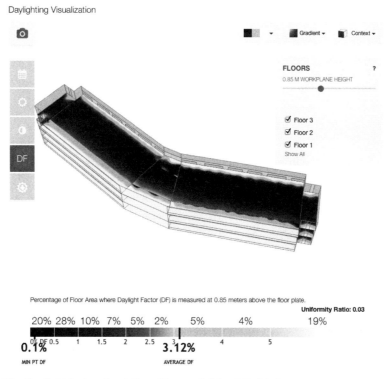

Figure 6.10   Daylight factor simulation. (*Source:* Sefaira, Trimble.)

Table 6.3 Annual Simulation Daylight Metrics

Daylight Metric Name	Threshold Input	Measured at	Describes
Spatial daylight autonomy (sDA)	Minimum level of light required annually (e.g., 300 lux)	A point	Percentage of hours that the measurement point meets a daylight threshold
Annual sunlight exposure (ASE)	Level of daylight considered too high for acceptable use	A point	Number of hours that the threshold can be exceed (often it is pass or fail based on an allowable number of hours)
Lux-hours	Maximum number allowable	A point	The sum of illuminance intensity at each hour step; used to test things like damage to artwork
Useful daylight illuminance (UDI)	Maximum and minimum daylight thresholds; frequency limits	A point	Whether the point exceeds the minimum daylight threshold (sDA) without exceeding the maximum daylight allowance (ASE)

6.7.2.3   Controlling or Collecting Direct Sun

With some exceptions, annual daylight calculations generally do not quantify whether the space will have good visual comfort (usually defined in working environments as limiting glare and direct sun; often defined for residential environments as providing direct sun).

There are lots of ways glare and direct sun can be calculated. However, most fall under three categories:

- Excessive daylight measured on a floor plane similar to annual daylight thresholds;

- Glare as experienced from a viewpoint, represented either as a point in time or over a seasonal or annual time period; or

- Direct sun exposure in a plan view measured as an average frequency of direct sun during a seasonal or annual time period

6.7.2.4   Over-Lit Hours (or Excessive Daylight)

The idea of over-lit hours is to set a maximum illuminance threshold of illumination on a surface and count any hour when that illuminance is exceeded as over-lit (and therefore not properly daylit). The concept has some merit because the threshold can be set to count only time steps where someone might expect there to be direct sun or some kind of glare condition. To this end, it is an improvement on daylight factor or spatial daylight autonomy because it encourages design to control excessive daylight while also providing enough to cross a minimum threshold. The U.S. Green Building Council's LEED standard uses this calculation method. Figure 6.11 provides an example of a daylight analysis showing occurrences of over-lighting and under-lighting.

Incorporating over-lit hours into daylight calculations helps to prevent making excessively large windows and can also be used to help design shading that controls too much light without reducing minimum daylight. Testing shading options for

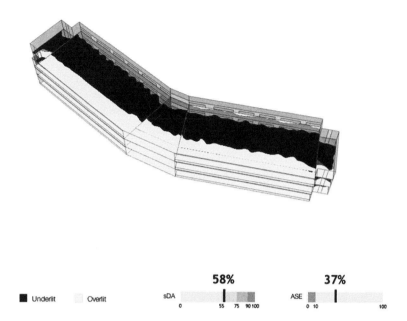

Figure 6.11 An example of daylight analysis showing over-lit and under-lit hours. (*Source:* Sefaira, Trimble.)

the total percentage of the floor area that is neither over-lit nor under-lit is a good way to quickly get design guidance on the usefulness of different shading strategies.

Although this method is an improvement on simpler minimum lighting thresholds, it has drawbacks because glare is caused predominantly by contrast perceived by the viewer rather than by brightness on a large surface such as a floor plate. Therefore, although this standard can help guide a daylight design measured primarily by minimum light levels on a surface, it does not help identify where the design may be struggling with visual comfort issues.

6.8 Glare Analysis

The main drawback with an over-lit hours approach is that glare caused by contrast in the view is not effectively captured. This kind of glare is caused when some objects in the field of view are substantially brighter than others. Direct sun is the most common example, but another common cause might be sun reflected off a nearby light-colored building. Over-lit hours do not capture these kinds of events, which tend to be the worst causes of glare.

Although there are no strong standards around using analysis to measure glare, fairly good tools are available for making comparable studies. Quite a few metrics exist, most of which try to quantify the impact of the relative brightness of objects within the field of view. Daylight glare probability is probably one of the more commonly adopted methods.

Glare calculations are determined based on a point in space combined with a view direction and a moment in time. Most seek to attribute a probability of glare or glare score within different angles of the field of view. This has two challenges:

- Determining the correct point in space plus view direction plus time of day to study glare is an artform. Most studies could only cope with a limited number of data points and so the viewpoints need to be selected for risk of glare *and* for their suitability to test design options.

- The data for each viewpoint analysis is substantial and without a pass/fail benchmark. To this end, options can only be compared, not signed off.

6.8.1   A Simple Methodology for Using Glare Calculations

Probably the most common and useful application for a glare calculation is to try out different blind or shade cloth materials. Here is a step-by-step guide to using glare to compare blind materials:

Step 1. Conduct a direct sun analysis of the building floor plate to identify where the areas are that often get direct sun.

Step 2. Look at surrounding buildings for each orientation (if they exist) and consider which building is likely to be the worst source of glare. (*Hint:* Buildings to the north that reflect sunlight from the south [Northern Hemisphere] are usually the worst.)

Step 3. Set up two viewpoints (with view angle and time of day) when the viewer is going to be looking into the sun with an azimuth of ideally around 45 deg.

Step 4. Set up two viewpoints when the viewer is looking at the offending reflecting building.

Step 5. Run glare calculations from each viewpoint + angle + time of day with all of the blind options that you would like to consider.

Step 6. Use the relative glare performance of the different options in the view condition to make a decision about the relative merits of the blind options.

Figure 6.12 provides examples of glare simulations.

6.8.2   Direct Sun

In many applications a good substitute for glare analysis is direct sun analysis. This is because a lot of the worst glare conditions are the cause of direct sun, so if you know how much direct sun exists in a space, you can often get a feel for whether there is likely to be any glare.

There are many ways to look at direct sun. Two ways that are pretty easy to do and that can provide really good design guidance are (1) stereographic (sun path) diagrams and (2) average direct sun exposure over a season.

6.9   Sun Path Diagrams

Imagine your view as a hemisphere. Now imagine you are lying under a tree looking straight up into the sky. Some parts of the sky will be obscured, some you will see. The sun tracks a path across your view of the sky and at certain times it will

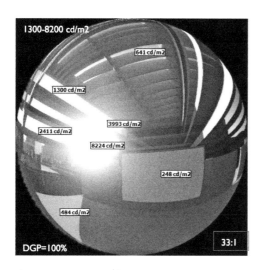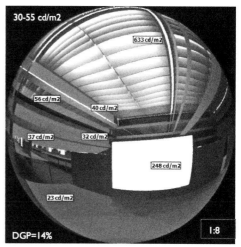

Figure 6.12 Example of two glare simulations in Radiance, without blinds (left) and with blinds (right). (*Source:* WSP | Parson's Brinkerhoff.)

probably shine in your face. A sun path diagram shows this view with the sun path overlaid so you can see when that would happen.

In other words, a sun path diagram is essentially a way to show the time of direct sun exposure across an entire year for a single point in space. Because the diagram is able to not only show the times of day but also the angle and orientation of the sun's position at the time direct sun, it is an extremely useful design tool. This means you can see if direct sun:

- Happens at a time of day that is critical,
- Happens for a continuous period or not, and
- Happens in summer or winter.

Before the advent of 3D modeling, sun path diagrams were often used by architects to assist in the design of shading devices. Now that they can be developed in 3D, however, it is generally faster and more intuitive to make changes to a design and see the impact on direct sun than to generate the diagram and work out the optimum design by hand.

Many 3D modeling software tools have a facility to generate a sun path diagram at a particular point in space. An example of a sun path diagram is shown in Figure 6.13.

6.9.1 How to Use Sun Path Diagrams as a Design Tool

Consider a situation in which there are two sun path diagrams: one with and one without shading. The shading in the 3D model can be adjusted until there is no direct sun showing on the diagram. To this end, different shading options can very quickly be tested for their ability to control direct sun (see Figure 6.14).

Sun path diagrams do have some limitations. The main issue is that each diagram represents only a single point in space. To consider a whole room and check

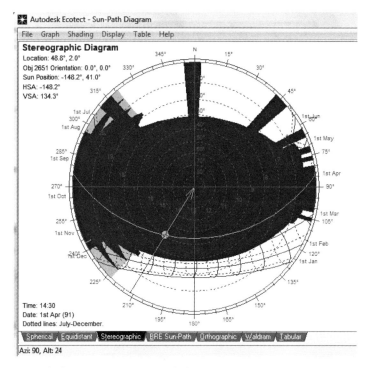

Figure 6.13 Sun path diagram. (*Source:* Autodesk Ecotect.)

the impact of shading on a room, it is usually necessary to look at multiple sun path diagrams at different positions.

6.9.2   Seasonal or Annual Average Direct Sun

Although sun path diagrams provide a lot of detail for a single point, another useful design tool is an assessment of the average number of hours of direct sun over a nominated period of time (say, a day, season, or year). Typically, a designer might be working toward goals like these:

- No direct sun during working hours at any time of the year,
- At least 3 hours of direct sun in midwinter, and
- Less than 2 hours of direct sun in summer and early autumn.

This sort of analysis is generated very quickly by software tools like Sefaira. This means that different options can be quickly assessed for the suitability of hitting a goal. An example is shown in Figure 6.15.

6.10   Computational Fluid Dynamics (CFD)

As described earlier, most analyses considering natural ventilation and comfort look at a bulk zone and take the average condition in that zone. While this is usually enough to effectively design a building, sometimes in the design process it is good

POINT 7

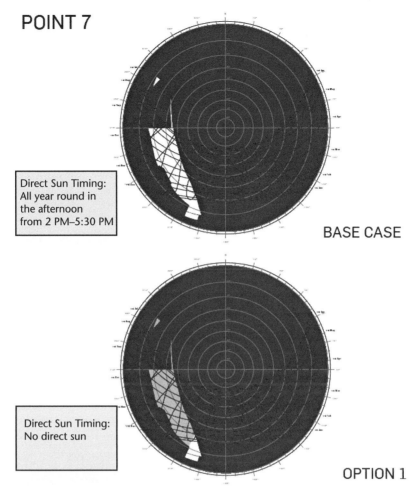

Direct Sun Timing:
All year round in
the afternoon
from 2 PM–5:30 PM

BASE CASE

Direct Sun Timing:
No direct sun

OPTION 1

Figure 6.14   Using sun path diagrams to evaluate shading impact. (*Source:* WSP | Parson's Brinker-hoff Built Ecology Analysis.)

to know in more detail how a space can be expected to feel in terms of comfort and air movement. For example, you might want to know whether a specific air diffuser model is likely to cause a draught. Or whether the distribution of air through an underfloor plenum is causing it to pick up too much heat from the floor below. CFD is the best tool for these circumstances.

CFD is one of the less accessible analysis methods and will usually involve some kind of building physics specialist to generate results. It is still good to know some of the limitations and outputs you can expect to see.

6.10.1   How CFD Works

CFD creates an array of finite elements and iterates toward a steady-state condition for each of those elements. In other words, it measures temperature, comfort, air movement, and so forth, at many points in space, enabling a contour map to be generated of variations in comfort across a space. Because it is an iterative calcula-tion, the right inputs and enough time needs to allowed for the calculation to reach

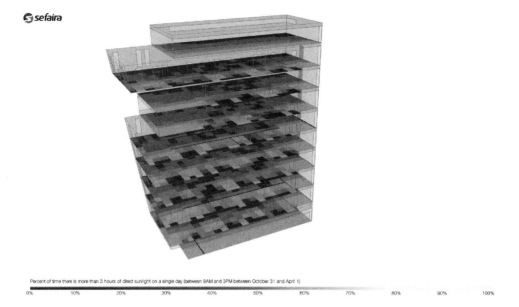

Figure 6.15   Seasonal/annual average direct sun. (*Source:* Sefaira, Trimble.)

a steady state. An example of the sort of output you could expect to get is shown in Color Plate 20. This image shows thermal decay through a raised floor and temperature distribution in the occupied zone.

6.10.2   CFD Limitations

It is easy to get caught up in thinking that a CFD model is a perfect prediction of what will happen, but many limitations remain regarding the validity of the results. For example, most software assumes heat loads and users are sedentary. This might be a reasonable assumption for an office but it is not a realistic assumption in a space like a shopping mall or train station.

It is also very difficult if not impossible to properly model a specific diffuser or detailed equipment characteristics in CFD. For this reason, it is more useful at testing relative spacing of diffusers and the risk of draught than at validating actual comfort.

References

[1]   Sefaira, http://sefaira.com (July 2016).

[2]   Corney, A., et al., "Performance Analysis Methods for Passive Downdraft HVAC Systems, in *Proc. Building Simulation 2011: 12th Conference of International Building Performance Simulation Association,* Sydney, 14–16 November, 2011, pp. 177–184, http://www.ibpsa.org/proceedings/bs2011/p_1179.pdf (July 2016).

CHAPTER 7

Water: Efficient Use, Sustainable Waste Water Treatment, and Management

For every drop of water you waste, you must know that somewhere on earth some-one is desperately looking for a drop of water!

—Mehmet Murat ldan

7.1 Design for Water-Efficient Buildings

Population growth, water scarcity, industrial and agricultural pollution, and over-development that reduces runoff have rendered water a precious resource. Moratoriums have been placed on areas where water and waste water services are limited. Focus has developed from a concentration on the embodied energy and carbon of products and materials into consideration of embodied water in manufacturing and system operations. Integrated water-efficiency solutions must follow a pattern similar to that previously discussed for energy systems: reduction of water demand, minimizing waste water generation by adopting efficient servicing strategies, and finally responsible exporting of the surplus generated from the site, including waste treatment.

Green building assessment schemes recognize these needs by including criteria for efficient water-consuming equipment, controls, monitoring, and servicing strategies. In some especially vulnerable areas, such as India and the Emirates, local iterations of rating schemes place as much emphasis on water credits as they do on energy credits. In addition, all LEED v4 projects must commit to sharing water usage data with USGBC for a 5-year period as part of its water efficiency prerequisite, *Building-Level Water Metering*, hence affording efficient water consumption the same focus as energy. Net-zero water consumption, as required by the Living Building Challenge certification, requires buildings to set demand limits based on availability of water from annual precipitation and reuse strategies.

An optimal integrative system will follow the natural water cycle as closely as possible, allowing it to pass through and service the building before returning to its natural state. For example, rainwater captured from a green roof (which slows down runoff, thereby maximizing harvesting potential) can be treated for use within handwashing basins; the gray water treated and recirculated for use in flushing toilets; and the black water finally sent to an on-site waste water treatment plant (WWTP) that separates solids for treatment and returns clean water to the ground

147

drip irrigation network. Clearly this type of solution is not appropriate for every application; however, the principles of efficiency can be applied to the majority of building types.

7.1.1   Reducing Demand

Reduce demand through the specification of low-flow sanitary fittings, for example, dual flush or composting toilets, siphonic or waterless urinals, low-flow shower and aerated tap fittings, and low-consumption appliances and equipment. Controls such as push taps and infrared sensors avoid unnecessary wastage. Labeling schemes such as the EU Water Label and the EPA's WaterSense Label are used to communicate water consumption of fittings and fixtures to customers, designers, and specifiers. Usability is also a factor; particularly in spaces with transitional users, such as schools, hotels, commercial, and retail facilities, fittings must be specified that are clear and simple to use, to avoid wasting water while, for example, running a tap or shower to reach desired temperature. Modern fittings achieve the same performance using fewer resources; and often water savings will also carry ancillary savings since using less hot water results in the use of less energy, smaller HVAC systems, and fewer maintenance requirements.

Specification of finishes and equipment that will affect the cleaning and maintenance schedules can also reduce water consumption through a building's lifetime, for example, opting for durable concrete or carpeted floors over vinyl or tiles. Maintenance of external areas can also be water intensive, with hard landscaping that requires pressure washing and green spaces requiring irrigation. Consideration of these whole life impacts during the design phase should lead to the use of alternative finishes such as permeable surfaces and drought-tolerant or indigenous planting to reduce the need for potable water (known as *xeriscaping*).

7.1.2   Efficient Servicing Strategies

Water recycling systems, such as gray water and rainwater harvesting systems, can substantially reduce potable water consumption and reliance on municipal water supplies and volatile utility prices—providing the parameters exist to make the systems economically viable. Consider the opportunity for incorporation into design proposals as early as possible, since the decision to pursue could affect excavations for tank storage and building layout. Gray water reuse refers to storing waste water from showers, washbasins, and cooling system condensate for a limited time so that it can then be accessed for nonpotable uses such as toilet flushing and laundry washing. System design can be optimized by stacking gray water sources vertically across floors to shorten the recirculation pipework and reduce pump specifications (and therefore energy requirements).

Rainwater harvesting involves the collection of rainwater for, depending on the level of purification required to meet local codes, a variety of nonpotable uses. For fully integrated systems to be economically viable, a correct ratio of rainfall, roof catchment area, storage capacity and demand must be achieved. Rainwater harvesting can also help to alleviate the effects of storm water runoff and flooding and, if designed appropriately, can continue to supply water in periods of drought.

Challenges to adopting these systems focus primarily on cost and on the balance of supply and demand. With so many variables to consider, it is difficult to determine a standard rule of thumb for projecting costs. Monitoring the exact site for rainfall data for as long as possible, rather than relying on average data, will ensure that the system is not over- or undersized. This will have a large impact on return on investment. Life cycle cost analyses must consider rising utility prices as water resources come under increasing pressure. Introducing any type of water recycling into a project will be simpler for new developments than retrofitting to existing facilities; therefore, the best opportunity to achieve water efficiency is to incorporate recycling into the early design stage proposals and integrate all systems supplying and requiring water. Some of the case studies in Chapter 10 have achieved closed-loop systems through this approach.

Reclaimed water, such as from a WWTP, is safe for a variety of nonpotable uses including landscape irrigation, toilet flushing, industrial processes, and even fire protection systems. Whichever of these options is pursued, it is extremely important to ensure that sufficient filtration systems are specified, to ensure effectiveness and minimize maintenance requirements.

7.1.2.1 HVAC Systems

In HVAC systems, water savings can be achieved through specification of efficient equipment and processes and use of a regular maintenance regime. Properly sized boiler and steam systems and appropriate setpoints will reduce wasted water (and heat). Leak detection systems identify issues early on to enable immediate repairs, preventing flooding and damage to building structures. Recirculating hot water systems and insulation on hot water pipework will reduce heat losses, thus reducing the need to run water taps wastefully before hot water arrives.

Automated building controls ensure that water-based cooling systems are only used when required. Smart metering and submetering, connected to a building management system, can alert building users of anomalies in consumption, for example, out of hours, that might be caused by a system or fitting fault.

7.1.2.2 Cooling Towers

Cooling towers can be a huge consumer of water, particularly within warmer climates. The amount of water circulating through the system is a function of the cooling load; this should therefore be reduced initially via passive techniques described in earlier chapters. Heat is rejected to the atmosphere by cooling a water stream to a lower temperature, raising the air temperature and dissipating the steam, and recirculating the water to absorb more heat. A typical commercial building with an evaporative cooling system can use 2 to 3 million gallons of water in a season to "make up" water lost through evaporation and the blowdown cleaning cycle (a control process whereby water is discharged from the system to remove minerals, chemicals, and bacteria, which improves the efficiency of the cooling process).

Ways to improve water consumption include the following:

- Use alternative sources for the make-up water (subject to feasibility, required pretreatment requirements, and compliance with local authorities) that would otherwise be diverted to drains, for example, air handling unit (AHU) condensate recovery or rainwater:

- 2013 study into the feasibility of condensate recovery in humid climates suggests that up to a 30% savings in make-up water can be achieved through the practice, and that "the large cost of implementing a recovery system is still justifiable for buildings with high fresh air percentage in countries with a hot, humid and arid climate" [1].

- Introducing clean rainwater to the system can also increase cycles between blowdown (which can be responsible for 25% of cooling tower water usage), because rainwater contains fewer dissolved solids than potable water.

• Reduce interstitial losses, such as drift (droplets in the evaporated air), overflow, leaks, backwash processes, excessive pipe pressures, and cleaning processes, through good system design. As with any active system, preventive maintenance is an essential part of ensuring optimal performance.

• Use an alternative treatment. Cooling tower systems require treatment to prevent buildup of scale, biological growth, and corrosion, all of which lead to lower performance efficiencies through reduced flow rates and increased head pressure, high maintenance, and health hazards. Chemical treatments can be dangerous to manage, because often a combination of hazardous chemicals is required to treat the system, and dosing systems require frequent monitoring for optimum levels. Nonchemical treatments for cooling towers such as pulsed electromagnetic technology (under certain water compositions, such as low chloride levels, and in conjunction with a sophisticated monitoring system for biological growth) also eliminate chemicals in cooling tower discharge to main sewer systems.

More information on water efficiency in cooling towers is available at the Office of Energy Efficiency and Renewable Energy [2] and the EPA's WaterSense at Work program [3].

7.1.3 Other Considerations

7.1.3.1 Desalination

In especially hot climates prone to periods of drought and in isolated locations such as islands, desalination plants are becoming increasingly viable. Reverse osmosis processes remove salt from seawater to produce drinking-quality water. Modern systems are increasingly less energy intensive, with solar desalination plants also in development, and ultimately rely on an abundant source of seawater. The process's brine by-product must be carefully controlled to mitigate against damage to marine life when redispersed to the ocean. In 2015 the International Desalination Association reported that over 300 million people rely on fresh water from more than 18,000 plants in 150 countries. This number is expected to rise significantly within the next 5 years with new megaplants being constructed in the Middle East and the United States.

Building-level desalination plants are often cost prohibitive; however, some vulnerable island resort locations such as Indonesia and the Maldives have adopted the process to produce drinking water for their guests, avoiding the need to import bottles and process the plastic waste, and for water security in drought conditions.

7.1.3.2   Education and Awareness

Awareness campaigns are important to ensure installed fittings and systems are used optimally, since most involve human interaction for utilization or maintenance. For example, double flushing of ultra-low-flush toilets may result in more water consumption than older, single-flush devices. Training courses for facilities managers on complex systems, for example, are useful. However, an integrated strategy should ensure that use of everyday water fittings is intuitive—enhancing, not inconveniencing, user experience. For existing buildings with retrofitted systems, or innovative and demonstration initiatives, point-of-use signage, displays with real-time consumption information, or internal newsletters are useful to ensure the systems achieve their maximum savings potential.

For facilities with other high-water-consuming areas or equipment, opportunities for reduction and integration with reuse strategies must be evaluated on a case-by-case basis.

7.1.4   Water Efficiency in Domestic Properties

Kemi Adeyeye, University of Bath, U.K., and Kenneth Ip and Kaiming She, University of Brighton, U.K.

The common fittings and fixtures in buildings are toilets, urinals, taps (handwashing basins in baths and kitchens), showers, bathtubs, dishwashers, and washing machines. Water use for flushing toilets accounts for nearly 22% of domestic consumption and offers significant potential for saving (see Figure 7.1). A simple option of using a 4/2.5 l dual-flush unit in a dwelling can save 26 m³ water a year for an average household, but a further reduction to 1.5 l per flush could be achieved if power- or air-assisted products were used [4]. Table 7.1 illustrates the typical performance of fittings and fixtures, with examples of available options considered appropriate for high-efficiency practice, and the performance of baseline practice for comparison [5].

7.1.4.1   Integrated Design of Water Supply to Homes

To attain sustainable use of water resources, the water supply system must be designed at the building level in an integrated manner that combines centralized (mains water) and decentralized supplies. Mains water supply meets the potable water standards suitable for all general purposes including drinking. Decentralized systems, which include rainwater collection and gray water recycling systems, can be used to augment the mains water supply, thereby negating the need to use potable water for nonpotable functions.

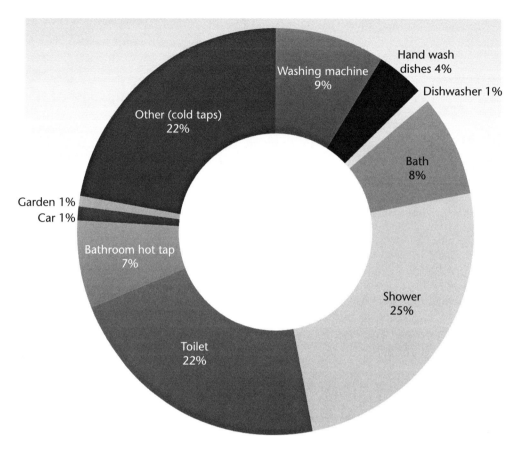

Figure 7.1 Breakdown of domestic water consumption. (*Source:* Energy Savings Trust 2014, reproduced with permission.)

Table 7.1 Baseline and High-Efficiency Fixtures and Fittings for Water Consumption in Dwellings

Fittings/Fixtures	Baseline Practice	Options	High-Efficiency Practice
Toilet	6 l/flush	Dual-flush, pressure-assisted, power/air-assisted toilets, vacuum, composting	≤3.5 l/flush
Shower	8 l/min	Aerating, laminar flow shower heads or flow regulators	≤6 l/min
Tap (basin)	Up to 12 l/min	Spray tap, sensor-activated faucet, push tap or tap flow restrictors	≤4 l/min
Tap (kitchen)	12 l/min		≤6 l/min
Urinal	3.8 l/bowl/flush	Hydraulic valve, passive infrared sensor, timed flush, waterless urinals	≤1.5 l/bowl/flush
Bathtub	200 l capacity (excluding body mass)	Lower capacity bath tubs, or removal	≤155 l capacity (excluding body mass)
Washing machine	10 l/kg dry load	Low water specifications	≤7 l/kg dry load
Dishwasher	1.2 l/place setting	Low water specifications	≤0.7 l/place setting

7.1.4.2   Rainwater Harvesting

In homes, rainwater may be harvested for use instead of potable water in toilets and washing machines or for gardening and irrigation purposes. Australia has a long history and wide use of rainwater harvesting; a comprehensive document on the use of rainwater tanks is available from the Australian government [6]. Figures 7.2a and 7.2b show a simple configuration for a rainwater collection system coupled with the mains water supply. The outlet of the pump is directly connected to the appliances and utilities in this setup and is referred to as a direct system. An alternative is an indirect system in which the water is pumped from the water tank into a loft tank to create a conventional gravity system (Figures 7.3a and 7.3b). An indirect system is less demanding on the pump specification and related controls and is thus likely to be more cost effective. The pressure, however, is limited by the loft height relative to the appliances and utilities.

7.1.4.3   Gray Water Recycling

Gray water recycling systems in homes normally collect used shower, bath, and tap water and recycle it for toilet flushing. Other uses of gray water include watering green roofs and vegetative façades and garden plants (not recommended for fruit or

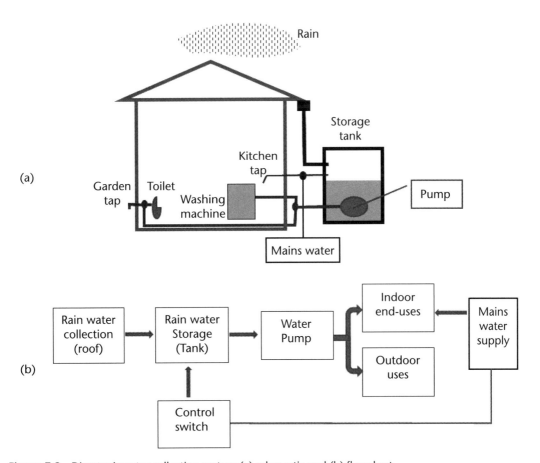

Figure 7.2   Direct rainwater collection system (a) schematic and (b) flowchart.

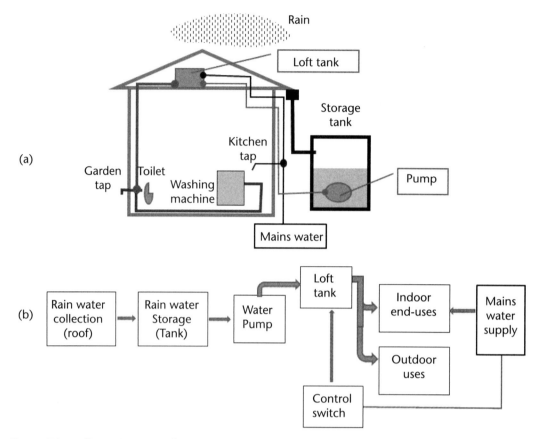

Figure 7.3 Indirect rainwater collection system (a) schematic and (b) flowchart.

vegetable plants) and washing clothes. Apart from watering garden plants, recycled gray water must be treated according to guidelines published by relevant authorities. In the United Kingdom, the British Standards Institution (BSI) [7, 8] defines the code of practice for six types of gray water systems:

1. Direct reuse systems: No treatment is involved and the water is normally collected via a diverter from the drainpipe and then used for plant irrigation.
2. Short retention systems: A simple basic filter is used to collect surface debris. The treated water may be stored for a short time only.
3. Basic physical/chemical systems: A simple filter is used to remove debris and solids, and chemical disinfectants such as chlorine and bromine are then applied to bacterial growth. The treated water may be stored for a longer period of time.
4. Biological systems: Gray water is treated by means of aerobic or anaerobic bacteria digesting unwanted organic material.
5. Biomechanical systems: In addition to biological treatment, the solids are removed via a physical process.
6. Hybrid systems: Combinations of above.

Figure 7.4a show the schematic of a popular and cost-effective gray water reuse system and Figure 7.4b shows the flowchart.

As in the case of rainwater systems, the mains supply must be connected with appropriate controls to ensure continuous supply of water to the utilities in case of insufficient recycled water. Both rainwater and gray water systems are effective in reducing the water demand from the water mains but they require local storage, water treatment, and regular maintenance. Detailed guidance on rainwater and gray water treatment, testing, and maintenance can be found in BSI documents [7, 8].

The complexity, life cycle impact, and cost of such systems should be carefully considered before selecting a system for a specific application.

7.2   Sustainable Drainage Design for Developments

Jane Shields, Director, Living Water Ecosystems Ltd.

Foul drainage is an essential but unglamorous side of building design. Although drainage design is fundamental and a key component of all developments, since it is mostly underground the client often undervalues this key and indispensable aspect of building design. Many projects cannot proceed without adequate provision for foul and surface water drainage.

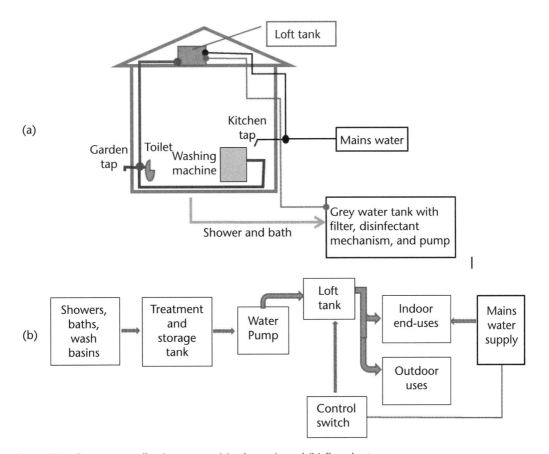

Figure 7.4   Gray water collection system (a) schematic and (b) flowchart.

7.2.1 Composition of Foul Drainage

Most buildings situated within an urban, suburban, or semirural area are within a 10-mile radius of a WWTP and under these circumstances there is a legal requirement to send foul drainage to the mains sewer. All new developments must manage and attenuate surface water on site to prevent flooding downstream.

Where management and treatment of foul drainage via the mains sewer is not an option, an alternative type of drainage must be provided. Section 7.2.3 deals with the design, operation, and regulation of such systems.

7.2.2 Problems with Present Practice

In older urban drainage systems, surface water is conducted via land drains and culverts into the foul drainage system. Such discharges are known as combined sewage outfalls (CSOs). Large volumes of surface water thus become contaminated by sewage. The additional water overloads the WWTP, delivering volumes it was not designed to handle. During sustained wet weather this causes overflows to land and watercourses, with the associated possibility of disease. A further problem with surface water entering a WWTP is that it makes the processing of foul water less efficient, leading to higher levels of nutrients and suspended solids reaching watercourses. Although some progress has been made in recent years to reduce the volume of CSOs or their impact, this remains a major source of pollutants to our watercourses.

When new developments are proposed in locations where the local WWTP is receiving surface water, a condition known as *drainage block* occurs. In these circumstances, surface water is consuming the capacity in the sewage works that could be used to treat sewage from housing or effluent from other developments. Consequently, new developments become impossible. In recent years legislation has been introduced that requires new buildings and developments to have separate strategies and pipework for foul and surface water drainage. However, the majority of older WWTPs are still receiving surface water. In such cases, three possible solutions exist.

7.2.3 Solutions

The first possible solution is to work with the Water Authority to exclude or minimize surface water drainage to the WWTP, thereby maximizing the fraction of the input that is domestic or other effluent and minimizing the problem of overflows. This necessarily involves the renewal of drainage infrastructure and separation of combined drainage pipes from houses and businesses; consequently, it is often considered an expensive and impractical option. In these older systems surface water draining from roads and motorways also enters the WWTP, which is usually located at the lowest point in a catchment. In some cases, removing road drainage from the flow to the WWTP will be sufficient to enable a development to proceed. Where this option is adopted, legislation requires that the surface water thus excluded be attenuated before discharge to a watercourse, for which land must be available.

The second option is to build an ecological treatment system on the Water Authority's or the developer's land to receive and treat the wet-weather overflow, which can contain a significant fraction of the total foul load. In these cases a

Hydrobrake or valve needs to be installed at the start of the WWTP to allow only the design volume to enter the WWTP. The remaining flow is then diverted to the ecological treatment system, which has been designed to treat the volume and loading of the combined sewage overflows. Working with Water Authorities is slow, difficult, complex, and time consuming and many developers cannot wait long enough for this process to happen.

The third solution is to obtain permission from local authorities to treat domestic effluent privately on the developer's land. When an existing WWTP is available (even one that has drainage block), it is very difficult to obtain permission to build a private treatment system, even though the quality of treatment would be higher than that delivered by a WWTP.

7.2.4   The Design of Ecological Treatment Systems

To design an ecological system to treat sewage or other effluents, it is essential to consider the parameters discussed next.

7.2.4.1   Topography

A topographical survey is needed to ascertain the relative levels of the development and the site of the proposed treatment system.

- Drainage pipes need to be sufficiently (at least 1m) below ground level to minimize the risk of damage and freezing.
- The slope of the drainage run needs to be at least 1 in 70 to allow movement of liquid and prevent settling of solids.
- Ideally the drainage line should run by gravity from the building to the treatment system, so that no power or pumping is required.
- The simplest and most common way of managing solids is to collect the effluent initially in a septic tank or other, similar vessel such as a mechanical treatment plant (MTP). Solids then settle out, where they are slowly broken down by bacteria and other microorganisms that view the solids as a nutrient. In an MTP, aeration is added, which enhances and speeds up treatment. Any solids that remain are later removed by suction tanker, usually on an annual basis. These solids are then taken to a WWTP for treatment.

In both septic tanks and an MTP, a liquor remains that contains nutrients and suspended solids that require further treatment. This outfall is conducted (preferably by gravity) to the ecological treatment system, where natural processes result in a clear, high-quality discharge that meets local environmental authority standards and can be sent to either watercourses or land.

7.2.4.2   Sizing and Design of an Ecological Treatment System

In sizing a treatment system, we need to know the values of two key parameters: the volume and the biological load, that is, the amount of nutrient the plants and microorganisms will be asked to absorb and digest.

British Water, in collaboration with U.K. environmental agencies, has produced a code of practice that tabulates the volume and load that will be discharged by populations of different sorts, from households to offices, kitchens, dormitories, public conveniences, and other common groupings[9].

To evaluate the loading, one must consider all activities that will produce waste water in addition to sewage. These may include effluent from business/industry, laundry, swimming pools, kitchens, restaurants, and so forth. How the volume and loading are distributed throughout the day will depend on whether there is full- or part-time occupancy or, for a business, full- or part-time staff and visitors. It is useful to know whether an existing population needs to be included in the treatment system and if the site will be a mixed development or community.

When designing an ecological system for the treatment of other effluents arising from businesses or industry, a full chemical analysis of their effluent—their volumes and flow rates—is required in order to assess the size of system needed to treat it (see Figure 7.5). As long as all the parameters and waste streams are assessed and included, it is possible to design a system that can treat a mixed effluent stream.

7.2.4.3 Design Considerations

The treatment system is lined with a robust, waterproof liner, so that the effluent remains isolated from the land and watercourse. Only after treatment is it discharged according to regulations.

Where possible, three cascading wetland beds are built in series, each planted with a carefully selected range of species, thus maximizing diversity and treatment capacity. Ecological systems are among the most adaptive on Earth and their species distribution will adapt to the nutrients present, in the process becoming more efficient and increasing the system's treatment capacity.

Figure 7.5 Ecological system at a factory for the attenuation and treatment of surface water contaminated with magnesium oxide. (*Source:* Living Water Ltd.)

If land is available and there is sufficient slope, it is best to set each bed into the slope to make the best use of land.

Depending on the effluent and the level of suspended solids, the treatment system may consist of a series of components, each utilizing a different technique.

7.2.4.4   Future Proofing

Future proofing should be allowed in the design so that there will be a comfortable period before a new or enlarged treatment system is required. However, if the population equivalent (PE) is likely to increase dramatically within the planned lifetime of the system (e.g., 50 to 100 years), it is better to design a full-size, modular system and install only the first phase. Modules can be added as necessary as the development progresses.

For reasons of treatment efficiency, septic tanks and MTPs cannot be oversized at the outset. Therefore, if the PE is likely to increase dramatically, it is best to install an additional septic tank with each expansion phase.

7.2.5   Types of Natural Treatment Systems

A number of different natural treatment systems are available to treat sewage and effluent, but they must be sized, designed, and planted correctly in order to achieve full treatment. The type of system used will depend on the volume, flow rate, loading, chemical and physical composition of the effluent, topography of the site, and land availability.

Although the design of the natural treatment systems can be completely different, the terminology used in the public domain is confused and people refer to reedbeds or constructed wetlands as a generic term because they are unfamiliar with the field. However, it is necessary to choose the type of natural system that is most suited for the site, volumes, and loadings and that can achieve a high-quality discharge.

The main types of systems currently in use for the natural treatment of foul drainage are summarized here:

- Ecological treatment system: Complex ecologically, using up to 60 native plants. Substrate is comprised of graded aggregates, usually 500-mm depth, drainage and surface pipework, maximizing air rather than effluent in the bed, aerobic, can be utilized to remove complex and high loadings, can receive high flows, system may include wetland cells, willow soakaway, and wetland scrape. Can operate with no additional energy. Land required is approximately 3 m²/PE.

- Reedbed: Horizontal flow underneath the surface, substrate can be soil or aggregates, flow through gabion, usually 1m deep, planted with Phragmites australis (common reed), can be aerobic or anaerobic, best utilized after primary loading removed, can receive high volumes. Can operate with no additional energy. Land required is approximately 5 m²/PE.

- Vertical flow wetland: Vertical flow is distributed across a sand layer before draining through aggregates. usually 1m deep. Mainly planted with

Phragmites australis (common reed), is aerobic, flow must be dosed and is less able to process high volumes quickly. Can operate with no additional energy. Land required is approximately 3 m^2/PE.

- Overland flow wetland: Mainly planted with Phragmites australis (common reed), although sometimes one or two more species of wetland plants is used (e.g., Iris pseudacorus, Typha latifolia) is aerobic. Flow is over the surface and can have a soil or aggregate substrate. Can operate with no additional energy. Land required is approximately 4 m^2/PE.

- Aerated reedbed or constructed wetland: Horizontal flow underneath the surface, substrate can be soil or aggregates, flow through gabion, usually 1m deep, planted with Phragmites australis (common reed), can be aerobic or anaerobic, best utilized after primary loading removed (although this system can process a higher loading than those without aeration), can receive high volumes. The main difference is the addition of aeration into the treatment system, which reduces the nutrients, but uses much more energy for the aeration process and pumps. Land required is approximately 3 m^2/PE.

- Treatment pond: Lined ponds usually consist of three ponds in series, the first receives raw sewage, which degrades mainly anaerobically; the second and third ponds have additional oxygen. Long retention times over 30 days remove pathogens. Most treatment ponds require additional aeration or recirculation so will have an added energy input. Land required is approximately 10 m^2/PE.

- Willow plantation/soakaway: Planted mainly with Salix (willow species), although some other trees (e.g., poplar) that can tolerate water and are able to be coppiced can be used. Substrate is usually "as dug," which is what is locally found. Willow species are not perennial and therefore can only be used for sole treatment during the growing season.

In an ecological treatment system, in addition to the bacteria and microorganisms, invertebrates, insects, plants, trees, and birds are all involved in consuming nutrients and turning them into biomass, leaving the water clean and ready for discharge. Wetland plants are perennial and can provide treatment throughout the year. One or a combination of the above natural treatment systems can be used in one integrated treatment system (see Color Plate 21).

Usually a primary treatment system is required to remove gross solids or reduce the loading before a natural treatment system can be utilized. Examples of a primary treatment process may include a septic tank, package treatment plant, aeration, anaerobic digestion, activated sludge, or composting.

The chemical and physical characteristics of the particular effluent must be assessed in order to match the ecology of the system to the task it is being asked to perform. One must select plants that can break down the particular contaminants and turn them into food and hence into biomass. Much later in the life of the treatment system this biomass can be removed and appropriately composted.

The treatment system needs to be designed to treat the maximum volume and load arising in the course of a single day, and have a detailed and specific maintenance plan to suit the particular application.

Color Plate 1 The environmental impact of the built environment is profound . (*Photo:* Joshua K. Jackson CC0 License.)

Color Plate 2 Green building councils in 2013. (*Source:* IREBS Regensburg University.)

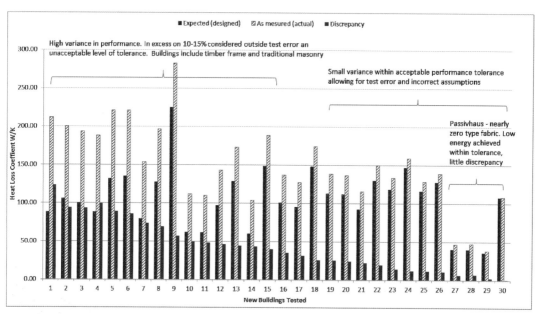

Color Plate 3 Coheating tests—whole building heat loss test results (in order of discrepancy in performance). *Note:* Some houses have a measured actual heat loss of over twice the design heat loss. (*Credit:* Gorse, C. A., et al., Leeds Beckett University, Chapter 2, Ref. [8]. Reproduced with permission.)

Color Plate 4 Portcullis House, London. (*Photo:* David Strong.)

Color Plate 5 Daylight and a visual connection with the natural world improves academic attainment. (Photo courtesy of UWC South East Asia in Singapore, http://www.uwcsea.edu.sg.)

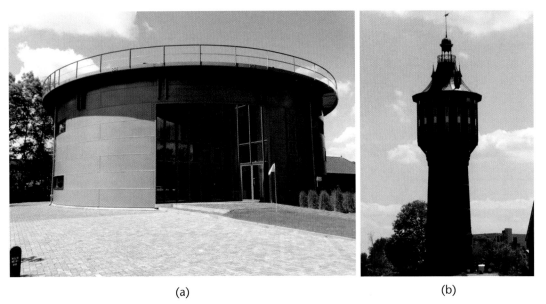

(a) (b)

Color Plate 6 Examples of redundant structures given a new life. (*Source:* David Strong.)

Color Plate 7 (a) Climate-excluding tower blocks in Shanghai. (b) Toronto. These represent very different climates, but both require air conditioning and in the case of the Shanghai building, a new power station! (*Source:* (a) Jerryang Shanghai Tower CC BY-ND 2.0. (b) David Strong.)

Color Plate 8 Wind towers (*badghirs*) providing natural ventilation Iran. (*Photo:* Badghirs (wind towers), Yazd Andrea Taroni, CC BY-ND 2.0.)

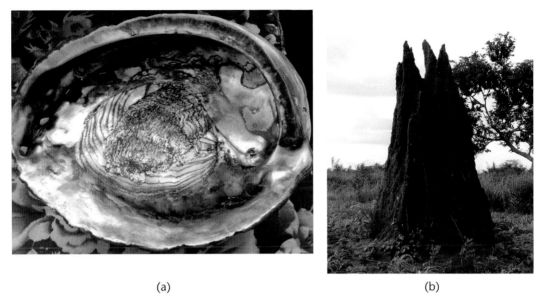

(a)   (b)

Color Plate 9   (a) Abalone shell (see Section 4.2.4). (Photo: Abalone shell, Lisa Ann Yount, public domain.)
(b) Termite nest , capable of self-regulating temperature, ventilation, and humidity in extremely hostile/extreme climatic conditions. (*Photo:* Termite, Jeff Attaway, CC BY 2.0.)

Color Plate 10   Biodiverse extensive green roof at Abbey Hive, Abbey Road, London. (*Copyright:* BugLife—The invertebrate conservation charity.)

Color Plate 11 Namba Parks, Osaka, Japan. The dynamic rooftop gardens of the office and shopping complex over eight levels incorporate tree groves, rock gardens, waterfalls, ponds, and outdoor terraces. (Image courtesy of JERDE, Design Architect, Los Angeles.)

Color Plate 12 The Park Royal at Pickering, Singapore. WOHA Architects' "hotel-in-a-garden." The greenery spans 15,000 m^2 of sky gardens, waterfalls, planter terraces, and green walls (see Section 4.3). (Image courtesy of Skyshot Pte. Ltd.)

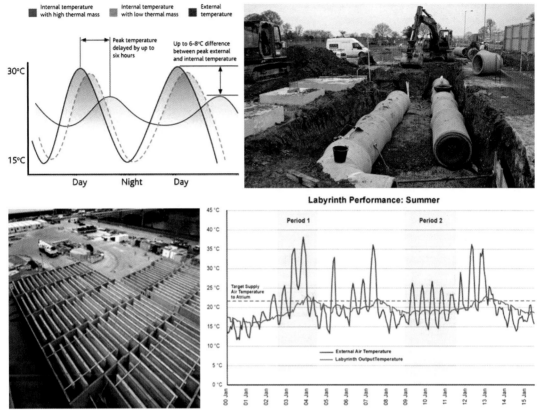

Color Plate 13 Clockwise from top left: (a) Impact of high and low thermal mass on internal temperature. (Courtesy of MPA, The Concrete Centre.) (b) Earth ducts being installed at Butterfield Office Village, Luton. (c) Graph of external temperature vs. labyrinth outlet temperature. (d) Labyrinth under construction at Federation Square, Melbourne, Australia. (Images (b), (c), (d) courtesy of Atelier Ten. Reproduced with permission.)

Color Plate 14 Naturally ventilated, thermally adaptive school. (*Photo:* Courtesy of Breathing Buildings.)

Color Plate 15 Beaufort Court, Kings Langley, U.K. Net-zero energy refurbishment of the former Ovaltine egg farm into office accommodation. (*Photo:* Courtesy of Fusion/RES. Reproduced with permission.)

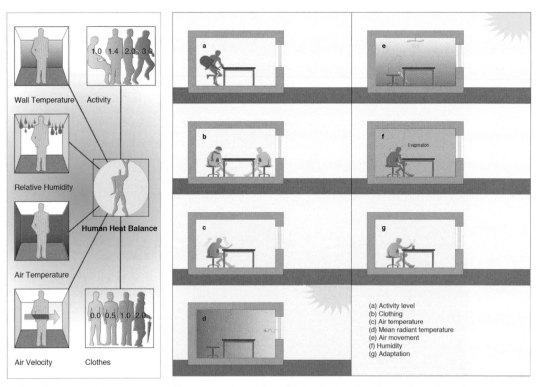

Wall Temperature

Activity

1.0 1.4 2.0 3.0

Relative Humidity

Human Heat Balance

Air Temperature

Air Velocity

Clothes

0.0 0.5 1.0 2.0

a

b

c

d

e

f Evaporation

g

(a) Activity level
(b) Clothing
(c) Air temperature
(d) Mean radiant temperature
(e) Air movement
(f) Humidity
(g) Adaptation

Color Plate 16 (a) Parameters affect thermal comfort. (b) Designing for thermal comfort. (*Source:* Green Vitruvius, University College Dublin. Reproduced with permission.)

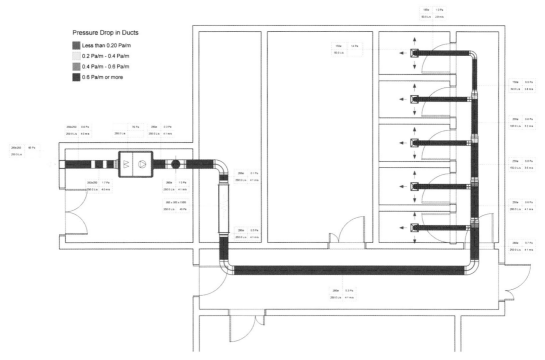

Color Plate 17 System A: Typical/conventional ductwork layout and component specification. (*Source:* e3 Consulting Engineers.)

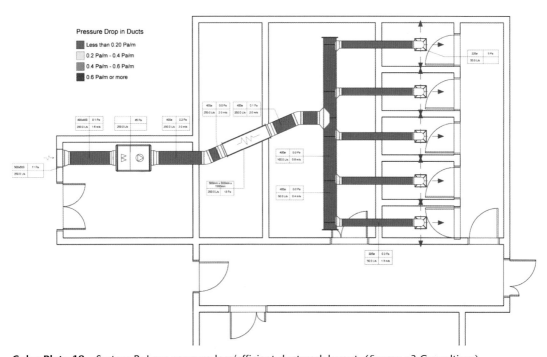

Color Plate 18 System B: Low-pressure-loss/efficient ductwork layout. (*Source:* e3 Consulting.)

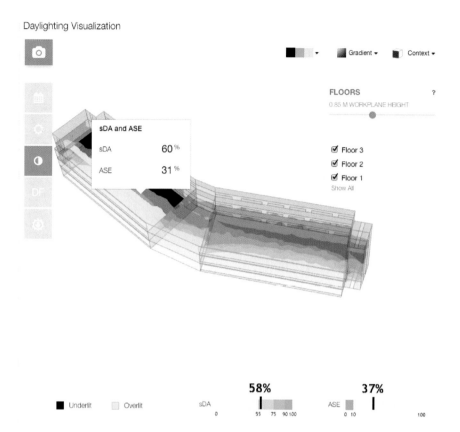

Color Plate 19 Spatial daylight autonomy and annual sunlight exposure for a specific zone. (*Credit:* Sefaira, Trimble.)

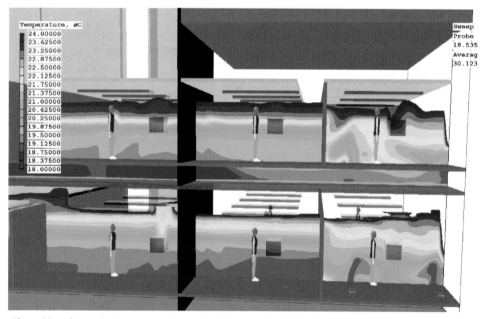

Color Plate 20 Thermal decay through a raised floor and temperature distribution in the occupied zone. (*Credit:* Corney et al., Building Simulation 2011: Performance Analysis Methods for Passive Downdraft Systems.)

Color Plate 21 *Top left to bottom right:* Examples of a willow coppice, pond, planted swale, and wetland treatment system at various locations. (*Source:* Living Water Ltd.)

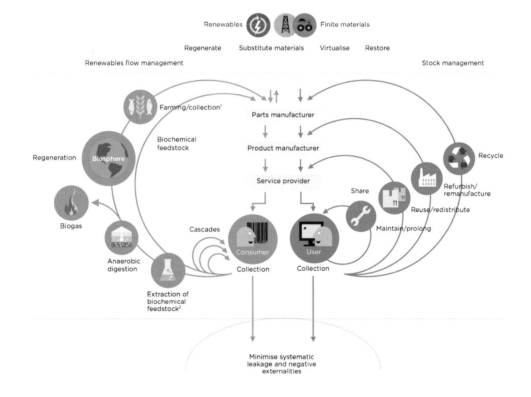

1. Hunting and fishing
2. Can take both post-harvest and post-consumer waste as an input

SOURCE: Ellen MacArthur Foundation, SUN, and McKinsey Center for Business and Environment; Drawing from Braungart & McDonough, Cradle to Cradle (C2C).

Color Plate 22 The circular economy—an industrial system that is restorative by design. (*Credit:* Ellen MacArthur Foundation.)

Color Plate 23 Pompidou Centre, Paris, 1979; detail of the exposed structure and services described as a "maintenance nightmare." The building reliance on HVAC is the antithesis of a sustainable, eco-minimalistic, low-impact, low-energy building! (*Photo:* Centre Pompidou, Jeanbaptiste M, CC BY 2.0.)

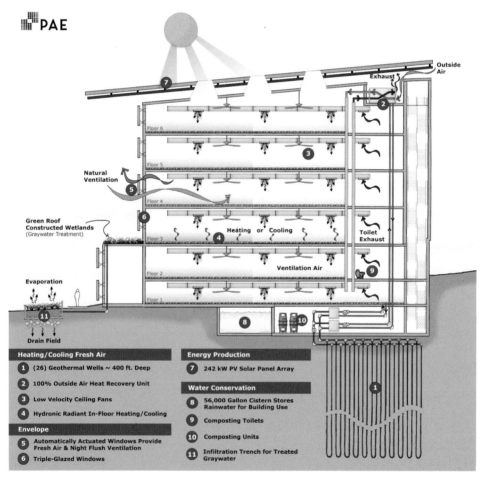

Color Plate 24 Bullitt Center environmental strategy highlighting the key features and integrated strategies. (*Source:* PAE.)

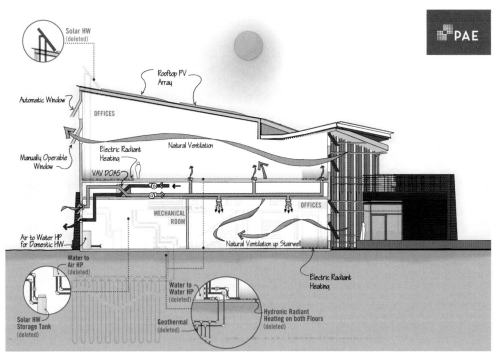

Color Plate 25 RMI Innovation Centre: servicing strategy showing eliminated systems following redefinition of thermal comfort parameters. (*Image:* PAE.)

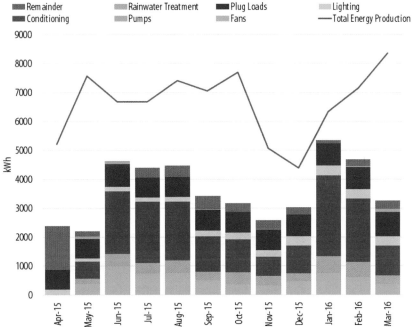

Color Plate 26 Brock Environmental Center energy consumption and production comparison chart. (*Source:* SmithGroupJJR.)

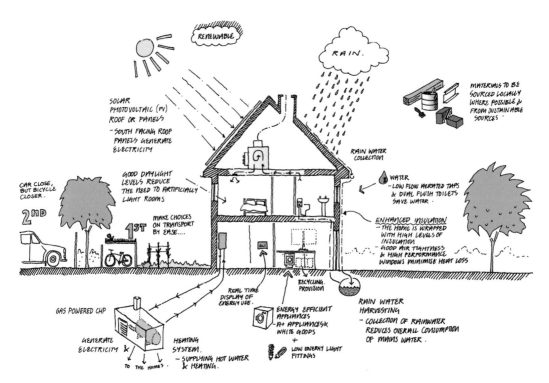

Color Plate 27 Environmental strategy for Elmsbrook Village including key features for net-zero carbon strategy. (*Source:* Courtesy of Farrells. Reproduced with permission.)

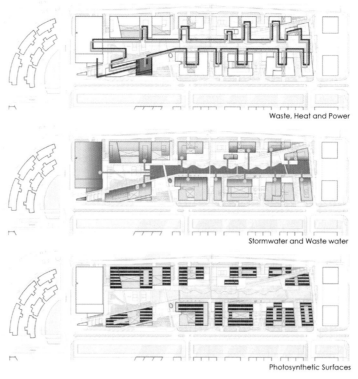

Waste, Heat and Power

Stormwater and Waste water

Photosynthetic Surfaces

Color Plate 28 Park 20|20 masterplan strategies for closed–loop, fully integrated energy, water, and waste management systems. (*Source:* William McDonough + Partners.)

Color Plate 29 (a) Hotel Verde's aquaponics garden supplies herbs and vegetables to the restaurant kitchen. (b) Hotel Verde's low maintenance natural pool does not require energy-intensive filtration or pumps. (*Photo:* Hotel Verde.)

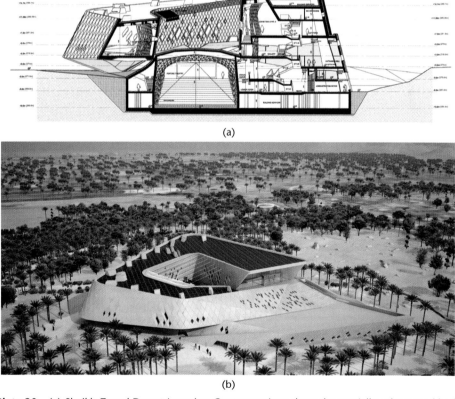

Color Plate 30 (a) Sheikh Zayed Desert Learning Center sections show the partially submerged building as part of the cooling strategy. (b) Rendering showing the rooftop photovoltaic panels. (*Source:* Chalabi Architekten & Partner.)

Color Plate 31 KTPH greenery and biodiversity in circulation spaces emulate the principles of biophilic design. (*Photo:* CPG Consultants Pte Ltd.)

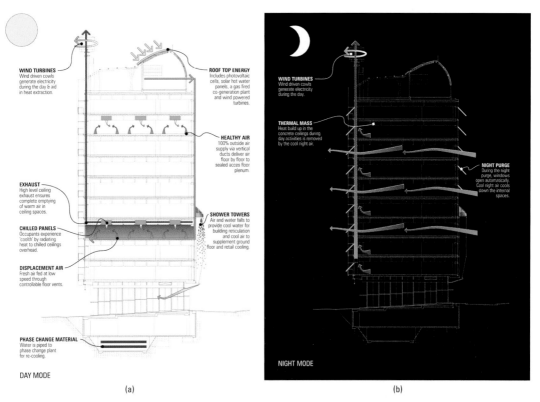

(a)   (b)

Color Plate 32 Council House 2 environmental strategy features (a) at daytime and (b) at nighttime. (*Source:* DesignInc.)

The standard of discharge required is laid down by the relevant environmental authority, who will take into account local geographical, geological, and hydrological considerations to ensure that the discharge does not degrade the watercourse or local ecology. Occasionally, local conditions will militate against a discharge of any kind and in these circumstances a willow plantation can be installed after the treatment system, to take up and transpire the treated water.

Discharge of sewage or effluent will require a license, setting the quality conditions necessary before the water can be discharged to either a watercourse or to land. Business and industries that have a variety of effluents or are processing hazardous materials will require a waste management license.

Further information on constructed wetlands can be found in [10].

7.2.6   Natural Solid Waste Treatment

Sewage solids (septage) that have been captured and settled in either a septic tank or in a packaged treatment plant need to be removed by a tanker operated by a waste management operator or Water Authority to a WWTP. Depending on the size of tank or manufacturer's instructions, these tanks will normally need to be emptied once or twice per year.

A closed-loop system optimizes the on-site treatment and recycling of as many of the effluent and solid waste inputs and outputs as possible. The natural treatment systems described above provide a sustainable way to treat effluent and contaminated surface water. Composting, bioremediation, and phytoremediation provide a natural process to transform solid waste into a landscaping material (soil) that can safely be applied back to land (see Figure 7.6). Local organic materials would be blended in until the material has a consistency and composition suitable for healthy fungal and bacterial colony formation. Note that composting and bioremediation processes require a waste management license.

The British Composting Association has established an industry standard for composts (BSI PAS 100) that is certified by the British Standards Institution. The specification covers the entire process from raw material and production methods through to quality control and certification. For green waste and nonhazardous biodegradable waste from a known source, the output quality of the composting process needs to achieve a BSI PAS 100 standard before it can be used as a compost on land for gardens or as a landscaping material.

For green waste, nonhazardous, or hazardous biodegradable waste arising from a mixed or unknown source, the PAS 100 standard is not applicable. In this case, it is possible to achieve a compost-like output (CLO), which on reaching a landscaping standard can only be used within the site or within its own operations. The waste management license would determine where this material could be used.

On a business park, industrial site, or site where solids are arising within surface water through site operations, the solids must be captured and managed to prevent them from entering a watercourse where the solids can pollute and negatively impact organisms living in a watercourse or pond.

The solids can be managed and reduced in the following ways:

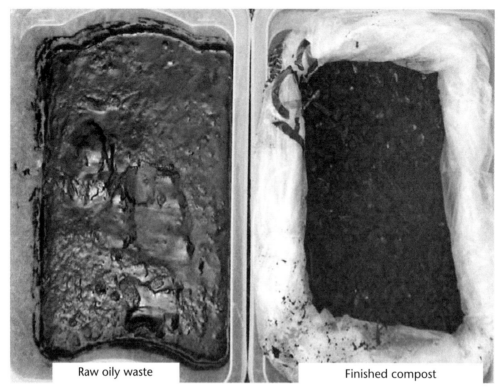

Raw oily waste   Finished compost

Figure 7.6   Bioremediation of a mixture of (a) pipeline piggings, tank bottom sludges, and gully waste at an oil terminal. The final product was (b) landscape quality. (*Source:* Living Water Ltd.)

- Install or utilize existing underground catchpits/gullies located in the drainage line from, for example, a vehicle washing facility to capture and store solids.

- Use the gullies and pumping chambers to settle and store solids prior to pumping.

- Sweep and brush excess solid materials arising on site.

- In situations where there is a high volume of water containing suspended or gross solids, use proprietary in-line centrifugal filters or curbing (i.e., Copa Surfsep or Hydro International Downstream Defender, Akko Drainage).

- Discharge to an ecological treatment system or swale that can filter and degrade solids.

7.2.7   Surface Water Attenuation, Management, and Treatment

Over time, populations have grown and the amount of land that has been developed or covered by tarmac and roads has increased dramatically. Land that previously allowed water to percolate away has been covered over so that surface water runs off quickly from roofs and hard surfaces, causing increased downstream flooding.

Developers must manage, attenuate and treat all surface water arising on site, so that no more surface water runs off than before the development (see Figure 7.7).

(a)   (b)

Figure 7.7   (a) Surface water attenuation and treatment system. (Source: Living Water Ltd.) (b) Treatment of contaminated surface water containing oil, petrol, diesel, metals, and salt for a 25 hectare oil terminal. (*Source:* Living Water Ltd.)

The Environment Agency and the Department for Environment, Food & Rural Affairs (DEFRA) have produced a comprehensive report [11] that can be referred to for more in-depth study and design.

Sustainable drainage aims to mimic natural drainage by:

- Storing surface water runoff and releasing it slowly (attenuation),
- Allowing water to soak into the ground (infiltration),
- Transporting (conveying) water slowly on the surface,
- Filtering out pollutants, and
- Allowing sediments to settle out by controlling the flow of the water.

Normally, implementation of a combination of techniques and measures is required to achieve a sustainable drainage strategy for a given site. The term given to such designs and techniques is sustainable urban drainage systems (SuDS).

7.2.8   Key Principles of SuDS

7.2.8.1   Impact and Principles of Attenuation

The aim of surface water attenuation measures is to achieve a greenfield equivalent runoff rate for the site once development is complete. This value matches the natural surface water runoff for the site prior to development, ensuring that the downstream land and watercourses will not flood, especially during storm events.

Water originating from roofs is considered to be surface water and, together with runoff from access roads and pavements, needs to be managed because almost 100% is pure runoff; that is, there is no infiltration to ground. If not attenuated, such water quickly adds to peak flows downstream of the development, where it has the potential to cause serious flooding problems. In contrast, surface water runoff from undeveloped land, porous pavement, and natural treatment systems has only a 30% runoff rate, similar to the value for the site prior to development.

The environmental agencies impose a general requirement to attenuate for at least half an hour to prevent storm flows from peaking at the same time as the rest of the drainage in the neighboring area. Three volume or flow rate criteria should be met:

- Interception: No runoff for up to 5 mm of rainfall,
- 1-year return period flow control: Aimed at morphological protection of receiving streams, and
- 100-year return period flow and volume control: Aimed at flood protection of those living downstream.

A number of measures are in use that can provide several hours of retention time for surface water, thus achieving the above requirements. These include attenuation ponds, wetland, swales, planted soakaways, rainwater harvesting, underground storage boxes, and porous surface materials. Porous pavements provide filtration and treatment of surface water as well as attenuation. Proprietary structured infiltration boxes are able to store and slowly release captured water after the storm event.

The U.K. SuDS website [12], authored and managed by HR Wallingford Ltd., provides estimation tools for the design and evaluation of surface water management systems and sustainable drainage systems.

A rainwater harvesting system (RWHS) can be used to collect water from rooftops for reuse in flushing, garden watering, etc. All RWHS storage tanks require a high-level overflow to a surface water drain. Therefore, although it is a sustainable use of water, be aware that an RWHS can generate a surface water flow during periods of high rainfall or low usage and must be taken into account in the drainage calculations.

Measures that can be included in a SuDS strategy include the following:

- Porous pavements: Used for car parks but also sometimes on less-used roads or pavements,
- Petrol interceptors: Used for car parks and trafficked hard standing areas or where machinery is used,
- Attenuation ponds,
- Swales: Wide-bottomed ditches, planted with grasses or wetland plants, that conduct water across a site,
- Wetlands: Can include ecological treatment systems and constructed treatment wetlands,
- Wetland scrapes: Shallow, planted depressions that detain and evaporate water,
- Grasscrete paving: Supportive grids whose cells contain grass or other plants,
- Underground infiltration and storage boxes, and
- Oversize pipework for attenuation: Use of drainage pipework to store storm flow surges.

The complementary measures described above can form a drainage strategy to capture, attenuate, and treat surface water so that it can discharge clean water and be released slowly without exacerbating downstream flooding. For further information regarding SuDS see The SuDS Manual by CIRIA [13].

7.2.9   The Need for Treatment of Surface Water

The surface water draining from a development or industrial site that has tarmac or concrete hard standing for cars, lorries, or other vehicles is not clean. It contains diesel, petrol, oil, and other hydrocarbons, and if the area is used for vehicle washing, detergents will also be present. The regions around houses contain cat and dog excrement that will find its way into surface water drains, and hard areas can also be contaminated by soil or other detritus. Any surface water management strategy, therefore, needs to include treatment of these contaminants. Once the water has been treated, it can be recycled and used for secondary uses.

If the surface water treatment system includes natural systems such as ponds, wetlands or swales, it has many advantages in addition to complying with regulations. It is beautiful to look at and it provides habitat for species of insects, birds, bats, and reptiles not normally found in urban environments. It also makes a powerful statement about an organization's environmental awareness and commitment.

7.2.9.1   Design Considerations

A SuDS system is designed to cope not only with everyday rain and drainage events but also with storms of various strengths. HR Wallingford Ltd. produces U.K. sustainable drainage guidance and tools for the estimation of the greenfield runoff rate for all locations in the United Kingdom [14]. These figures are available for different storm strengths: once in 10 years, once in 30 years, and so on, and recently a factor of +20% has been introduced to account for the very severe events of the past 10 to 15 years. SuDS designers are tasked with designing systems that can cope with at least a once-in-30-years storm event and on occasion (particularly where there is a risk of downstream flooding) the requirement is for a once-in-100+20%-years storm event.

Although one must design for the maximum storm event, it is essential to design a system that can cater to smaller storm events and can also function during dry weather. This is particularly important when the SuDS system includes an amenity pond or other habitat that forms part of the site's landscaping. Swales, wetland scrapes, and ponds can all be designed to function well during both strong storms and dry weather.

7.2.9.2   Key Points

- The system needs to include water storage, to provide damp habitat for plants and other creatures when there is no rainfall.
- Water needs to be attenuated, thus the design needs to incorporate a freeboard, that is, a difference between normal water level (NWL) and top water level (TWL). Functionally, the total volume of water is less important than the capacity of the freeboard, because it is the difference between NWL and TWL that provides the attenuation. However, if the pond is being designed

for wildlife, it is necessary to have sufficient depth (of at least 1m) at its deepest point to allow cold water at all times, and to maximize the circumference and planted marginal shelf to provide habitats for fish and other pond life. There also has to be sufficient freeboard to attenuate storm flows without the need to disturb the water at NWL, which will contain much of the pond life.

- There needs to be a throughput so that the water remains fresh and oxygenated.
- SuDS ponds and features usually operate by gravity and need to be placed so that they receive all the surface water that drains from the site. The drainage engineer will normally incorporate this requirement into the design.
- The system can be designed to receive surface water from the whole site, or from specific portions of it, as dictated by the topography. In the latter case several different surface water attenuation features may be needed.

Figure 7.8 illustrates examples of SuDs swales and ponds.

7.2.10 Construction

After clearing the site and getting it ready for construction, installing the drainage infrastructure for both foul and surface water is one of the first tasks to be completed on a building site.

Drainage engineers liaise closely with those designing the ecological systems for the management and treatment of both foul and surface water to achieve an integrated design that flows by gravity to a low point. To facilitate construction, detailed design drawings are prepared to exact specifications.

The foul drainage pipework draining the development to the low point will be connected to either the mains sewer, a septic tank, or a mechanical treatment plant. The discharge from the septic tank or MTP would discharge to a lined ecological system for further treatment before discharging to either a watercourse or land. The surface water drainage can discharge directly or via a swale to an attenuation pond or natural treatment system.

Figure 7.8 Examples of SuDs swales and ponds. (*Source:* Living Water.)

The treatment systems are lined to prevent untreated effluent from entering the groundwater. It is also important to ensure that there are no stones under the liner that could cause damage and leaks.

Topsoil should be stripped off and set aside to be used for forming the sides of the cells and/or for later landscaping. It is essential to manage the site so that no soil or debris reaches the watercourse during construction. As much recycling as possible should be employed with site materials, plants, soil, and so forth.

References

[1]   Hassan, N. M., "Feasibility of Condensate Recovery in Humid Climates," *International Journal of Architecture, Engineering and Construction,* Vol. 2, No. 4, December 2013, pp. 271–279, http://www.iasdm.org/journals/index.php/ijaec/article/view/202/116 (July 2016).

[2]   Office of Energy Efficiency and Renewable Energy, *Best Management Practice #10: Cooling Tower Management,* http://energy.gov/eere/femp/best-management-practice-10-cooling-tower-management (August 2016).

[3]   U.S. Environmental Protection Agency, *WaterSense at Work: Best Management Practices for Commercial and Institutional Facilities,* https://www3.epa.gov/watersense/commercial/docs/watersense_at_work/#/1/zoomed (August 2016).

[4]   National House Building Council, *NF20 Water Efficiency in New Homes: An Introductory Guide for Housebuilders,* 2010, NHBC Foundation.

[5]   Mudgal, S., et al., Study on Water Efficiency Standards: Final Report, July 2009, European Commission (DG Environment) report, BIO Intelligence Service, Paris, http://ec.europa.eu/environment/water/quantity/pdf/Water%20efficiency%20standards_Study2009.pdf (July 2016).

[6]   Australian Environmental Health Committee, *Guidance on Use of Rainwater Tanks,* https://www.health.gov.au/internet/main/publishing.nsf/Content/0D71DB86E9DA7CF1CA257BF0001CBF2F/$File/enhealth-raintank.pdf (August 2016).

[7]   British Standards Institution, *Code of Practice: Greywater Systems,* 2010, BS8525-1:2010, British Standards Institution, London.

[8]   British Standards Institution, *Gray Water Systems—Part 2: Domestic Gray Water Treatment Equipment—Requirements and Test Methods,* 2011, BS8525-2:2011, British Standards Institution, London.

[9]   British Water, *Code of Practice: Flows and Loads—4: Sizing Criteria, Treatment Capacity for Sewage Treatment Systems,* 2013, http://www.google.co.uk/url?sa=t&rct=j&q=&esrc=s&source=web&cd=1&ved=0ahUKEwjRzKqFwf3NAhVILMAKHRoYBXMQFggjMAA&url=http%3A%2F%2Fwww.britishwater.co.uk%2Fmedia%2Fdownload.aspx%3FMediaId%3D72&usg=AFQjCNEtQbH8m3p7dX-8aHWsMu8iowFxNA&sig2=cV6TYx5oORIzmvJ61-3SbQ (July 2016).

[10]   U.S. Environmental Protection Agency, *Constructed Wetlands,* https://www.epa.gov/wetlands/constructed-wetlands.

[11]   Department for Environment, Food & Rural Affairs, Environment Agency, *Rainfall Runoff Management for Developments,* Report SCO30219, https://www.gov.uk/government/publications/rainfall-runoff-management-for-developments_(August 2016).

[12]   http://www.uksuds.com (July 2016).

[13]   Construction Industry Research and Information Association (CIRIA), *The SuDS Manual,* 2015, CIRIA Report C753, http://www.ciria.org/Memberships/The_SuDs_Manual_C753_Chapters.aspx (August 2016).

[14]   HR Wallingford Ltd., *Greenfield Runoff Estimation for Sites,* http://www.uksuds.com/greenfieldrunoff_js.htm_(July 2016).

CHAPTER 8

Construction Phase Opportunities

Sustainable development is development that meets the needs of the present without compromising the ability of future generations to meet their own needs.
—The Brundtland Commission, 1987

8.1 Embracing Change

The global construction market is set to grow by 85% by 2030, with China, the United States, and India accounting for 57% of all global growth [1]. Yet as one of the largest environmental-impacting and resource-consuming industries, the construction industry is renowned as the most resistant to change, favoring traditional methods or financial concerns over alternative, more sustainable solutions. To ensure that the design intent is realized and the building performs accordingly, the construction phase must play its part and embrace the concepts of integrative design.

Sustainable construction has a positive impact on the entire life cycle of a project. Reducing resource consumption, waste production, pollution, and wider impacts on the surrounding environment will create buildings that provide healthy, comfortable, and fit-for-purpose spaces that provide longevity through quality of construction and future proofing. The challenge lies in delivering a product that satisfies all of these criteria while still delivering value for all stakeholders. The key to success is in collaboration, innovation, and finding efficiencies in "business as usual" processes.

Rethinking the approach to construction can improve effectiveness and prevent costly redesign or value-engineering processes. Although many methods are available to reduce the impact of the construction phase, as discussed later in this chapter, incorporating sustainability into the construction phase begins long before the first shovel hits the ground.

The opportunity to implement sustainable construction practices is defined by design decisions and must be considered as early as possible. Aspects such as the location (including weather profile) will directly affect the construction process, logistical arrangements on site, and supply chain options. Contractors are typically limited in their ability to control decisions regarding sustainable construction techniques, because decisions around building form and material selection are made during the design phase. Therefore, the involvement of contractors in the design phase so that they can advise on buildability, material selection, and construction technique is invaluable to achieving the design's intent: improving on-site coordination, reducing redesign and abortive works, and contributing toward a safer and more efficient construction process.

8.2 Legislative Drivers and Statutory Obligations

Increasing regulation in areas such as carbon emissions and waste and also client demands for responsible approaches to design and construction are forcing organizations to improve their processes. Corporate social responsibility (CSR) is about improving the way that businesses respond to the needs of stakeholders and ensure the long-term viability of their activities.

The U.K. government's *Strategy for Sustainable Construction* [2], launched in 2008, represents a commitment from the industry to work toward this vision by reducing its carbon footprint and consumption of natural resources, while creating a safer and stronger industry by training and retaining a skilled and committed workforce. The *Construction 2025* strategy, published in July 2013, includes a vision for "An industry that has become dramatically more sustainable through its efficient approach to delivering low carbon assets more quickly and at a lower cost, underpinned by strong, integrated supply chains and productive long term relationships" [3].

In the United States, the *2013 California Green Building Standards Code* [4] sets out mandatory and voluntary standards for low-impact development, including criteria for on-site development practices and deconstruction of existing buildings for reuse and recycling. Its earlier iteration, *CALGreen 2010*, was the first state-wide green building code.

In 2014, Singapore's Building Construction Authority launched its third *Green Building Masterplan* [5] with key strategic goals of (1) continued leadership, (2) wider collaboration and engagement, and (3) proven sustainability performance. Codes for mandatory energy disclosure effective from 2013 not only drive improvement in existing building stock performance, but also shift the emphasis of new-build projects to in-use performance compared to design targets. Three real estate and development companies are listed in the Corporate Knights' 2016 Global 100 Most Sustainable Corporations in the World—all based in Singapore [6].

Early sustainable construction practices have largely been driven through the use of green building certification schemes that include criteria to mitigate environmental impacts, driven by green building councils across the world, and often incorporated into regional planning conditions or codes. However, seeing beyond the marketing opportunities that the certifications or resultant awards can offer, contractors can distinguish themselves with a holistic and ambitious approach to sustainable development.

Through a combination of increased awareness, building codes at regional, state, and national levels, and the recognition of competitive advantage, the construction industry is gradually responding. Most construction companies now produce corporate social responsibility or sustainability reports, have sustainability policies, and/or employ dedicated sustainability managers. With a lack of consistent and coherent global government policy, the industry must demonstrate the way forward.

8.3   Procurement

A multidisciplinary integrated project must adopt procurement routes that define parameters reflecting the agreed-on targets; ensure appropriate project stage involvement for all disciplines; and provide space for flexibility and innovation while sharing risks. Contractors may promote a progressive approach to sustainable development through previous project performance and company policies; however, these must be aligned with project and client targets, otherwise one or more will inevitably be compromised.

For example, a contractor with a zero waste-to-landfill target or lean construction policy will struggle to deliver these ambitions on a project including design features that will generate waste only destined for a landfill or that specify high waste volume generating construction techniques.

This approach commands outside-the-box thinking, and continuous challenging of traditional working methods. Why should it be normal practice to make design choices that are inherently resource wasteful? Since the contractor is often not involved in, or responsible for, the operating building and its costs, there is little incentive to scan the market for alternative options that will provide value to the end user. The tender documents must clearly stipulate what the expectations of success are to the project stakeholders. The conversation must not be restrained by capital costs and impacts on schedule.

The general or principal contractor must be involved much earlier in the project process than traditionally appointed. The introduction of design and build (D&B) contracts, for example, has facilitated this, thus enabling the contractor to be in a position to influence design decisions and identify buildability issues. However, under these procurement models responsibilities often remain siloed and they do not incentivize the collaborative working necessary to achieve performance targets. D&B contracts are also often implemented to pass on risk, save money, and reduce delivery time, which is not conducive to fostering innovation.

Integrated project delivery (IPD) introduces an element of accountability that contractors and their supply chain are often not comfortable with, whereby the entire project team shares the risk opportunities and benefits of cost savings, but also bears some of the deficit when the budget is exceeded or anticipated operational cost savings are not achieved. This type of contract encourages efficient working and greater control of on-site procedures to ensure targets are delivered, extending focus into a shared interest in the whole life performance of the building.

8.4   Construction Documentation

The tender documents must clearly define the project parameters: design intent, sustainability and operational performance goals, and any green building certification objectives. Aspects relating to sustainability and sustainable construction must be clearly integrated into all construction documentation, including contracts and specifications. This ensures they are completely agreed on, understood, and acknowledged by all parties as an integral part of the project. This reduces the tendency for them to be viewed as "bolt-on" and secures their status as core principles. This is especially important for any innovative or unconventional aspects. They must reflect the client's design intent and project targets, and eliminate conflicts. For example, if the target is achieving the Living Building Challenge [7], but polyvinyl chloride (PVC), a Red List [8] item, is specified for the project, then the project's objectives and commitment to the final result will be undermined.

All members of a project team must be aware of any green building certification scheme such as LEED, BREEAM, or a regional equivalent that is being targeted, particularly with respect to expectations for documentation, which can be a large and often underestimated part of the certification process. A regular review of the project's predicted performance against criteria is important to track progress. At the design stage, a 10% to 15% contingency over the targeted certification level score is recommended to allow for any unavoidable loss of credits during later design development and construction phases.

Expectations for construction phase activities can be communicated in the form of a suite of detailed plans, allowing contractors, subcontractors, and the supply chain to be fully informed. These must be detailed and achievable to avoid lengthy negotiations, and most importantly there must be no room for interpretation. These should include, as a minimum, the following:

- *Sustainability action plan:* Outline the overall sustainability strategy for the project, and how activities on site contribute toward it. This is particularly useful to provide context (e.g., corporate and project targets, regulations) and where conditions affect the supply chain, for example, local and/or responsible sourcing.

- *Green building certification preassessment report:* Outline the strategy for targeted credits, including statements of any targeted certification level, responsibilities, and target action dates.

- *Site waste management plan (SWMP):* Include requirements for waste segregation and all areas of the waste hierarchy and adherence to the project's audit trail reporting requirements, including waste licenses and waste transfer notes, to demonstrate responsible handling of waste between a project site and destination. Require all tendering contractors to provide information on how they plan to reduce waste through the supply chain and site activities. Estimate waste stream volumes to feed into on-site management strategy.

- *Resource efficiency plan:* A document outlining the project's measures to reduce the use of energy, water, and fuel, and expectations of these on the subcontractor, including reporting requirements.

- *Environmental control plan:* Often combined with a health and safety plan, this document outlines control measures expected of the subcontractor to minimize impact on the surrounding environment, including hazardous substances and mitigation measures for specific site risks.

Request sustainability initiatives from the tenderer that will complement the overall sustainability strategy for the project. As experts in their field, they may be aware of innovations or alternative methods that could enhance the project, and should be given the opportunity to discuss them while they can still influence the design. The procurement process should be efficient, but flexible enough to accommodate a review period for these proposals—particularly if it will ultimately benefit the project.

Some projects allow for substitutions of products or systems where those originally specified are not available or when the subcontractor is aware of a superior (or cheaper) alternative. If this is permitted, ensure the process is valuable: the technical specification must be explicit about the sustainability or performance attributes that have contributed toward the selection of a particular element to enable these to be used as a basis of evaluation for potential substitutes. The approval process must involve review by all key stakeholders to ensure any impacts on other interrelated systems are captured and fully understood, and that the performance targets established during the design process are not affected.

There may be a perception on the part of some contractors that high-performance building approaches to construction are more costly, resulting in higher bids. This can be avoided by prequalifying contractors with experience in green design or by providing clear guidance on how costs can be maintained at standard levels. Indeed, an integrated approach should reduce overall project costs. A sustainability section must be incorporated into the prestart meeting minutes for all subcontractors in order to reinforce the project requirements.

8.5 Waste Management

Management of waste is one of the greatest challenges on a construction site. The logistics, space, and resources required to ensure that the strategy is efficient, valuable, and compliant with minimal impact on construction activities must strike a fine balance.

As the Waste and Resources Action Programme (WRAP) [9] identifies, two different types of waste arise from the construction phase of a development project [10]:

1. *Waste generated as a result of design and specifications:* This can occur when design solutions are proposed that prioritize aesthetic quality over other considerations, when unsuitable materials are specified, or when unusual design layouts or space sizes require on-site manipulation of materials.
2. *Waste generated by construction activities*: Poor workmanship, storage of materials, lack of coordination, or overordering can cause unnecessary waste generation.

8.5.1 Waste Management Versus Waste Reduction

Waste is about more than just disposal costs—those are just the tip of the iceberg. Waste is wasted resources, embodied carbon, and hidden costs (Figure 8.1). The true cost of waste includes the cost of raw materials, energy, labor, and so on, which can never be truly recovered.

Long before work begins on site, all parties must evaluate lean construction techniques to design out waste. Consider the root causes for waste, be informed by analysis of waste generation figures from other project sites, and schedule works with consideration for weather, watertightness, and deliveries.

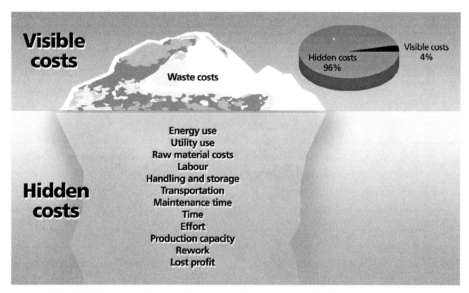

Figure 8.1 The hidden cost of waste. (*Source:* Envirowise, WRAP [11].)

All trades must see waste as a resource, in order to encourage efficient working practices and prevent wasteful habits, promoted through strong financial incentives. For example, if subcontractors were paid only for the quantity of materials being installed in the final building, any additional materials purchased as a result of required rework, damage caused during construction, or poor storage, would be charged to them or penalties applied. Contingencies built into the financial arrangements that allow for losses of materials do not incentivize resource efficiency. The cost of any additional materials as a direct result of their own actions should be borne by the subcontractor.

The contingency for additional resources should be tapped into only in extreme and/or uncontrollable circumstances—which are rare as most scenarios can be managed. For example, the cost of replacing water-damaged insulation due to poor storage on site should not result in additional cost to the client; the cost of replacing water-damaged insulation caused by flooding of properly stored materials, however, would be covered by a contingency. This will result in less waste being produced due to poor working practices and greater respect for the materials. It will also encourage take-back schemes other than those providing financial incentives—to avoid financial penalties—rather than taking the easy route of using the nearest waste skip.

Where work packages are procured per building element, the commercial team, or quantity surveyors, can quantify materials by individual subcontractors or tasks; when those same materials are in skips as waste it is impossible to trace back to the originator. By that point, it is no longer a waste reduction issue; it is a waste management issue. Without analysis of the amount of waste generated relative to the works installed, individual subcontractors can never know their efficiency rates; and as long as the cost is not attributed to them, they will have no desire to. Table 8.1 lists the various sources of waste.

Subcontractors willing to be accountable for their waste generation may also have an advantage during tender processes, as clients become increasingly aware

Table 8.1   Sources of Waste

Waste Generated as a Result of Design and Specifications	Waste Generated by Construction Activities
In-situ cutting of materials such as plasterboard, studwork, brick and blockwork, flooring, insulation, tiles etc., to fit room layouts, wall heights and openings, building services, etc.	Inaccurate or surplus ordering of materials that do not get used
	Damage through handling errors, inadequate storage, or poor coordination with other trades
Inefficient use of materials, lack of opportunity for reuse (limited standardization)	Rework due to low quality of work
	Temporary works materials (e.g., formwork, hoarding)

Adapted from WRAP.

of the true cost of waste, which extends beyond the cost of hiring a skip into transport, labor, original cost of wasted materials, and potential credit rates for valuable or recyclable materials.

A successful waste management strategy will reduce landfill rates, improve recycling rates, and drastically reduce costs. A designated waste coordinator, specifically or as part of a wider role (depending on the scale of the project), is responsible for promoting and monitoring the waste management strategies, adjusting where necessary, and educating the workforce on what, how, and, most importantly for universal buy-in, why. The waste coordinator should also regularly review the waste documentation, including waste transfer notes, invoices, and waste transfer facility records, to constantly review performance against targets and identify improvement areas. Could a waste stream destined for incineration be diverted to an alternative recycling route? Recognizing where an initiative is not working, or where the resource required outweighs the overall benefit, is just as important as identifying new opportunities.

Waste treatment facilities will often charge lower rates for segregated materials, because such materials require less post-collection sorting. Recyclable or valuable items may carry a zero cost or credit rate; the reduction in cost often justifies the additional cost and logistics involved in segregation before it leaves the construction site. It is extremely important to understand the destination of all waste streams from a project site. Aside from the implications of potential illegal fly-tipping and irresponsible disposal of waste or unlicensed carriers, knowing what happens to waste at a treatment facility focuses efforts on where segregation is beneficial.

One major area of influence is space. Space is often limited on construction sites, particularly in city center locations. Exploring options for increasing waste capacity on site will have both spatial and cost benefits, reducing the number of containers required and their associated rotations and, therefore, transport charges. Some readily available options include:

- *Compactors:* These are especially effective when waste segregation is simple, for example, cardboard or clear plastics, and well managed to avoid cross-contamination.
- *Balers:* These are useful for reducing void space in a container; however, the labor required to manually tie bales must be taken into consideration.

- *Roll packers or screw compactors:* Typically used on sites generating a significant amount of timber waste, these have impressive compaction rates and can reduce transports by up to 60%; however, they have a large energy requirement and specially adapted containers that might affect cost efficiency.

- *Take-back/donation schemes:* Where suppliers do not offer take-back schemes, research the local area for companies that offer buy-back schemes for particularly bulky items such as pallets or cable drums. Alternatively, offer such items to local charities, schools, or art groups that embrace the "industrial" look. Dry organic waste might be useful to a local farmer, and untreated timber off-cuts useful to a local operative with a wood burner.

Safety aspects should also be considered. Poorly stored materials or waste can be hazards and cause slips, trips, or falls—the most common cause of major construction-related injuries according statistics for 2013–2014 [12].

Subcontractors bearing waste removal costs individually, and therefore the financial benefits of segregation, will be incredibly adept at sorting waste streams. However, this approach is spatially inefficient and a paperwork nightmare! In centralized waste solutions, the rate of segregation at source (i.e., in work areas where the waste is produced) rapidly drops. This requires resource-inefficient double handling to ensure segregation rates. Measures to streamline the process and encourage best practice could include labeled or colored bins and skips in convenient locations, along with models linking financial incentives to sitewide segregation rates, and performance league tables whereby construction managers track and score monthly performance between subcontractors to encourage competition.

Online monitoring websites, such as the Building Research Establishment's SmartWaste [13], are useful for tracking waste and generating metrics, graphics, and analyses actual waste production against targets. On large sites this can be quite data-entry heavy; however, if used optimally the trend analysis can be used to influence purchasing and design decisions on future projects.

8.5.2 The Waste Hierarchy

The European waste hierarchy included in the Article 4 of the 2008 *Waste Framework Directive* [14], required EU member states to adopt policies prioritizing the following waste management order: prevention (or reduce), preparing for reuse, recycling, recovery, disposal. Each of these, with practical on-site opportunities, are discussed in detail below. Fundamentally, a significant proportion of construction waste has residual value that should be explored through the hierarchy of options, in order of preference.

8.5.2.1 Reduce

At an early design stage, a feasibility report should include an assessment of the impact of applying principles to design out waste on the project, including financial implications. These implications should also consider any potential financial benefits, such as savings from not removing waste from site, savings from avoiding demolition, or savings from avoiding the purchase of new materials [15].

Modularization and off-site construction solutions are increasingly being used. They reduce material use and waste (in a controlled environment) and transportation impacts, while guaranteeing improved building performance in terms of airtightness and quality of finish. Applications range from modern timber and light-gauge steel framing systems to tunnel form concrete casting to entire volumetric forms of construction (i.e., plantrooms), and they offer great potential for improvements to the efficiency of global construction. The potential exists for off-site construction, in collaboration with BIM (see accompanying box) and design coordination, to move some aspects of site activities from construction to assembly with multiple benefits.

Building Information Modeling

Building information modeling (BIM) can be used as a tool to realistically determine materials quantity and sequencing, and predict waste generation based on early scheme designs, enabling on-site waste management to be a part of early design conversations and development proposals accordingly. The 3D visualization provided by BIM helps identify coordination issues at early stages, complex engineering details, and potential installation challenges, thereby eliminating the need for costly and wasteful rework and improving on site efficiency [16]. The accuracy of BIM is entirely dependent on the quality of its inputs, and the more datasets the better. Collaboration between all project team members is imperative.

Implementing a just-in-time delivery process reduces volumes of waste produced by damaged materials caused by inclement weather or accidental damage from vehicles, and so forth. An off-site storage location or warehouse could also alleviate this issue. Good storage of materials is also a factor; for example, cover and raise absorbent materials such as plasterboard on a platform to prevent them from standing in water.

8.5.2.2   Reuse

A siloed approach to a construction project means that work packages and materials are procured individually. Overordering is a common strategy to reduce the risk of mistakes causing delays, and spatial pressures render it impossible to stockpile surplus materials on site until a use is identified. Successful reuse initiatives are identified through the coordination of works and cooperation of the subcontractors: one contractor's waste could be another contractor's resource.

Consider implementing a reuse station on site, whereby good-quality surplus materials are stored and made available to other contractors at zero cost. Hold coordination workshops to identify where works could be combined, therefore reducing waste production.

The most common applications of reused materials on-site are as follows:

- Reuse excavation materials to stabilize or backfill elsewhere on site.
- Process demolition materials using an on-site mobile crushing plant to provide aggregate for subbase layers.

- Use waste concrete, for example, in blocks for signposts or footpaths.
- Upcycle pallets and cable drums into furniture for canteen outdoor seating.
- Reuse timber off-cuts for site hoarding or signage.

Time, space, and equipment can often restrict opportunities for reuse; however, trying to reuse materials provides an opportunity to be creative. Reuse can also apply to reusing material from other locations in its original or adapted form, or donating materials from the project site to external sources for off-site reuse, such as community projects or local employees.

Capturing the quantities of waste reused on a project can be challenging, because sometimes it is happening more often than appreciated on an ad hoc basis. Subcontractors should be encouraged to report and document where possible, ideally with photos, where materials have been reused.

Case Study: Recycling and Improvisation, London 2012 Olympic Stadium [17]

Overordered material is generally collected and recycled efficiently, but of course it could also be resold. A high-profile example of this form of scrap diversion occurred during construction of the 2012 London Olympics.

The truss structure for the roof of the Olympic Stadium (see Figure 8.2) used 2,500 tons of "nonprime" steel tube, overordered from an oil and gas pipeline project. The original stadium design had specified large-diameter steel tubes, but the fabricator was concerned that the delays in purchasing new steel, and the difficulty of manufacturing these specialized sections, might delay construction. So the Olympic Delivery Authority (ODA) and Team Stadium chose to use this overordered stock to remove the risk of delays and to reduce the embodied emissions in the stadium.

The additional design time was modest, and despite having to overspecify some structural members, no additional weight was added to the structure. As a result of this action, 20% of the steel used in the stadium is diverted scrap. Although their motivation was to reduce project risk, and despite the additional design and testing effort, Team Stadium were delighted to find that reusing steel gave a small reduction in total project costs.

8.5.2.3 Recycle

Waste streams from a project that can be recycled into new materials are commodities; and this will be reflected in treatment costs. Ensuring segregation of, for example, metals, timber, plasterboard/drywall, glass, plastic and cardboard packaging, asphalt, concrete, and masonry, will generate the greatest returns. Negotiate credits rates with the waste transfer facility, and where possible arrange for diversion directly to recycling facilities to reduce transport impacts.

8.5.2.4 Recovery

Recovery is also known as energy recovery, waste to energy (WtE), or energy from waste (EfW). It offers a technologically advanced means of waste disposal while

Figure 8.2   London 2012 Olympic Stadium during construction. (*Photo:* Martin Cook.)

also generating clean, renewable energy, reducing greenhouse gas emissions, and supporting recycling through the recovery of metals. According to a 2012 white paper released by the Solid Waste Association of North America (SWANA) [18], EfW facilities "are economically sound investments that provide multiple financial and environmental benefits to the communities that utilize them" [19].

Energy waste is increasingly being recognized as its own waste stream, where waste to energy facilities exist. This can allow for reduced segregation requirements, in conjunction with a solid education strategy, whereby different waste streams would ultimately be combined at the waste transfer facility. Since treatment rates are directly linked to value, it is unlikely that further segregation would provide cost benefits for the on-site space and resources required.

This option should be ideally utilized only where alternative recycling options for a particular waste stream are not locally available.

8.5.2.5   Dispose

For the increasingly fewer materials that are not possible to reuse, recycle, or recover, the final option is a landfill. Landfill site resources all over the world are depleting, leading to a rise in alternative waste disposal methods such as recycling and energy recovery. Landfill can cause a negative impact on local communities and significant environmental damage, including pollution of the surrounding areas and generation of methane, a potent greenhouse gas, as organic matter decays. However, more modern sites operate responsibly, with active monitoring for landfill gas and groundwater contamination, and some collect and convert the gas into energy. The EPA's landfill methane outreach program (LMOP) strives to reduce methane gas emissions from landfill by encouraging the recovery and beneficial use of landfill gas (LFG) as a renewable energy resource [20].

To encourage resource efficiency and increase recycling rates, many countries have imposed penalties for landfill use, with a so-called "landfill tax" increasing year after year. Organizations including construction firms have set targets for diversion of their waste from landfill, with some also targeting diversion from incineration, of between 90% and 100%. Such a target requires designing out landfill waste, thoroughly reviewing all waste generation figures and waste streams to determine which are going to less desirable locations, and researching of the market for alternative suppliers where necessary. The greatest challenge lies in diverting contaminated demolition materials from landfill.

Case Study: Deconstruction of IOC Headquarters, Lausanne

The International Olympic Committee (IOC), based in Lausanne, Switzerland, is embarking on a ground-breaking project whereby the old headquarters, which has been the base for IOC operations since 1968, will be dismantled rather than demolished [21]. It is anticipated that at least 75% of the masterials can be re-used or recycled.

The IOC, in partnership with École Polytechnique Fédérale de Lausanne (EPFL), will evaluate the potential for materials from the deconstruction to be reused in future projects and explore the barriers to adopting this process. Deconstructing the building, rather than demolishing it, is a challenging undertaking that will maximize reuse and recyclability of materials and minimize landfill impact. The project began in Spring 2016 and will be closely monitored by the team involved.

The decision to adopt this innovative approach and explore the opportunities and implications for sustainable architecture demonstrates the IOC's commitment and vision toward sustainable development and will also provide insights for the industry.

8.5.3 Strategy Success

Waste management should be a regular item on meeting agendas, from the boardroom to the workers' committee meetings, to encourage dialogue and increase awareness, promoting sustainable behavior and choices. Performance against targets should be reported in monthly project reports and displayed on notice boards. Initiatives to promote good waste segregation and reward good behavior could include internal subcontractor or interproject league tables, or canteen meal vouchers for those who are most proactive in compliance.

Waste management is an important issue that cannot be ignored. The World Bank predicts a 70% global increase in urban solid waste between 2012 and 2025, from 1.3 billion to 2.2 billion tonnes per year [22]. Much of the increase is attributed to developing countries with scarce financial resources, rising populations, and limited capacity to manage environmental issues. The construction industry has an obligation, therefore, as one of the world's largest generators of industry waste, to influence the way waste is handled and capitalize on the opportunities to collaborate and share successes.

The chart shown in Figure 8.3 [23] outlines the four key areas that must be addressed for a successful waste management strategy for a construction site.

8.5.4   Circular Economy

A circular economy is one that is restorative and regenerative by design, aiming to keep products, components, and materials at their highest utility and value at all times [24].

The construction industry is guilty of following the linear take–make–dispose economic model. With increasing pressures on natural resources and mechanisms in place to encourage more responsible disposal, more organizations are exploring circular economy strategies to optimize on secondary resources as a way to reduce costs and sustain operations. It requires entirely rethinking business as usual operations; carrying out an in-depth review of all processes within an operation or manufacturing process including whole life cycle impacts such as transport and disposal; and challenging every element to identify opportunities to increase efficiencies and find value in what may have previously been considered waste, or where use can replace consumption.

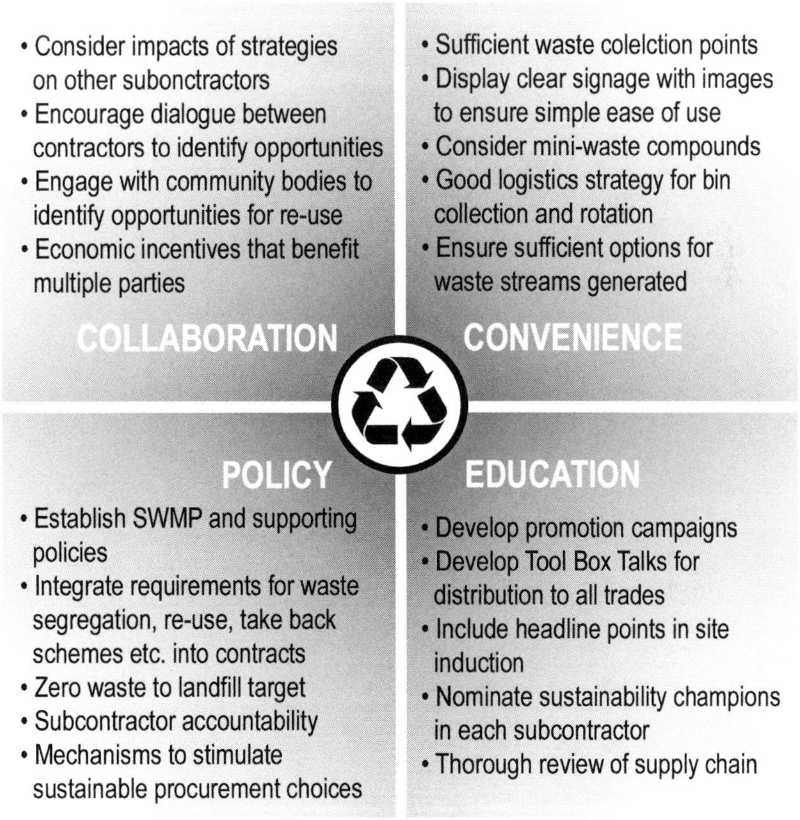

COLLABORATION
- Consider impacts of strategies on other subonctractors
- Encourage dialogue between contractors to identify opportunities
- Engage with community bodies to identify opportunities for re-use
- Economic incentives that benefit multiple parties

CONVENIENCE
- Sufficient waste colelction points
- Display clear signage with images to ensure simple ease of use
- Consider mini-waste compounds
- Good logistics strategy for bin collection and rotation
- Ensure sufficient options for waste streams generated

POLICY
- Establish SWMP and supporting policies
- Integrate requirements for waste segregation, re-use, take back schemes etc. into contracts
- Zero waste to landfill target
- Subcontractor accountability
- Mechanisms to stimulate sustainable procurement choices

EDUCATION
- Develop promotion campaigns
- Develop Tool Box Talks for distribution to all trades
- Include headline points in site induction
- Nominate sustainability champions in each subcontractor
- Thorough review of supply chain

Figure 8.3   Keys areas of on-site waste management.

The European Commission's *Circular Economy Strategy* [25] contains revised legislative proposals on waste focusing on closing the loop of product life cycles through greater recycling and reuse in an effort to stimulate Europe's transition toward a circular economy. This aims to "boost the European Union's competitiveness by protecting businesses against scarcity of resources and volatile prices, helping to create new business opportunities and innovative, more efficient ways of producing and consuming.... At the same time, it will save energy and help avoid the irreversible damages caused by using up resources at a rate that exceeds the Earth's capacity to renew them in terms of climate and biodiversity, air, soil and water pollution" [25]. Perhaps the greatest barrier to identifying circular economy solutions is the misalignment of priorities for all parts of the supply chain. A successful initiative must benefit the manufacturer, the contractor, and the recycling industry—and their respective agendas and commercial interests.

Building demolition accounts for around 450 million to 500 million tonnes of waste per year, one-third of the total volume of waste produced annually in Europe. A shift from demolition to dismantling of buildings would facilitate circular economy opportunities.

The Ellen Macarthur Foundation, a registered charity with the aim of inspiring a generation to adopt the framework of a circular economy, states that the circular economy rests on three principles [26], each addressing several of the resource and system challenges that industrial economies face:

> *Principle 1: Preserve and enhance natural capita* . . . by controlling finite stocks and balancing renewable energy flows. Use of renewable or better performing resources enhances natural capital by encouraging flows of nutrients within the system and creates the conditions for regeneration.
> *Principle 2: Optimize resource yields* . . . by circulating products, components, and materials at the highest utility at all times. Extend product life and optimize reuse through closed-loop systems to preserve energy and other resources such as labor.
> *Principle 3: Foster system effectiveness* . . . by revealing and designing out negative externalities. This includes reducing damage to human utilities, and managing externalities such as land use, air, water and noise pollution, release of toxic substances, and climate change.

While providing a broad spectrum capable of application to a range of industry outputs, these principles can undoubtedly be applied to the construction industry and its supply chain. It encourages review beyond the initial consideration of a material, product, or building for its aesthetic or superficial qualities, into evaluation of its potential for infinite or renewable use, ultimately preserving natural resources and optimizing efficiency (see Color Plate 22).

Case Study: ArcelorMittal

As one of the world's leading integrated steel and mining companies, ArcelorMittal has pursued alternative production methods applying circular economy principles. This approach enables the company to focus on reuse of steel back into the production processes, drastically reducing its dependency on natural resources.

To maximize this concept, the balance of limited global scrap supplies must first be addressed. ArcelorMittal is tackling this issue by maximizing the sustainability benefits over the entire life cycle of steel products. Even if recycling rates were to reach 100%, the world would still need more steel [27]. Through working with their supply chain, the whole life benefits of steel can be communicated and can drive recycling of the product at every opportunity. Alternative business model approaches, such as leasing steel rather than selling it, and incentivizing reuse of materials, are also under development to facilitate a change in demand. Steel is essentially infinitely recyclable, making it the ideal subject for a circular economy process.

8.6   Efficient On-Site Operations

Although minimal compared to the resource demands of the facility being built over its operational life, the construction phase of a project does offer opportunities to improve efficient use of electricity, water, and fuel. Often the client picks up the tab for this phase and will appreciate efforts to reduce the bills. With the knowledge and technologies available to us, there is no need for construction activities to contribute to unnecessary negative impacts during this important phase of a new development.

The adage "you can't manage what you can't measure" also applies to the construction industry. As discussed in this chapter, data must be collated in order for metrics to be set for waste generation and segregation, but also for utility consumption and carbon emissions associated with the construction or demolition of buildings.

8.6.1   Energy

Construction site operations are energy intensive. Prepare an energy plan during the setup phase to predict the energy consumption profile for the duration of the project. This could be used to negotiate preferential tariffs with energy companies and manage grid supply connections as early as possible, and to accurately calculate on-site demand to reduce wastage from oversized generators. This is especially pertinent in remote locations where temporary power supplies have multiple implications, being volatile and expensive to operate.

8.6.1.1   Construction Zone

- *Temporary on-site power*: Consider submetering of supplies to various areas and equipment to monitor usage.
- *Diesel power generators*: Minimize the use of on-site diesel power generators with high associated energy costs, CO_2 emissions, and potential for environmental damage due to frequent fuel deliveries.
- *Efficient lighting systems*: Install time clocks or daylight sensors on external lighting, and movement sensors on safety and/or security systems to ensure they are only used when required.

- *Remote lighting:* Minimize the use of mobile diesel lighting towers required through advance planning of temporary electrics or replace with hybrid lighting towers.
- *Maintenance:* Procure the most energy-efficient plant and equipment, with regular maintenance schedules. This also reduces downtime for unscheduled repairs.
- *No-idling policy:* Implement a "no-idling" policy on site to reduce fuel wastage and harmful emissions (see Section 8.7.2).
- *Efficient heating:* Use efficient internal heating systems with time clocks and ensure they are suitably spaced apart.
- *Scheduling:* Consider the impacts of weather in project programs or construction methods to reduce drying out during wet weather periods that place extra demand on space heating and welfare facilities.
- *Reduce demand:* Limit out-of-hours work to seasons with longer daytime hours or to essential work only to reduce nighttime lighting demands.

8.6.1.2   Site Accommodation and Welfare

During procurement of the site accommodation (i.e., office units and welfare facilities) integrate energy efficiency measures into the specification, and carry out cost/benefit analyses as necessary for each aspect. Some will be more effective than others dependent on the scope, scale, and length of the construction phase:

- *Energy-efficient, high-frequency lighting:* High lamp lumens per circuit watt (lm/cW) are conducive to a healthy working environment.
- *Absence detection sensors:* Best use is in cellular offices, toilets, and meeting rooms.
- *Lighting zones in open plan offices:* Ensure that lighting is only used as required during low occupancy; allows for user flexibility.
- *High-efficiency air-conditioning units:* Invest in high-performance units, particularly for large open plan spaces. Educate users on the effect that opening doors and windows when air conditioning is in operation has on efficient performance.
- *Time clocks on heating units:* Ensure employees are educated on the efficient use of heating units to avoid the temptation to overcompensate for internal conditions.
- *High-efficiency hand dryers:* Use high-efficiency dryers or omit dryers entirely (or a proportion of) in favor of recycled paper towels.
- *Solar panels:* Dependent on the demand, solar availability, and payback. May be used on remote lighting towers or site signage.
- *Insulation:* Use high thermal performance insulation, zero ozone depleting potential (ODP) and global warming potential (GWP), in walls, floors, and roof.

- *Double-glazed windows:* Openable or with large vents for natural ventilation, and blinds to reduce glare and solar gain.
- *Appliances:* Specify A+ or A Energy Star rated appliances for kitchen areas, and use on-demand hot water heaters that use lower energy to maintain hot temperatures in lieu of overuse of kettles.
- *Power down:* Fit high-energy usage equipment with out-of-hours settings.

8.6.2   Water

Construction site cabins are temporary and therefore some water-saving solutions are not viable. However, some small specification changes may result in large savings or the opportunity for reuse elsewhere on site:

- *Dual-flush toilets:* Increasingly standard specification due to the payback in water savings and reduced demand on infrastructure are undeniable.
- *Low-flow taps and showers:* Low-flow taps and showers reduce water consumption without compromising on use. Taps must be auto-shutoff to prevent being left on for long periods.
- *Waterless urinals:* While often overlooked as a viable alternative, properly maintained waterless urinals can save significant amounts of water a day on a large construction site.
- *Rainwater collection:* Collecting water from the roofs of site accommodation for storage and reuse for dampening down the site in dry conditions, in lieu of using potable water.
- *Rainwater harvesting systems:* For more established or long-term projects, or a satellite office with limited access to the mains infrastructure, a self-sufficient rainwater harvesting system can result in significant savings in terms of the water required for flushing toilets or for wheel wash systems.
- *Cleaning:* Install shoe cleaners between site and welfare/office areas to reduce cleaning demands.

A combination of the solutions outlined is likely to provide the most benefit, depending on the specific requirements of each site. Metering and submetering on electricity and water supplies provide automatic or manual readings, and results can be used to identify where further savings might be made.

8.6.3   Site Logistics

A site's logistical arrangements also have an important part to play in reducing the unnecessary waste of resources:

- *Deliveries:* Adopt a delivery management system to ensure deliveries are staggered to limit the number of waiting vehicles. Deliveries from the same supplier should be combined where possible, reducing carbon emissions associated with part loads.

- *Alternative transportation:* Give precedence to rail or water transport over road deliveries.
- *Site transport:* Stagger working shifts to reduce impacts on local residences and businesses.
- *Resource management:* Anticipate low resource levels to avoid expensive last-minute orders of fuel or water.
- *On-site fuel storage:* On large sites, a dedicated fuel contractor and delivery area will attract preferential supply rates; ensure safe operations, reducing the likelihood of spillages and fire risk; and enable accurate tracking of fuel usage.
- *Out of hours:* Conduct system checks across the construction zone and site accommodation to ensure equipment is not left on unnecessarily.

8.7 Pollution Prevention

Sufficient consideration of the risks and impacts of a construction project can mitigate the effect on surrounding areas, and implementation of clear and appropriate control measures will ensure the building is completed without causing irreparable damage.

Some of the most common sources of construction-related pollution include fuel storage and delivery area spillages, vehicle maintenance faults and improper chemical storage. Consequences can include groundwater contamination, soil or watercourse pollution, human health problems, and serious damage to plants and animal life. In some cases, environmental damage can lead to large fines or prosecution.

8.7.1 Water Pollution

A water pollution prevention plan contains policies and control measures to reduce the chance and effect of spillages. These must be incorporated into methods of working and must be identified in the job hazard analysis (JHA), the job saftey analysis (JSA) or risk assessment method statement (RAMS) documents. Control of substances hazardous to health (COSHH) extends across any product that holds a material safety data sheet (MSDS or SDS) from the manufacturer, because some materials and products can have health implications during usage or environmental impacts if not handled correctly. Working methods must therefore always consider the correct storage, movement, handling, and disposal per the manufacturer's recommendations. This includes use of appropriate personal protective equipment (PPE) to prevent personal injury, secondary containment (or *bunding*) and storage to contain spills of hazardous substances, and responsible disposal of empty containers and used spill kits.

Refueling policies must call for the use of dedicated refueling teams to prevent spillages associated with refueling of plant and equipment and require the use of automatic shutoff nozzles, and drip trays. Regular checking and maintenance of the equipment can prevent issues before they occur.

Fully stocked fuel, oil, and chemical spill kits must be distributed across the construction site, in areas of high vehicle or machinery usage and vulnerability, such as open drains or watercourses, and work areas handling fuel and chemicals. All operatives should have a basic level of training for handling hazardous substances and spill responses in the event of, for example, a plant hydraulic line failure. A dedicated on-site spill response team should have specialist training (and be easily identified and contactable in the event of an incident) to ensure appropriate containment of spills, protection of surrounding areas, and facilitation of cleanup. Establish a connection with a local spill response company to provide assistance in the event of a large or uncontrollable spill.

Regular monitoring of nearby watercourses, groundwater, and drainage systems may be required to ensure the site is operating within permit conditions, and identify any issues that may be caused by on-site activities.

8.7.2   Air Pollution

Air pollution can be affected by the plant, machinery, and vehicles associated with on-site activities and transportation of personnel and deliveries to site. To reduce the impacts from construction activities, an air quality management plan can address ways to reduce harmful fumes on site, for both health and environmental considerations. Measures can include:

- *Preventive equipment maintenance:* All subcontractors should keep registers of inspections and certifications and carry out necessary repairs to ensure plant and equipment are fit for purpose. Instigate preuse inspections to identify any issues before use, such as leaking connections or valves, or filters requiring replacement.

- *Reduce the need for diesel:* Evaluate opportunities to replace diesel plant or equipment with alternative sources or fuels.

- *Emissions standards:* Implement emission standard requirements (U.S. EPA, EU directive or local equivalent), ensuring that equipment is suitable for use on site. Where newer equipment is not available, require exhaust filters or retrofit newer, cleaner engines to reduce particulate emissions.

- *No-idling policy:* Implement this type of policy in vehicle holding locations and on site to reduce nuisance impacts on local neighbors, emissions, and wasted fuel. As a building becomes airtight, exhaust emissions will affect the cleanliness of internal ventilation systems—requiring additional cleaning and filters and possibly affecting performance and indoor air quality. Locate loading bays and generators away from air intakes and building openings, and prohibit the use of diesel-fueled vehicles inside the building in favor of electric-powered vehicles. This requirement must be considered during sequencing workshops.

- *Cleaner fuels:* Use biofuels, electricity with green energy supply contracts (e.g., from wind generation), on-site solar, and so forth.

8.7.3   Other Pollution Sources

Impacts from construction site activities can also include noise, dust, and light pollution:

- Foundation piling and other noisy activities are often restricted by development permits to within specific time limits to reduce impacts on neighboring properties. Strict working hours, scheduling of work, and alternative construction methods can help in reducing the impact.

- Dust from construction work (e.g., resulting from demolition and building work on site and vehicle movements on the approach) can have a dramatic effect on the immediate and local surroundings. There is an obvious visual impact, but dust also presents problems for public health and wildlife. Dampening down the site in dry weather, ideally using captured rainwater with a mist sprayer rather than potable water, can reduce the effects. Cover loaded skips to prevent dust and debris en route to the waste facility.

- Light pollution, particularly from sites allowing out-of-hours work, can have a negative affect on nearby properties. Restricting the site to essential lighting only, using time clocks or presence sensors, and installing light fittings that restrict the arc of light can reduce nuisance overspills of light from the construction zone.

8.8   Other Considerations

The spectrum of sustainability as it applies to the construction phase is broad, and many other opportunities exist to help ensure that the development will have a positive impact throughout its life cycle. The project should also have the flexibility to adopt sustainability initiatives during the construction phase as the inspiration arises.

8.8.1   Community Engagement

A construction site has an unavoidable impact on its surrounding area. Beyond the site boundaries are communities affected by the development through increased traffic, noise, light, or dust. While the physical impacts can be mitigated, there are opportunities to have a positive impact, some of which can leave a legacy long after the project is finished. For example, through the duration of the project, consider a quota for employment of local staff and internships or partnerships with local colleges. This provides inclusion, increases local perception, and offers education. When undertaking charity events, consider donating a portion of the proceeds to a local school or community center, or host an information event to discuss the project. Newsletters are a good way to communicate news about a development and inform those affected by upcoming changes; however, personal engagement will develop acceptance of the project and help ensure that the new occupants will be welcome.

8.8.2   Biodiversity

In June 1992 the Convention of Biological Diversity was signed by 159 governments at the Earth Summit, which took place in Rio de Janeiro, establishing a legal framework for global biodiversity conservation. Natural habitats are often a casualty of new construction developments. As brownfield land is in short supply, the boundaries of developed areas encroach onto previously undeveloped greenfield sites.

Legislation and green building rating systems promote responsible development, and in many areas biodiversity plans or environmental impact assessments (EIAs) are early project stage requirements. These require extensive research into the site conditions and existing ecological features to inform early design options and advise on any protected species identified through on-site surveys. Protection and enhancing of biodiversity are valuable from both an ecological point of view and also a well-being perspective for the occupants of the future building.

Dependent on the findings and recommendations of the EIA (or equivalent), the following measures can be taken:

- Construction should be scheduled at an appropriate time of year so as to minimize disturbance to wildlife. For example, avoid site clearance work during nesting season. Removal of an active bird's nest is illegal in some countries.

- Provide protection measures for all existing ecological features on the site. For example, any protected plant species or watercourses should be protected with fencing and signage.

- Provide guidance on actions to take if any live animals are found on site.

- Include protection of ecology within the site induction, and raise awareness of any site-specific issues.

- Appoint a biodiversity champion to ensure all legislation with respect to biodiversity protection is met.

Where impact on biodiversity is unavoidable, offset the impact by investigating alternative off-site projects that would benefit the local community. Enhancing biodiversity should be aligned with social and economic benefits that are less quantifiable, such as well-being, productivity, and health, so that it can be considered more than an architectural feature.

8.8.3   Transportation

Construction sites will inevitably cause pressures on local transport systems, with personnel and deliveries relative to the project scale and program. Green transport plans can identify ways to both reduce transportation costs and alleviate congestion. Car pooling, minivans, staggered shift patterns, and the use of greener transport options such as public transport or offering cycle-to-work schemes (with required infrastructure such as cycle lanes, parking, and shower facilities) can reduce pinch points.

8.8.4 Cloud Collaboration

The effective coordination of design information, and the tracking of design changes and communications against regular reviews of project targets, is an important element a multidisciplinary collaborative construction projects. To facilitate the smooth transfer of information between project team members, the construction industry is moving into the 21st century. Traditionally a very paper-intensive industry, with reams of paper and ink used in printing (and archiving) everything from lengthy contracts to every drawing revision, it is embracing the digital age and adopting cloud collaboration and storage systems.

Platforms allow for communication, sharing, real-time editing, tracking, reductions in server space, and digitizing of the document and drawing review process. These platforms improve the efficiency of information exchange, the approvals process, and defects management. These systems also enable communications across multiple locations and time zones, and with the support of video conferencing, virtual teams are possible. This has a particular impact on the construction phase, whereby changes in design can be reviewed and incorporated without causing significant delays.

8.8.5 Achieving Buy-In

Sustainability in the construction industry is still relatively new, and it requires a significant shift in perceptions and attitudes to ensure its success. While the project objectives can be clearly laid out in the tender documentation, a program of awareness at the project delivery level is also required.

Previous experiences and impressions of sustainability have resulted in the concept being seen as more of a nuisance than a provider of value. Perhaps someone has worked on a "green" project that resulted in significant increased costs or failed to achieve a green building certification target due to a poor strategy. Or someone had a poor experience with an innovative system that did not perform as promised or handled a project guilty of greenwash. Therefore, for an initiative to be successful, its benefits must be clear, tangible, and undeniable. Several highly successful initiatives will foster more buy-in and support than multiple low-impact ones.

A strong communication strategy will undoubtedly assist with buy-in. A sustainability notice board, used to communicate to all stakeholders actual performance against targets, will help illustrate the bigger picture and encourage cooperation. Signage around the site, for example, on waste segregation or environmental controls, should contain carefully selected images to communicate the intent clearly, transcending language and levels of literacy. If text is required, it should be short and punchy, and in the nominated site language(s). When preparing communications, always consider the target audience, and ensure the question of "Why should I?" is addressed. On construction sites there can be layers and layers of rules and regulations. To avoid something being "just another rule," use signs to explain, for example, that segregated plastic waste is recycled into new products, or that biowaste is collected by a local pig farmer, or that turning off the lights saves carbon and money.

Site bulletins or a sustainability newsletter are another effective way of communicating initiatives and the successes—or otherwise! They provide a high-level context to the requirements being implemented at the site level and demonstrate involvement in the bigger picture. They can and should be used to thank operatives and their delivery team regarding the successes of the project.

Buy-in from everyone on the project at all levels is essential to maximize success and provide longevity to new initiatives past the initial novelty period, embedding them into the construction phase as business as usual, and providing value on multiple levels.

8.8.6   Training and Education

To ensure that the project sustainability requirements are communicated through to the project delivery level, clear and regular training should be encouraged. Key objectives and initiatives must be communicated through site inductions, ensuring that every worker and visitor attending the site is well informed.

General contractors should develop a suite of Toolbox Talks covering specific areas of interest such as waste segregation, energy conservation, water conservation, hazardous substances, protection of biodiversity, spill response procedures, timber certification, materials sourcing, and green building certification schemes. These must be short and informative and circulated regularly to ensure communication is as widespread as possible in a high-turnover environment.

Employee recognition or incentive schemes are a good way to inspire cooperation. Suggestion boxes are frequently used to allow an employee to raise awareness about a pending environmental issue, demonstrate good actions to avoid environmental damage, or propose an innovative sustainability initiative. This could be coupled with canteen meal vouchers or monthly prize draws to encourage participation.

Subcontractors should be encouraged to identify sustainability champions who are tasked with identifying or communicating the environmental and sustainability requirements of the project to their colleagues and feeding back suggestions or alternative proposals.

The general contractor should ensure that the delivery management team has a minimum level of environmental awareness and is encouraged to recognize potential on-site issues or areas for improvement.

8.8.7   Commissioning and Testing

Often misinterpreted to focus solely on testing during the end of the construction phase, commissioning is actually a collaborative process for planning, delivering, and operating buildings that work as intended. As stated in [28], "Commissioning is a holistic process that spans from pre-design planning to post-construction operation and can be thought of as a checks-and-balances system". Subcontractors should be given incentives to accept accountability for their installations by linking payments or bonuses to commissioning test results. In addition, include requirements for commissioning, recommissioning (1 yr later), and training and education of operations and maintenance staff.

Overall building performance will include a requirement for airtightness as a measure of how effective the building fabric is at preventing interstitial leaks. This will require a formal airtightness test, the results of which will be directly impacted by the quality of installations. This is one of many reasons why defects management should occur throughout the entire construction phase, not simply be left until the final few weeks before completion, to enable continuous review of installation quality. A robust quality plan and clear performance specification will help achieve this.

In the final rush to hand over a building, all too often construction stage commissioning is not undertaken with sufficient rigor. The risks associated with inadequate commissioning should be identified early in the design process and they way they are to be mitigated form a key element of any Soft Landings protocol. Construction stage commissioning should be seen as the first stage in a process of continuous commissioning to be undertaken on a regular basis over the life of the building (see Section 9.4).

8.9   Green Building Certification Schemes

The green building certification schemes discussed elsewhere in the book, often contain three types of credits as related to the construction phase: (1) design or specification elements requiring management, (2) credits specifically related to construction practices, and (3) credits used to promote innovation outside of the scope of standard points.

A major drawback of these systems is that they are often very linear. Achieving some credits affect the ability to achieve others (it is therefore impossible to achieve 100%!), and thresholds for credit awards are strictly adhered to (as is required to establish a robust governance system). In an all-or-nothing approach, gut feeling or previous experience overrules—often to the detriment of a genuinely viable alternative or innovative solution. There is little incentive to carry out a feasibility study or invest in research if the end options might be rejected by the client on a cost basis or otherwise. The client willing to pay for this indulgence of time is a rare one; but sometimes, the resulting solutions may just be worth it, given the incentive and latitude to take the plunge.

For the certification process to provide value, it must be applied effectively and the practice of chasing credits (or, worse, buying credits) must be avoided in order to achieve a particular certification level. Each point or credit scoring initiative or feature must be evaluated for its merits and the benefit they bring to a building and its occupiers. Statements such as "If we do that we will lose a credit?" or "How many credits will that get us?" are unfortunate by-products of the green building certification process, and this does not create truly sustainable buildings. They should be applied in the way they are intended—as assessment schemes, not design tools. As previously discussed, a building that achieves a certification level may not live up to the expectation, and leaves a poor legacy for the client. And indeed, perhaps a building that achieves a lower certification level may perform better in operation than its neighbor with a more glitzy certificate in the lobby.

It is tempting for a green building certification scheme to assume that the construction stage-related points will be achieved iwthout truly appreciating the nuances of the compliance requirements. A good practice to prevent the loss of credits previously targeted during the construction phase is to generate a roadmap for the project, outlining the credit targets and the actions that must be taken at different stages of the project schedule. Some schemes require actions to be taken and documented at specific times of the design phase in order for construction-related items to be achieved. Failure to do this, and simply mark a credit as the contractor's responsibility, may render some credits unachievable and therefore the final score will not reflect the actual practices on site. Worse, if it affects a prerequisite credit, the entire certification is unachievable.

For example, both LEED and BREEAM require a 10-yr management plan to be written for the ecological habitat features of the site. This should be done by the landscape architect, in consultation with a qualified ecologist, to reflect (and ideally influence) the landscaping strategy for the site. If this critical element is not completed, the credits may not be achieved, despite the development having well-thought-out and well-managed external areas. These can be expensive and/or time-consuming mistakes to rectify.

8.10 Collaboration Is Key

Sustainable practices on a construction site must be a collaborative effort, ultimately ensuring that the project is completed while minimizing its demand on natural resources and impact on the environment. They must be commercially viable, practical, and beneficial to the project and its wider context to achieve buy-in: from the cleaner who turns off lights and heaters at night, to the operative reusing timber off-cuts to make a sign, to the quantity surveyor encouraging a tenderer to consider alternative suppliers with FSC or ISO 14001 certification, and finally to the design manager feeding back to the client measures to reduce waste through design changes. Lessons from what has worked and, just as importantly, what has not worked must be captured and fed into each of the stakeholders' future projects until it becomes common practice. The measures discussed in this chapter should be a core part of the construction process, and not hampered by the traditional priorities of site management: embrace new innovative technologies but also know when tried and tested methods really are the best solution.

Regular meetings must be held during the construction phase between the client and contractor, in order to keep lines of communication open. Any potential risks or deviations from the agreed-on scope, specification, or targets must be identified early, perhaps via a risk register. Using a roadmap to guide discussions and remind the team of core principles will focus discussions.

For the construction phase to deliver a whole system building successfully, the conditions of success are as follows:

- Have clear goals, targets, and visions for the project.
- Establish required systems, processes, and contractual environments in which they can be delivered.
- Align all team members and supply chain toward the goals.

There is no one-size-fits-all approach. The secret is in finding synergies between different site processes to deliver a quality product efficiently, while ensuring the aspirations of the project's stakeholders are upheld. In different locations the solutions implemented will vary depending on the social, economic, and environmental benefits that the project can bring to the local community. However, the underlying principles will remain the same, and the greater the coordination of all aspects of this complicated process, the greater the results.

References

[1]   Global Construction Perspectives and Oxford Economics, *Global Construction 2030*, November 2015, http://www.globalconstruction2030.com (August 2016).

[2]   HM Government, *Strategy for Sustainable Construction*, June 2008, http://webarchive.nationalarchives.gov.uk/+/http:/www.bis.gov.uk/files/file46535.pdf (August 2016).

[3]   HM Government, *Construction 2025—Industrial Strategy: Government and Industry in Partnership*, July 2013, https://www.gov.uk/government/uploads/system/uploads/attachment_data/file/210099/bis-13-955-construction-2025-industrial-strategy.pdf (August 2016).

[4]   *2013 California Green Building Standards Code*, California Code of Regulations Title 24, Part 11—California Building Standards Commission, http://www.documents.dgs.ca.gov/bsc/CALGreen/2013-California-Green-Building-Standards-Code.PDF (August 2016).

[5]   Singapore Building Construction Authority, *3rd Green Building Masterplan*, https://www.bca.gov.sg/GreenMark/others/3rd_Green_Building_Masterplan.

[6]   Corporate Knights, *The Global 100*, http://www.corporateknights.com/reports/global-100/#requestReport (August 2016).

[7]   Living Building Challenge, http://living-future.org/lbc (August 2016).

[8]   Living Building Challenge, *Red List*, http://living-future.org/redlist. (August 2016). The Red List represents the "worst-in-class" materials, chemicals, and elements known to pose serious risks to human health and the greater ecosystem.

[9]   Waste and Resources Action Program (WRAP) is a U.K.-based charity focusing on the promotion of waste management and resource efficiency. http://www.wrap.org.uk.

[10]   Waste and Resources Action Program (WRAP), *Reducing Material Wastage in Construction*, 2007 http://www2.wrap.org.uk/downloads/Reducing_Material_Wastage_in_Construction.95823cfa.4711.pdf.

[11]   Envirowise, *Waste Minimisation for Managers*, Report GG367, 2002, http://www.wrap.org.uk/sites/files/wrap/GG367.pdf (August 2016).

[12]   Health and Safety Executive (HSE), *Slips and Trips and Falls from Height in Great Britain*, 2014, http://www.hse.gov.uk/statistics/causinj/slips-trips-and-falls.pdf.

[13]   Building Research Establishment, *SmartWaste*, http://www.smartwaste.co.uk (August 2016).

[14]   European Commission, *Waste Framework Directive*, Directive 2008/98/EC, http://ec.europa.eu/environment/waste/framework (August 2016).

[15]   Waste and Resources Action Program (WRAP), *Designing Out Waste: A Design Team Guide for Buildings*, http://www.modular.org/marketing/documents/DesigningoutWaste.pdf (August 2016).

[16]   Waste and Resources Action Program (WRAP), *Resource Efficiency through BIM: A Guide for BIM Users*, February 2013, http://www.wrap.org.uk/sites/files/wrap/Resource%20efficiency%20through%20BIM%20-%20a%20Guide%20for%20BIM%20Users.pdf (August 2016).

[17]   Extract from Allwood, J. M., and J. M. Cullen, *Sustainable Materials: With Both Eyes Open*, 2011, http://www.withbotheyesopen.com/index.html (July 2016).

[18]   Solid Waste Association of North America, *Waste-to-Energy Facilities Provide Significant Economic Benefits*, http://swana.org/portals/Press_Releases/Economic_Benefits_WTE_WP.pdf (August 2016).

[19]   Covanta, *Understand How Energy-from-Waste Works*, http://www.covanta.com/sustainable-solutions/energy-from-waste.aspx.

[20]   U.S. Environmental Protection Agency, *Landfill Methane Outreach Program*, https://www3.epa.gov/lmop/index.html.

[21]   IOC Olympic House: Deconstruction and Reuse, https://www.olympic.org/olympic-house-new/deconstruction-and-reuse. Last accessed October 2016.

[22]   World Bank, *What a Waste: A Global Review of Solid Waste Management*, 2012, http://go.worldbank.org/BCQEP0TMO0.

[23]   Adapted from FCM Green Municipal Fund, *Getting to 50% and Beyond: Waste Diversion Success Stories from Canadian Municipalities*, 2009 https://www.fcm.ca/Documents/tools/GMF/Getting_to_50_percent_en.pdf (August 2016).

[24]   Ellen Macarthur Foundation, *Circular Economy,* http://www.ellenmacarthurfoundation.org/circular-economy (August 2016).

[25]   European Commission, *Circular Economy Strategy: Closing the Loop—An EU Action Plan for the Circular Economy*, December 2015, http://ec.europa.eu/environment/circular-economy/index_en.htm (August 2016).

[26]   Ellen Macarthur Foundation, *The Principles of a Circular Economy,* https://www.ellenmacarthurfoundation.org/circular-economy/overview/principles (August 2016).

[27]   ArcelorMittal, *Efficient Use of Resources and High Recycling Rates,* http://corporate.arcelormittal.com/sustainability/2014-report/resources (August 2016).

[28]   "Roadmap for the Integrated Design Process, Summary Guide and Reference Manual, BC Green Building Roundtable," complied by Busby Perkins + Will and Stantec Consulting, 2007. http://www.greenspacencr.org/events/IDProadmap.pdf. Last accessed October 2016.

CHAPTER 9

Post-Construction

Bad architecture is, in the end, as much a failure of psychology as of design
—Alain de Botton, *The Architecture of Happiness*

9.1 Post-Construction Evaluation: Closing the Gap Between Design Intent and Actual Performance

Bill Bordass, The Usable Buildings Trust, U.K.

9.1.1 Introduction

Clients are increasingly interested in specifying buildings by output performance. Unfortunately, however, building performance assessment has not been a routine—or even a familiar—activity for most clients, designers, and builders, so everybody is on a steep learning curve. This applies to a great extent all around the world. Although one might expect designers, builders, and project managers to be experts on the in-use performance of the buildings they make, this is not what they have been trained to do, and seldom are they commissioned and paid to do it. They are appointed to create or to change buildings, not to follow things through into operation, so they go away when their work is physically complete.

If clients have their own building professionals, they often do the same thing: Their job description is to procure the facility, not to breathe life into it. Even where things might appear to be more integrated—as in third-party funded design, build, and operate projects—under the surface one can often find the same old processes and divisions of labor, sometimes in an exaggerated form, for example, with a more constrained role for the designers. In spite of the rapid growth in facilities management, creative involvement of building operators in briefing and design decisions has also proved difficult to achieve.

9.1.2 The Need for Project Feedback

Of course, a lot is known about aspects of how buildings perform: research, publicized failures, and personal and organizational interest and involvement create all sorts of feedback loops. However, most of these are not closely connected to the delivery of an individual project. Nor are they good at detecting minor problems, which can be advance warnings, or just low-level but nevertheless real impediments to a building and its occupiers achieving their potential—so the same shortcomings can often recur in project after project.

Meanwhile, the insights of organizations with large stocks of buildings have often become less precise as their design, maintenance, and technical services departments have been outsourced, thus breaking some of the feedback loops they used to take for granted.

9.1.3   Post-Occupancy Evaluation

To get better information on in-use performance, interest has been growing in post-occupancy evaluation (POE). In the past, POE was largely research based and often covered a limited range of issues (in particular, thermal comfort, energy performance, and environmental psychology), albeit sometimes in considerable detail.

For various reasons, integration of POE with everyday practice has proven difficult. Reasons for this disconnect seem to include the following:

- *Different priorities of building projects and researchers*—so a real-world approach is required.
- *Timescales of building projects*—so techniques need to be applied and analyzed rapidly.
- *Uncertainty about the utility of results*—so proven techniques and benchmarks are important.
- *Uncertainty about costs and cost effectiveness*—so robust, low-cost methods are helpful.
- *Fears by designers of uncovering problems*—so start with a no-blame approach.
- *Fear by designers of affecting their professional indemnity insurance*—so insurers may need to be consulted.
- *Worries about being wise after the event, when all decisions have been made, the budget spent, and nothing much more can be done*—however, feedback information can often be applied at little cost, to the benefit of the individuals and buildings concerned.
- *Uncertainty about whether the learning would be used*—certainly knowledge management systems in the industry can be creaky, but the people directly involved definitely benefit.
- *Reluctance of clients to pay for something they felt should be taken for granted*—but some clients do now seem more prepared to invest, and the costs will be recouped by better performance.

9.1.4   Making Feedback and POE Routine

In recent years, as a result of greater use, better analysis software, and the Internet, POE techniques have become faster, cheaper, and more robust, which has helped to overcome many of the barriers to their use. Clients are also more interested in understanding and improving building performance and occupant satisfaction and productivity, and leading design and building teams are beginning to realize its importance to their future credibility.

However, there is a long way to go, progress is slow, and the dangers of being wise after the event remain. So POE should be seen as part of a continuous improvement process for all of the parties involved: incorporated into a broad framework of developing insights, setting and managing expectations, providing follow-through and feedback throughout the life cycle of a building and of a project, and informing and learning from related projects.

9.1.5   What Range of Techniques Can Be Used?

While a universal, standard technique has its attractions, several recent studies confirm that one size will not fit all. A balanced approach to suit the specific needs of the project and the client makes more sense. To be of interest to senior management, it may also be important to link what is examined to business drivers, for example: How is the building affecting our staff? What is its effect on their perceived productivity and can it be improved further? What is its environmental impact? How could we get better value for money next time? From the perspective of the design and building team, however, it is also necessary to focus on the things over which they have a direct influence.

9.1.6   What Should We Be Thinking About?

Often people ask "Did the building meet our requirements?" This question is often difficult to answer because usually both the requirements and the actualities have changed since the project was initiated. Often a more useful set of questions is "How well is the building working? How well does it compare with its peers? Where can it be improved? What lessons can be learned?"

Another important question for any organization is "Is it delivering its business benefits?" The answer, however, can be a complex mixture between the culture and management of the organization; its effect on the psychology of the users; the design, operation, and use of the building; and other aspects such as information technology support. When looking at in-use performance, it is often helpful to concentrate on the issues that are within the remit of the design, building, and management team.

9.1.6.1   Start at the Beginning If You Can—Ideally, When a Project Is Initiated

Introducing POE techniques at the start of a project will help you get the brief straight because these techniques can help you understand the actual performance of the facilities you want to replace or of other buildings you feel you could learn from. It is then possible to establish and calibrate some of the briefing requirements against achieved realities; to express them in a form that can be kept under review as the project develops; and to assess outcomes on the same basis, once the building is in use.

9.1.6.2 Changing the Process

Starting at the beginning also allows the client to require the design and building team not just to commit to a POE of the outcome, but to operate a management system that is performance driven, constantly reviewing likely outcomes against client and design aspirations, managing expectations, and making the maximum use of feedback throughout the procurement process. Soft Landings (see Section 5.3) can help clients, design, and building teams to do this; in particular, they help ease the transition from construction project into operation including organization, communication, fine-tuning, support during initial occupation, and checks of energy performance and occupant satisfaction using POE techniques. It is usually impossible to retrofit something like Soft Landings after people have been appointed, owing to the difficulty and expense of changing habits and management systems in the middle of a job. However, there are many opportunities for using feedback and POE techniques at almost any stage in the life cycle of a building.

9.1.6.3 A Possible Starter Pack

Some people get interested in POE, want to examine everything, and then grind to a halt owing to the complication, expense, and information overload. Experience suggests it is better to do a few things, gain confidence in them, and then move on to further use of a POE if there is a case for doing so. Information on a number of techniques by subject, building type, and stage of development can be downloaded from the Usable Buildings Trust website [1]. Here is our suggested starter pack:

- *An occupant survey:* This allows one to determine what occupants think and feel about their building. A number of surveys are available with different emphases, for example, on the building and the internal environment, the workstation and the working environment, or on the perceived productivity. As a set of general-purpose questionnaires, the BUS methodology is widely used [2].
- *An energy survey:* This throws light on much more than one might think; not just energy performance and greenhouse gas emissions, but specification, build quality, commissioning, control, management, maintenance, record keeping, and occupant satisfaction.
- *A walk-through survey:* This allows the building to be examined by experts in discussion with users and building management.

These three techniques formed the backbone of the successful Probe series of published POEs (plus a pressure test for air infiltration, now required under building regulations). They can be augmented by design quality indicators [3, 4] and by facilitated discussions, including:

- *Post-project reviews* on how the project went, for the client, design, and building team;
- *Post-implementation reviews* on the benefits the building provides for the organization;

- *Technical discussions* between managers and design team on how the building is performing; and

- *Focus groups* that include occupiers and other stakeholders, to help understand their perceptions and concerns.

A method developed by the Higher Education Design Quality Forum covers the four aspects in four separate sessions, held on a single day unless the building is very large and complex. It is potentially applicable to almost any building type. More detailed analysis is of course possible.

9.2   Design Quality Method

Martin Cook provides the following summary.

> The Design Quality Method (DQM) has emerged as an industry standard due to its fifteen-year legacy and extensive use in public buildings, for clients such as U.K. auditing authorities and many funding bodies. The DQM is an evidence-based approach that measures the whole performance of all building types, at design, construction and post-construction stages.
>
> Six strategic matrices with defined levels of quality and performance cover the key areas of architecture; environmental engineering; user comfort; whole life costing; detailed design; and user satisfaction. A seventh matrix is often added to cover specific aspects such as school grounds; safety and security in prisons; and clinical aspects in health buildings.
>
> The system is flexible enough to allow the addition of further matrices, as required. It represents a triangulation of expert opinion, scientific evidence and occupant satisfaction—supported by a database of over 200 buildings over the last 15 years.

For further information regarding DQM, see Ref. [4].

9.3   Optimize Operational and Maintenance Practices

Rob Bolin [5] provides the following advice regarding optimizing operational and maintenance practices:

> Incorporating operations and maintenance considerations into the design of a facility will greatly contribute to improved work environments, higher productivity, and reduced energy and resource costs. Designers are encouraged to specify materials and systems that simplify and reduce maintenance requirements; require less water, energy, and toxic chemicals and cleaners to maintain; and are cost-effective and reduce life-cycle costs.
>
> - *Preventative Maintenance*—building occupants and operators should be appropriately trained in a comprehensive preventative maintenance program

to keep all building systems associated with the building functioning as designed.

- *Environmentally Preferred Cleaning Products*—institute a policy for the purchase and use of resource-efficient and non-toxic cleaning products, supplies and procedures for all building elements.

For further information regarding facilities operations and maintenance good practice see the *Whole Building Design Guide* [6] and the CIBSE's *Guide M—Maintenance Engineering and Management* [7].

Color plate 23 shows the Pompidou Centre, Paris, described as a "maintenance nightmare" [8]. The building's reliance on HVAC and exposed structure and services is the antithesis of a sustainable, eco-minimalistic, low-impact, low-energy building!

9.4 Continuous Commissioning

Prof. David E. Claridge, Ph.D., PE, PCC, Director, and Mitch Paulus, Charles Culp, and Kevin Christman, Energy Systems Laboratory, Texas A&M Engineering Experiment Station

Commissioning an existing building has been shown to be a key energy management activity during the past two decades, often resulting in energy savings of 10%, 20%, or sometimes 30% without significant capital investment. Commissioning is more often applied to new buildings today than to existing buildings, but the energy manager will have more opportunities to apply the process to an existing building as part of the overall energy management program. The process for commissioning existing buildings was initiated about 25 years ago by the Energy Systems Laboratory (ESL) at Texas A&M University with Continuous Commissioning® and CC® being registered trademarks of the Texas A&M Engineering Experiment Station. (*Note:* The registration symbol is not used subsequently to improve readability.)

Applying the CC process to an existing building provides several benefits in addition to being an extremely effective energy management strategy. It typically provides an energy payback of 1 to 3 years. In addition, building comfort is improved, systems operate better, and maintenance costs are reduced. Commissioning measures typically require no capital investment, though the process often identifies maintenance that is required before the commissioning can be completed. Potential capital upgrades or retrofits are often identified during the commissioning activities, and knowledge gained during the process permits more accurate quantification of benefits than is possible from a typical energy audit. Involvement of facilities personnel in the process can also lead to improved staff technical skills.

9.4.1 Continuous Commissioning Stages

A successful CC process has four major stages:

1. Preliminary Investigation,
2. Detailed Investigation,
3. Implementation, and

   4. Keeping the commissioning continuous.

9.4.1.1 Use of Software

Software plays an important role in the success of the complete CC process. To apply CC as efficiently as possible, specialized software has been developed for use in each stage of the process.

The ESL has developed the following suite of software tools for use in the CC process. *Opportunity Assessor* is a tool that quickly identifies high potential savings opportunities employing a limited set of inputs, including monthly utility bills and answers to other basic questions about the building that can be assembled in minutes. During the second step of the initial investigation stage, *WinAM* is used, which is a detailed, hourly building energy simulation engine specifically engineered to estimate savings from CC energy-saving measures. In the implementation phase, *Implementer* is used to collect and store building automation system (BAS) trend data, and then analysis routines are run to find issues and verify that commissioning measures are operating as intended. Then, *Validator* is an automated measurement and verification tool that can produce a monthly energy and dollar savings report using procedures laid out in ASHRAE Guideline 14 within seconds. Finally, *Implementer* and *Sustainer* are used to track performance and indicate when follow-up is needed.

Software allows the CC professional to focus on creative solutions to operating the chosen building as optimally as possible rather than spending time on setting up manual spreadsheet calculations or dealing with managing gigabytes worth of BAS trend data.

9.4.2 The CC Process

9.4.2.1 Preliminary Investigation

The preliminary investigation stage consists of selecting buildings that have sufficient potential to benefit from CC to merit conducting an on-site assessment of the potential benefits gained by implementing the CC process (see Figure 9.1).

Step 1: Screen Buildings for CC Potential

The objective of this step is to determine whether a building is a good candidate for the CC process. This may be indicated by excessive energy consumption or poor thermal comfort. A building is normally screened using *Opportunity Assessor* to determine whether it has the potential for significant savings from the CC process. *Opportunity Assessor* goes far beyond simple EUI analysis in estimating the potential for savings.

The CC process can be effectively implemented in buildings that have received energy efficiency retrofits, in newer buildings, and in existing buildings that have not received energy efficiency upgrades. Virtually any building can be a potential candidate for CC.

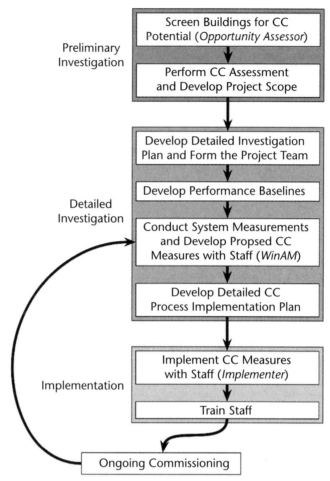

Figure 9.1 Outline of the continuous commissioning process.

Step 2: Perform CC Assessment and Develop Project Scope

Objectives:

The objectives of this step are to:

- Define the owner's current facility requirements (CFR).
- Identify major CC measures.
- Estimate potential savings from CC process implementation and costs to implement.

Approach:

The CFR is determined. This may be done through a formal process that includes interviews with stakeholders in the building, but is more often defined informally by the owner's representative (often the facility manager) and any other facility personnel present at a meeting with the CC project manager at the beginning of the CC assessment. The CFR will address the expectations and interest of the building owner in comfort improvements, utility cost reductions, and maintenance cost reductions. The initial meeting also seeks information on persistent comfort problems or other operational issues. After this discussion, a walkthrough must be conducted to identify the feasibility of the owner expectations for comfort performance and improved energy performance. During the walkthrough, CC professionals will identify major CC measures applicable to the building. An in-house technician should participate in this walkthrough to provide a local operational perspective and input. The project manager estimates the potential savings and the commissioning costs and prepares the CC assessment report that documents these findings as well as the owner expectations.

An initial simulation model of the building is created using a calibrated *WinAM* simulation to estimate the potential savings from potential CC measures. The *WinAM* calibration process often helps identify potential measures. Any available energy management control system (EMCS) trend data are examined and evaluated using *Implementer* software.

9.4.3 Detailed Investigation and Implementation Plan

After the initial assessment, the detailed investigation is conducted. The first step is to form the project team and develop a detailed investigation plan. The duties of each team member are made clear, and additional training for in-house staff may be necessary.

Performance baselines are created for comfort, systems and equipment conditions, and energy performance. Data used in the baselines may come from short-term or spot measurements, long-term sub-hourly BAS sensors, and/or utility bills.

Step 1: Develop Detailed Investigation Plan and Form the Project Team

Objectives:

- Develop a detailed investigation plan.
- Identify the entire project team.
- Clarify the duties of each team member.

Approach:
The project manager develops a detailed work plan for the detailed investigation that includes major tasks, their sequence, time requirements, and technical requirements. The investigation plan is then presented to the building owner or representative(s) at a meeting attended by the entire project team. During the meeting, the owner representative(s) and in-house technicians who will work on the project should be identified. In-house staff may require additional training. The investigation plan may need to be modified, depending on the availability and skill levels of in-house staff utilized.

Special Issues:
- Availability of funding to replace/repair parts found broken,
- Time commitment of in-house staff, and

- Training needs of in-house staff.

Step 2: Develop Performance Baselines

Objectives:

- Document existing comfort conditions.
- Document existing system conditions.
- Document existing energy performance.

Approach:
Document all known comfort problems in individual rooms resulting from too much heating, cooling, noise, humidity, odors (especially from mold or mildew), or lack of outside air. Also, identify and document any HVAC system problems including:

- Valve and damper hunting,
- Disabled systems or components,
- Operational problems, and
- Frequently replaced parts.

Room comfort problems should be quantified using handheld meters or portable data loggers. System and/or component problems should be documented based on interviews with occupants and technical staff in combination with field observations and measurements.

Develop a fully calibrated *WinAM* simulation model for use in the final evaluation of potential savings from CC measures considered for implementation.

Special Considerations:

- Use the maintenance log to help identify major system problems.
- Select a metering plan that suits the CC goals and the facility needs.
- Always consider and measure or obtain weather data as part of the metering plan.
- Keep meters calibrated.

Step 3: Conduct System Measurements and Develop Proposed CC Measures

Objectives:

- Identify current operational schedules and problems.
- Develop solutions to existing problems.
- Develop improved operation and control schedules and setpoints.

Approach:

The CC professional should develop a detailed measurement cut-sheet for each major system. The cut-sheet should list all of the parameters to be measured and all mechanical and electrical parts to be checked. The CC professional should also provide measurement training to the technician if a local technician is used to perform system measurements. The CC technicians should follow the procedures on the cut-sheets to obtain the measurements using appropriate equipment.

The CC professional conducts an engineering analysis using *WinAM* to develop solutions for the existing problems; and develops improved operation and control schedules and setpoints for terminal boxes, air-handling units (AHUs), exhaust systems, water and steam distribution systems, heat exchangers, chillers, boilers, and other components or systems as appropriate. Cost-effective energy retrofit measures can also be identified and documented during this step, if desired by the building owner.

Special Considerations:
- Trend main operational parameters using the EMCS, analyze with *Implementer* software and compare with the measurements from hand meters.
- Print out EMCS control sequences and schedules.
- Verify system operation in the building and compare to EMCS schedules using *Implementer*.

Step 4: Develop Detailed CC Process Implementation Plan

Objectives:
- Prepare detailed implementation plan.
- Obtain approval to implement for each measure recommended.
- Modify individual measures if necessary to obtain approval to implement.

Approach:

The project engineer should present the engineering solutions to existing problems and the improved operational and control schedules to the building owner's representative in one or more meetings. The in-house operating staff should be invited to this meeting(s). All critical questions should be answered. It is important at this point to get buy-in and approval from both the building owner's representative and the operating staff. The meeting(s) will decide the following issues:

- Approval, modification, or disapproval of each CC measure;
- Implementation sequence of CC measures; and
- Implementation schedules.

9.4.4 Implementation

Step 1: Implement CC Measures

Objectives:

- Implement solutions to existing operational and comfort problems.
- Implement and refine improved operation and control schedules.

Approach:

CC implementation should start by solving existing problems. The existing comfort and difficult control problems are the first priority of the occupants, operating staff, and facility owner. Solving these problems improves occupant comfort and increases productivity. The economic benefits from comfort improvements are sometimes higher than the energy cost savings, though less easily quantified. The successful resolution of existing problems can also earn trust in the CC professional from facility operating staff, facility management, and the occupants.

Implementation of the improved operation and control schedules should start at the end of the comfort delivery system, such as at the terminal boxes, and end with the central plant. This procedure provides benefits to the building occupants as quickly as possible. It also reduces the overall load on the system. If the process is reversed, the chiller plant is commissioned first. The chiller sequences are developed based on the current load. After the rest of the commissioning is complete, the chiller load may decrease by 15% to 30%, resulting in a need to revise the chiller operating schedules.

The CC professionals should develop a detailed implementation plan that lists each major activity. The CC technician should follow this plan in implementing the measures. They should closely supervise the implementation and refine the operational and control schedules as necessary and should also be responsible for the key software changes as necessary.

Following implementation, the new operation and control sequences must be documented in a way that helps the building staff understand why they were implemented. Maintenance procedures for these measures should be provided. If any measures have had their implementation postponed due to temporary impediments such as an out-of-stock part, recommendations for their future implementation should be included.

In some CC projects, the implementation is contracted to an external service provider rather than being implemented by the CC provider in cooperation with the building staff. If this approach is taken, careful coordination with the CC provider is needed to ensure that measures are properly and completely implemented. The external service provider lacks a full understanding of the measures being implemented, and hence is unable to modify them slightly to make them completely successful as can be done when the commissioning professional is part of the implementation process.

Special Considerations:

- Ensure that the owner's technical representative understands each major measure.
- Encourage in-house technician involvement in the implementation.
- Document improvements in a timely manner.

9.4.5   Summary

Commissioning of existing buildings is now recognized as one of the most cost-effective ways for an energy manager to lower operating costs, and typically does so without capital investment, or with a very minimal amount. It has been successfully implemented in several hundred buildings and provides typical paybacks of 1 to 3 years.

CC is quite different from new building commissioning, which ensures that the systems function as originally designed. CC focuses on improving overall system control and operations for the building as it is currently utilized and on meeting existing facility needs. During the CC process, a comprehensive engineering evaluation is conducted for both building functionality and system functions. The optimal operational parameters and schedules are developed based on actual building conditions. An integrated approach is used to implement these optimal schedules to ensure practical local and global system optimization and to ensure persistence of the improved operational schedules.

The CC process begins by conducting a thorough examination of all problem areas or operating problems in the building, diagnoses these problems, and develops solutions that solve these problems while almost always reducing operating costs at the same time. Equipment upgrades or retrofits may be implemented as well, but have not been a factor in the case studies presented. This is in sharp contrast to the more usual approach to improving the efficiency of HVAC systems and cutting operating costs that primarily emphasizes system upgrades or retrofits to improve efficiency.

The benefits of the CC process include:

- Simple paybacks under 3 years,
- Improved building comfort,
- Reduced maintenance costs,
- Identification of potential system retrofits/upgrades, and
- Improved technical knowledge of the in-house staff.

For further information on continuous commissioning see [9–11].

References

[1]   Usable Buildings Trust, *Feedback Portfolio: Techniques,* http://www.usablebuildings.co.uk/fp/index.html (July 2016).

[2]   *BUS Methodology*, http://www.busmethodology.org (July 2016).

[3]   *Design Quality Indicator*, http://www.dqi.org.uk (July 2016).

[4]   *Design Quality Method*, http://www.dqm.org.uk/DQM.html (July 2016).

[5]   Bolin, R., *Whole Building Design Guide: Sustainability of the Building Envelope*, November 2014, https://www.wbdg.org/resources/env_sustainability.php (July 2016).

[6]   Sapp, D., *Whole Building Design Guide: Facilities Operations & Maintenance*, September 2015, http://wbdg.org/om/om.php (August 2016).

[7]   Chartered Institution of Building Services Engineers (CIBSE), *GVM/14 Guide M: Maintenance Engineering & Management*, 2014, http://www.cibse.org/Knowledge/knowledge-items/detail?id=a0q20000008I7oZAAS (August 2016).

[8]   Brand, S., *How Buildings Learn: What Happens After They're Built*, 1995, New York: Penguin Publishing, ISBN 1101562641.

[9]   Turner, W. D., et al., "Persistence of Savings Obtained from Continuous Commissioning SM," in *Proc. of 9th National Conference on Building Commissioning*, Cherry Hill, NJ, 9–11 May 2001, pp. 20-1.1–20-1.13.

[10]   Claridge, D. E., et al., "Is Commissioning Once Enough?" in *Solutions for Energy Security and Facility Management Challenges: Proc. 25th WEEC*, Atlanta, GA, 9–11 October 2002, pp. 29–36.

[11]   Toole, C. D., and D. Claridge, "The Persistence of Retro-Commissioning Savings in Ten University Buildings," in *Proc. 11th International Conference for Enhanced Building Operation*, New York, NY, 18–20 October 2011.

CHAPTER 10

Case Studies

The only real mistake is the one from which we learn nothing.
—Henry Ford

The authors have carefully selected nine world-class sustainable buildings, each representing some of the concepts explored in previous chapters. Providing a global representation, the case study locations have different climatic and contextual challenges, and a specific core focus that offers learning outcomes to practitioners.

The case studies (see Figure 10.1) have been prepared in conjunction with key individuals from the project teams, who offer their unique perspective on the application of integrative processes and a whole systems approach. All projects have adopted a similar core approach of applying passive design strategies optimally for the site location to reduce energy and heating/cooling loads to be supplied by high-performance servicing systems, demonstrating that the principles are replicable across all climatic conditions.

Key learning outcomes are also similar across the selection: the importance of clear and defined performance targets; the benefits of integrated and collaborative design teams; the critical role of testing and commissioning to optimize performance; and the willingness to share lessons learned within the industry. While these projects represent a handful of exemplary case studies, the lessons learned and concepts developed can and should be rapidly incorporated into all building projects, which can help accelerate the process of high-performance buildings becoming standard industry practice. The benefits are unquestionable, the methodologies are proven, and the market is prepared to deliver.

10.1 The Bullitt Center, Seattle, Washington

Paul Schwer, President, PAE and Sara Calabro

10.1.1 Context

When design started on the Bullitt Center in 2010 (see Figure 10.2)—a six-story, 4831 m² (52,000 ft²) building in Seattle, Washington (see Table 10.1 for climate data)—some of the most energy-efficient buildings in the United States had annual energy use intensities (EUIs) of around 69.4 kWh/m² (22 kBtu/ft²). The project team set out to raise the bar, aiming for an EUI of 50.5 kWh/m² (16 kBtu/ft²). The

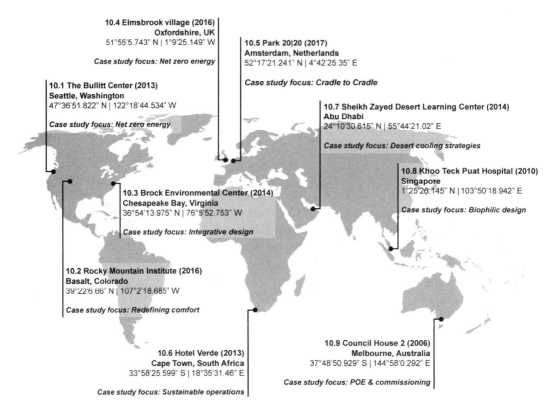

10.4 Elmsbrook village (2016)
Oxfordshire, UK
51°55'5.743" N | 1°9'25.149" W

Case study focus: Net zero energy

10.5 Park 20|20 (2017)
Amsterdam, Netherlands
52°17'21.241" N | 4°42'25.35" E

Case study focus: Cradle to Cradle

10.1 The Bullitt Center (2013)
Seattle, Washington
47°36'51.822" N | 122°18'44.534" W

Case study focus: Net zero energy

10.7 Sheikh Zayed Desert Learning Center (2014)
Abu Dhabi
24°10'30.615" N | 55°44'21.02" E

Case study focus: Desert cooling strategies

10.8 Khoo Teck Puat Hospital (2010)
Singapore
1°25'26.145" N | 103°50'18.942" E

Case study focus: Biophilic design

10.3 Brock Environmental Center (2014)
Chesapeake Bay, Virginia
36°54'13.975" N | 76°5'52.753" W

Case study focus: Integrative design

10.2 Rocky Mountain Institute (2016)
Basalt, Colorado
39°22'6.66" N | 107°2'18.685" W

Case study focus: Redefining comfort

10.6 Hotel Verde (2013)
Cape Town, South Africa
33°58'25.599" S | 18°35'31.46" E

Case study focus: Sustainable operations

10.9 Council House 2 (2006)
Melbourne, Australia
37°48'50.929" S | 144°58'0.292" E

Case study focus: POE & commissioning

Figure 10.1   Case study locations, completion dates, and focus areas.

Figure 10.2   The Bullitt Center, Seattle, Washington. (*Photo*: Nic Lehoux.)

Table 10.1 Key Climate Data for Seattle, Washington [1]

Altitude	158m (518 ft)
Climate	Maritime
Average Monthly Maximum	24.5°C (76.1°F) dry bulb 13.4°C (56.1°F) wet bulb 89.7% RH
Average Monthly Minimum	2.0°C (36.5°F) dry bulb –0.3°C (31.5°F) wet bulb 66.4% RH

building has surpassed all expectations, and is currently operating at an EUI of 34 kWh/m² (10.8 kBtu/ft²). After accounting for the renewable energy generated on site, it is net positive with an EUI of –21.7 kWh/m² (–6.9 kBtu/ft²) (see Figure 10.3).

Denis Hayes, president of the Bullitt Foundation, a nonprofit organization committed to safeguarding natural environments in the northwest United States, wanted to create a commercial office building that reflected the highest standards in sustainability and served as an example for what is possible in urban environments. Convinced that LEED and other green-building standards in the United States were not stringent enough, Hayes ultimately found what he was looking for in the Living Building Challenge (LBC).

10.1.2 Aligned from the Start

Project team members were informed at the very first meeting that the Bullitt Center would meet the LBC standard. It was not up for discussion or negotiation, which provided a sense of clarity that kept everyone focused from day one through completion. And it worked: on April 1, 2015, the Bullitt Center became the largest certified Living Building. It was the first office building and only the 23rd building in the world to meet the challenge.

Another unwavering target was also made clear: the Bullitt Center would last at least 250 years. This building would not be part of the throwaway economy, but rather, increase in value over time as resources diminish and net-zero buildings

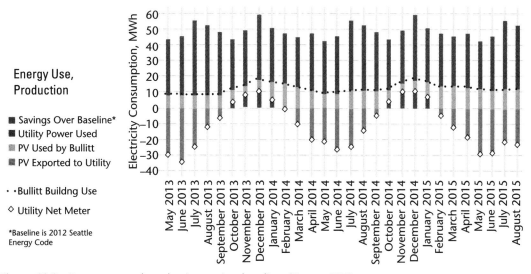

Figure 10.3 Energy use and production against baseline. (*Source:* PAE.)

become the norm. That meant a design with longevity in mind. The framework—made of heavy timber, concrete, and steel—is built to last the anticipated 250-year life span. The building's skin is easily replaceable and expected to be updated every 75 to 100 years, while its solar technology gets refreshed every 30 years.

The initial meeting for the Bullitt Center, included everyone—the owner (Bullitt Foundation), the developer (Point32), the architect (The Miller Hull Partnership), the engineer (PAE), and the contractor (Schuchart).

Involving the entire team in the up-front design process meant that everyone fundamentally understood the "why" behind the project; all were aligned with the owner's Living Building requirement as well as the reasons for all design decisions.

This saved time in two key ways: The architects and engineers were able to avoid rehashing things for a late-to-the-game construction team, and the construction team was able to provide real-time cost estimates. It is not uncommon in a more traditional scenario for the architect and engineer to agree on a solution only to have the contractor come back with a cost estimate that is 30% over budget. These kinds of pitfalls were avoided by taking an integrated approach from the start.

10.1.3 Replicability of Processes

The lack of solar resource in Seattle required a very efficient building design, including extending the solar panels beyond the roof edge to gather maximum energy. Additionally, Seattle's 866 mm (34 in.) of annual rainfall is less than the average rainfall in every city east of the Mississippi River in the United States. However, despite these challenges, the Bullitt Center achieves both net-zero energy and net-zero water (see Figure 10.4 for key specification information). Computer models of the Bullitt Center in other locations found that this performance could be achieved in the vast majority of cities in the United States, with similar results in most European cities as well.

Currently there are a limited number of net-zero energy buildings; people tend to assume that they are really difficult to design and build. Of course, net-zero energy buildings require a lot of thought and modeling; however, the technology involved is available off the shelf and, therefore, the performance is undoubtedly replicable in other buildings.

Anyone can buy the photovoltaic (PV) panels used on the roof—and for much less, since the cost of these systems has decreased so much since installation on the Bullitt Center. Anyone can buy the windows installed, and the same goes for the mechanical systems. In fact, designers and contractors have used these exact components in other buildings. The difference with the Bullitt Center is that these components were combined into one building in a fundamentally different way. Nothing new was invented to make this work.

Focusing on the basics (a high-performance envelope, extensive daylighting, and efficient computers) allowed the use of small mechanical systems that could easily be made very efficient. That approach (see Color Plate 24) led to a building that is extremely comfortable and, with the addition of PV, it generates more energy than it uses over the course of a year.

Other sustainability features of the building include:

DESIGN

Design Targets
- Lighting density — Design 0.4 W/sf (4.3 W/m²) — Operations 0.12 W/sf (1.29 W/m²)
- Installed computers/ appliances/ task lights/other plug loads — Design 0.8 W/sf (8.6 W/m²) — Operations 0.23 W/sf (2.48 W/m²)
- Installed mechanical loads 1080 sf/ton (28.6 m²/kWh)

HVAC System
- Closed-loop geothermal system
- (26) 400ft (122m) deep wells
- Water-to-water heat pumps
- Hydronic radiant-floor heating and cooling
- Heat-recovery central ventilation system

Orientation NW/SE

Gross Square Footage 52,000 (4830 m²)
Conditioned Space 50,142 (4658 m²)

Total Construction Cost $18.2 million
Cost per Square Foot $349

Annual Energy Use Intensity (EUI) (Site) 10.8 kBtu/ft² (34 kWh/m²)
Electricity (Grid Purchase) 2.3 kBtu/ft² (7.25 kWh/m²)
Electricity (On-Site Solar) 8.5 kBtu/ft² (26.8 kWh/m²)

WATER

Annual Water Use 50,442 gallons (191,000 L) 0.97 gallons/sf (39.5 L/m²)

Water Conservation Rainwater captured in 56,000 gallon (212,000 L) cistern for all building and site uses (potable use pending regulatory approval), Composting toilets

ENERGY

Annual On-Site Renewable Energy Exported 9.2 kBtu/ft² (29 kWh/m²)

Annual Net Energy Use Intensity -6.9 kBtu/ft² (-21.7 kWh/m²)

Annual Source (Primary) Energy 15.7 kBtu/ft² (49.5 kWh/m²)

Annual Energy Cost Index (ECI) $0/ft²

Annual Load Factor 45%

Savings vs. 2009 Seattle Energy Code Design Building* 79%

ENERGY STAR Rating 100

Carbon Footprint 0 lb CO_2e/ft²yr

Heating Degree Days (Base 65°F / 18.3°C) 4,615 °F days (2563 °C-days)

Cooling Degree Days (Base 65°F / 18.3°C) 192 °F-days (107 °C-days)

Annual Hours Occupied 2,500

BUILDING ENVELOPE

Roof: Type Styrene-butadiene-styrene (SBS) modified on wood decking, rubberized asphalt on concrete Overall R-value R-40 (RSI-7.05)

Walls: Type Steel stud, continuous exterior insulation Overall R-value R-25 (RSI 4.41) Glazing Percentage 40%

Windows:
Effective U-factor for Assembly 0.25 (1.42)
Solar Heat Gain Coefficient (SHGC) 0.32
Visual Transmittance 0.56
Air Tightness 0.19 cfm/sf @ 0.3" wg

*2009 Seattle Energy Code baseline approximately 10-20% better than ASHRAE Standard 90.1-2007

Figure 10.4 The Bullitt Center's key design and performance data. (*Source: PAE.*)

- Use of recycled materials in salvaged formwork and compliance with the LBC Red List (chemicals to avoid) and appropriate sourcing (distance radius limits, FSC certified, etc.);
- Daylight penetration approximately 20 ft into the space, exterior blinds provide glare control;
- "Irresistible stair" to encourage use in lieu of elevators; and
- Small green roof areas including constructed wetland for gray water treatment.

10.1.4 Challenging Traditional Concepts

Once moved into the Bullitt Center, PAE were in the unique position of being both designers and tenants of the building, allowing them to see how systems were functioning on a daily basis and to make post-occupancy adjustments as needed. Early on, occupants reported feeling cold in the morning on 32.2°C (90°F) summer days because the building had been "precooled" overnight to 19°C (66°F) by flushing it with cool night air, thus identifying a need to tweak the system. Once it was discovered how well the building held its temperature and that adding a small amount of chilled water to the radiant floor used very little energy, the night-flush setpoint was raised a couple of degrees. This kept people warm enough in the morning without getting too hot in the afternoon.

In winter, adjustments to the radiant floors increased comfort. The design model assumed that occupants would be comfortable if the offices were heated to 20°C (68°F); however, the exposed cold-concrete mass was making people cold. To achieve desirable comfort conditions, the slab temperature was increased by flowing slightly warmer water through it.

The Bullitt Center has composting toilets on all six floors [2]. When the stall is opened, the toilet foam-flushes once to lubricate the bowl and again to clear waste, using a total of just 148 ml (~5 oz) of water per flush. In the closed-loop system, 10 composters in the building's basement collect waste, which eventually gets treated and turned into fertilizer. The composters only need to be emptied of their fertilizer once every 18 months. Scentless composting toilets are just one of several innovative features of the Bullitt Center that have forced us to reimagine the future of sustainable building design.

The Bullitt Center envelope is tuned for passive operation that allows the building to operate without cooling systems and no central heating system to maintain comfort. Instead of just focusing on dry bulb temperatures, all comfort variables were considered: air temperature, relative humidity, air speed, metabolic rate, and mean radiant temperature.

> Before the Bullitt Center, we tended to focus just on energy modeling. But now we're looking at energy models alongside comfort models, daylighting models, and other factors in order to find the best solutions. For example, when we started working on the Bullitt Center, I was pretty convinced that it should include an atrium. But when we started modeling it, we realized it didn't work from a thermal, daylighting, or real-estate standpoint, so we went in another direction.
>
> —*Paul Schwer, PAE*

The Bullitt Center also inspired new thinking around how to finance the energy that gets saved—and in this case, generated—through energy-efficient buildings. The Bullitt Foundation negotiated a model that convinced Seattle's public utility to compensate the foundation for "nega-watts," or energy saved, from the Bullitt Center. Known as MEETS (Metered Energy Efficiency Transaction Structure) [3], the program is expected to generate USD $1.2 million over the next 20 years for the Bullitt Foundation instead of a one-time USD $84,000 utility incentive.

10.1.5   Endnote

On the outer edge of efficiency in sustainable design, a lot of preconceived notions start falling apart. The Bullitt Center project team discovered that problems can be solved in new and different ways, ones that allow creativity and innovation to blossom. Lessons learned from the process include the following:

- Set audacious, inspiring goals and never waver—then let your design team tackle them.
- When designing a great envelope and highly efficient HVAC systems, plug loads dominate. To control plug loads, bring the tenants into the process by introducing an energy budget into the lease.
- Give users control. Automated windows allow for after-hours night flushing, but having an occupant-override option is important for keeping tenants comfortable throughout the day.
- Simplicity drives aesthetics. Simple HVAC and lighting systems reduced ceiling clutter, and using fewer finishes in order to meet the Living Building Challenge's materials standard created a functional and comfortable interior.
- Net-zero energy can be achieved in virtually any location, regardless of climate.
- Verification is an ongoing effort. There have been some operational challenges with end-use submetering and data reporting as tenants continue to make changes throughout the building. Commission your metering system.
- Involve the building operator in the design process. So far, the Bullitt Center has required a full-time on-site building engineer to perform ongoing commissioning of the energy, water, and metering systems. While that role will diminish over time, having this person involved up-front in the design process would have ensured a seamless construction-to-occupancy transition.

The Bullitt Center has an operating EUI of 34 kWh/m^2 (10.8 kBtu/ft^2). Based on a typical occupancy of 220 people, this equates to 0.37 kW/Occ. before allowing for on-site PV generation (see Figure 2.8) and therefore falls comfortably within the green building quotient.

10.2   RMI Innovation Center, Basalt, Colorado

John Breshears, President, Architectural Applications

10.2.1   Context

The Rocky Mountain Institute (RMI), is a medium-sized, independent, and nonpartisan nonprofit that has been a leader in transforming global energy use since 1982. It focuses on advancing market-based solutions to address challenges in various sectors. The development of new, cost-effective methods to deliver higher-quality, lower-carbon footprint buildings is one such challenge.

Therefore, within the context of the Rocky Mountains climate (see Table 10.2 for climate data), a series of ambitious goals for the RMI's new Innovation Center (RMI IC) were set, including on-site net-zero energy; a passive, envelope-centric approach; a world-class convening space able to welcome visitors; and a growth-friendly, beyond-the-state-of-the-art office that, as RMI founder Amory Lovins wrote to the team, "will create delight when entered, health and productivity when occupied, and regret when departed" (see Figure 10.5).

Table 10.2   Key Climate Data for Basalt, Colorado

Altitude	2,015m (6,611 ft)		
Climate	High altitude, arid		
Average Monthly Maximum	30.1°C (86.2°F) dry bulb	8.5°C (47.3°F) wet bulb	50.9% RH
Average Monthly Minimum	−10.8°C (12.6°F) dry bulb	0.0°C (32.0°F) wet bulb	25.9% RH

Figure 10.5   Rocky Mountain Institute. (*Photo*: Rocky Mountain Institute.)

The positioning of the project within the construction market was also strategic. Approximately 90% of all commercial buildings in North America are less than 2,300m^2 (25,000 ft^2) in size—comparable in size to the RMI IC. The majority of these are occupied as offices, with approximately half being owner occupied. As such, RMI targeted a precedent-setting approach and outcomes that could be adopted as standard practice throughout a substantial portion of this sector. Much of the approach, including highly integrated design and construction, an expanded definition of thermal comfort, and a robust use of passive systems, is readily extensible to the design of higher-performing, lower-carbon buildings everywhere.

Ambitious certification goals included LEED Platinum Certification, International Living Future Institute's Living Building Petal Certification, Passive House Certification, and Net-Zero Energy Certification. Importantly, these goals were rapidly translated into a more detailed summary transformation dashboard and finally into the owner's project requirements (OPR) that set the project acceptance criteria.

Lovins' penchant for multifunctional solutions informed an axiom fitting for a holistic design approach: that every element had to form a part of multiple, interdependent systems and, as a result, serve to improve the building in multiple ways.

Located at an elevation of 2,015m (6,611 ft) above sea level, Basalt, Colorado, presents unique challenges and opportunities for passive design. The climate is substantially heating dominated, with 7,795 heating degree days (ASHRAE HDD65) and winter design temperatures that are well below –17°C (0°F). There is significant solar radiation availability, but also periods of cold temperatures with overcast skies and snowfall. The challenge of heating the building, therefore, needed to rely heavily on harvesting available solar radiation and managing it effectively, including storing it, retaining it, or rejecting it as required.

The cooling season is relatively short, with 950 cooling degree days and moderate relative humidity levels. Two strong climatic characteristics—the high diurnal temperature swings from day to night, and the prevailing wind patterns moving up-valley during the day and down-valley at night—created key opportunities for passive conditioning of the building during the cooling season.

10.2.2   Passive Design Strategies

10.2.2.1   Envelope

A parametric study of single-zone energy models oriented at various angles around the compass helped to determine the performance makeup of the optimal envelope for each primary exposure. This influenced materials and construction costs, floor-to-wall ratio, thermal and visual comfort, and building function, as well as aesthetics.

The opaque wall construction was targeted to achieve a U-value of 0.142 W/m^{2}K (R40), and the roof at R60. The structure of glue-laminated timber on a concrete foundation was enclosed with structurally insulating panels (SIPs). An air barrier applied to the outer layer required rigorous detailing and execution to ensure continuity of the air seal throughout the complex geometries. Metal panels and coursed local stone make up the outer weathering layer of the walls, while the roof is finished in standing seam metal beneath an extensive PV array.

10.2.2.2 Glazing Design

The elongated building form helped to minimize the challenges of widely vary-ing solar angles on the east and west facades, while maximizing and distributing natural sunlight. However the south-facing glazing system, as the largest conduit of energy flux through the façade, proved to be the most challenging.

During cold winter days, the glass needed to gather every available bit of solar radiation, and retain it within the building throughout the course of a cold night. The lack of a cooling building system meant that all direct solar radiation on the glass needed to be blocked during the summer days.

Ultimately, following extensive research on control devices and market-avail-able technologies, a layered system of control was selected for the south-facing glazed elements. Manually operated roller shades were used both above and below a series of cantilevered light shelves. The curtain wall framing consisted of extruded aluminum profiles with large thermal breaks and foam inserts designed to reduce conduction and convection through their various cavities. The operable windows could be automated and featured a positive latching system to ensure Passive House Institute US (PHIUS) airtightness levels when in a closed position.

The outermost layer is composed of a continuous scrim of automated alumi-num venetian blinds. The blinds are controlled during the cooling season to cut direct solar radiation from the glass while still reflecting considerable daylight on the interior. During the winter months, when snow and ice are a concern, the blinds are safely retracted into their head cases to prevent them from damage and allow direct solar radiation in (see Figure 10.6).

Heat Mirror Quad Pane glazing, an insulating glass unit (IGU) with two layers of low-E-coated Mylar film and three layers of gas between inner and outer glass, was able to prove the performance of a quad pane IGU at a fraction of the weight of an all-glass product and a thickness of 37 mm (1.5 in.). Parametric studies de-termined the exact composition of glass, film, and coatings tailored to the unique requirements of each exposure.

10.2.2.3 Natural Ventilation

Cross-flow natural ventilation is the primary form of cooling. Rules of thumb and preliminary calculations indicated that a large amount of window opening free area as a percentage of the floor area would be required to achieve the desired air flow. Following this approach would have increased the number and total cost of the operable window package. The team opted for a lower-cost casement window strategy tuned to take advantage of local wind patterns.

10.2.3 Thermal Comfort Design Parameters

With the building thermal loads reduced, a series of active systems optimized to meet the remaining demand was designed, within the project target of net-zero energy and the Living Building Challenge prohibition of fossil fuels. Focus was placed on paring down and, where possible, eliminating entire systems. Perimeter heating and any direct expansion cooling systems, for example, were omitted from the design.

Figure 10.6   RMI IC glazing and facade design. (*Photo*: Rocky Mountain Institute.)

At this stage, RMI chose to push the limits of current thinking and fully embrace the broad definition of thermal comfort. Human comfort has been characterized as a complex result of six measurable variables: air temperature, relative humidity, air speed, mean radiant temperature (the average temperature of the building surfaces surrounding the occupant), level of clothing insulation, and intensity of physical activity. Building operational standards in North America typically assume that only two of these six variables—air temperature and relative humidity—are monitored and directly controlled by the building conditioning systems. Current industry practice, therefore, is to control these two parameters within a fairly narrow range so that the other four uncontrolled factors may vary widely without risking occupant dissatisfaction.

Two primary shifts in thinking enabled a radical change to the system design and operation:

1. With proper monitoring and control of all six variables of thermal comfort, the air temperature and relative humidity of the interior can vary over a much greater range than conventionally believed while still maintaining comfortable conditions, thus reducing the required conditioning energy.
2. Heating and cooling the occupants directly, in contrast to conditioning the entire space they occupy, could be a more energy-efficient means of maintaining the expanded comfort criteria described above.

Localized heating and cooling was provided directly to the occupants via a new-to-market office chair [4], providing small amounts of heating directly to the body of the person via electric resistance elements sewn into the seat and back-rest, and convective cooling via small fans drawing air away from the sitter's body through the mesh fabric upholstery. Testing on the product suggested that seated occupants would remain comfortable through an expanded air temperature and humidity range and that this effect would endure for roughly 10 minutes after leaving the chair due to the thermal lag experience by the human body in adapting to its surroundings.

Equipped with this new comfort metric, the team redoubled its effort to pare back and simplify the active building systems (see Color Plate 25). All heat pumps and compressor-based technologies were excised from the project. Electric resistance heating was added in the form of undercarpet elements—a simple and flexible solution supplied the necessary heating, now reduced to nominal capacity used only during the coldest parts of the season.

The entire cooling system would now rely entirely on natural ventilation with nightly flushing of cool outdoor air. In addition to the cooling potential of the chairs, an array of ceiling and local desk fans was added to ensure every occupant control over air at their workstation. Finally, a phase-change material was added into certain interior walls and ceilings to increase the effective thermal mass of the spaces and to affect the drift of mean radiant temperature.

The building, completed and occupied in early 2016, was certified with an envelope air leakage rate of 0.3 ACH 50 (air changes per hour at 50 Pascals), making the building the largest yet certified by PHIUS and exceeding their exacting standard by threefold. At the time of writing, after less than a full year of operation, the EUI can be extrapolated to 53 kWh/m^2 (16.77 kBtu/ft^2). Further monitoring and tuning will be required as the building moves through its first year of operation; in particular, the summer months will test both the natural ventilation cooling effectiveness and the daylight strategies.

10.2.4   Endnote

The degree of replicability and, ultimately, the Innovation Center's impact on market transformation remain to be seen. However, the RMI IC has achieved or exceeded all of the prescriptive guidelines for net-zero building listed in Reinventing Fire [5] within the constraints of the project budget and schedule, supporting RMI's assertion of market-feasible net-zero energy buildings.

The redefining of thermal comfort [6] resulted in an entirely different solution, enabling huge latitude to reduce systems and save energy. Following the usual rules of thumb would have resulted in an oversized and overall more expensive servicing strategy, and is a core and transferrable outcome from the project.

Only with absolute trust between team members and faith in systems implemented can the project eliminate the redundancy of segregated disciplines and fully leverage the building as a whole system. Interdependence and integration are key. This process was facilitated by use of the integrated project delivery process, which is centered around collaboration, strong communication, creativity, and a shared risk and reward pool. It requires the right balance between streamlining the project process to keep costs down and having the breadth to innovate as demanded by the project brief.

Following the same Thomas Hartman process for determining predicted average annual occupant efficiency, the 1,450m^2 (15,610 ft^2) RMI IC has a design EUI of 53 kWh/m^2 (16.77 kBtu/ft^2) and a typical occupancy of 173. This equates to an estimated 0.22 kW/Occ. and therefore falls comfortably within the green building quotient.

10.3   The Brock Environmental Center, Chesapeake Bay, Virginia

Greg Mella, Vice President, SmithGroupJJR

10.3.1   Context

The Brock Environmental Center, located at Pleasure House Point, Virginia Beach, Virginia (see Table 10.3 for climate data), was completed in September 2014 (see Figure 10.7). It serves as an educational facility for the protection and restoration of Chesapeake Bay, intended to be a light-touch, low-environmental impact facility

Table 10.3   Key Climate Data for Chesapeake Bay, Virginia

Altitude	0m (0 ft)
Climate	Maritime—Humid
Average Monthly Maximum	32.4°C (90.3°F) dry bulb 21.7°C (71.1°F) wet bulb 89.8% RH
Average Monthly Minimum	−3.4°C (25.9°F) dry bulb −6.7°C (19.9°F) wet bulb 63.4% RH

Figure 10.7 The Brock Environmental Center (*Photo:* Prakesh Patel with permission by SmithGroupJJR.)

meeting the highest environmental standards. A community effort to save the site from commercial development of more than 1,100 new high-rise condominiums and townhouses preserved the land for open space and environmental education. The 975m² (10,500 ft²)high-performance center containing staff offices, meeting rooms, an 80-seat conference room, and an outdoor classroom is the result of a highly collaborative and engaging project, with resilience against future climate conditions and enhancement of the surrounding natural environment.

The building is water and energy independent, producing up to 90% more energy than it requires (see Color Plate 26). It has been certified as LEED Platinum and in May 2016 it achieved Living Building Challenge certification, demonstrating excellence in seven categories: place, water, energy, health and happiness, materials, equity, and beauty. This required an entirely holistic design approach.

The Brock team included a wide range of stakeholders, engaged from an early stage of the project, including the contractor. The team toured other LBC projects, meeting their teams to gather lessons learned. A full-day, predesign charrette was held on site, involving all design disciplines, local officials, community representatives, and outside experts, to formulate a shared vision for the project.

10.3.2 Iterative Design

The design was highly iterative, using simulation tools to validate each design decision, working toward the LBC net-zero goals for energy, water, and waste. Smith-GroupJJR, as both the appointed architect and MEP engineers working on a shared BIM model, facilitated integration. Early charrette topics included meeting the challenges of the LBC materials petal Red List criteria, and renewable energy sources, in which wind energy was uncovered as a potentially viable source (through collaboration with external parties, such the Center for Wind Energy at James Madison University, and with the U.S. Fish and Wildlife Services to ensure a bird-safe solution). Conversations with regulatory agencies began during early design and spanned throughout design and construction to enable discussions on more innovative proposals.

The building design was strongly influenced by the location and climatic conditions of the site: climate zone 3A, with hot, humid summers and varied winters. Extensive simulation modeling enabled the optimum building footprint, internal layout, and exterior envelope design (R-31 walls, R-50 roof, R-7 triple-glazed/argon-filled windows) to encourage year-round passive ventilation and daylighting, reducing demand on mechanical systems and renewable energy sources.

A combination of passive design features and smart controls enabled efficient operation for the ventilation strategy (see Figure 10.8).

> Bi-directional breezes are captured with low inlets and high outlets on both North and South facades. Airflow modeling predicts the building can effectively maintain comfort using only natural ventilation for 11% of the year. When sensors determine climate suitability, mechanical cooling shuts and automated controls send an email to staff alerting them to open windows, using a combination of hand-crank and motorized operators. Motorized windows allow night-flush of the interior to pre-cool the interior during cooling-driven months. [7]

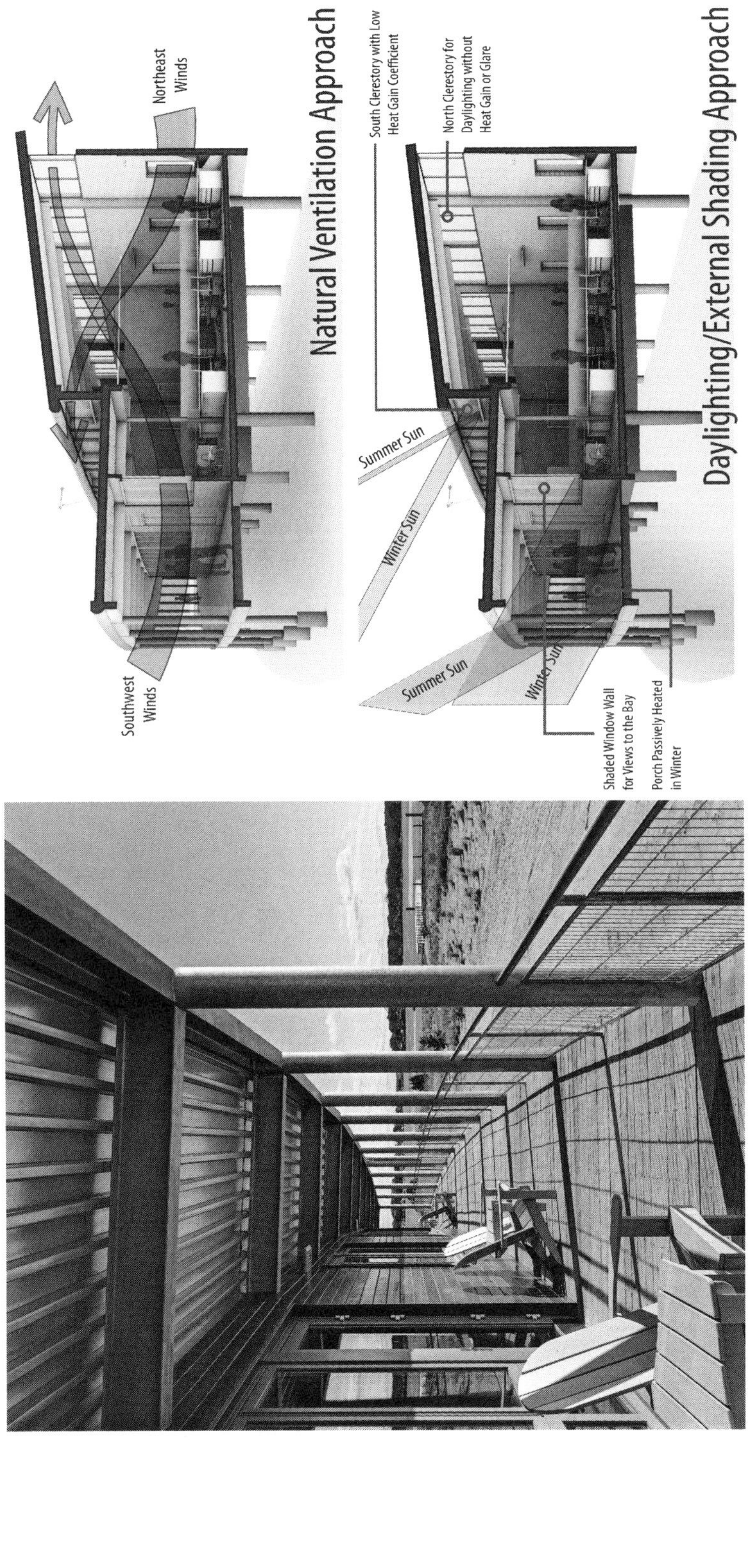

Figure 10.8   Passive design features. (*Source*: SmithGroupJJR.)

10.3.3   Active Systems

The mechanical system utilizes a variable-refrigerant flow (VRF) system with 18 ground-source 76m (250 ft) deep bores, harnessing the earth's stable temperature, improving heating and cooling efficiency. A geothermal piping loop provides the heat sink for the building ventilation and cooling and heating loads of the building. The load profiles and ground temperatures allowed the design to use water only and avoid glycol. The VRF system is coupled with a dedicated outside air system.

Occupancy/vacancy sensors control lighting, ventilation, and plugs (reducing parasitic "vampire" loads), and Energy Star copiers, computers, and appliances are used throughout. The photosensor lighting specifications and controls use 5% of the lighting energy typically used in an office building (CBECS 2003). These measures combined result in a remarkably low EUI of 48.9 kWh/m^2 (15.5 kBtu/ft^2/yr), approximately 80% less than a typical building of the same size.

The resulting energy demand is met and exceeded by grid-tied, on-site renewables. Two 10 kW wind turbines, predicted to generate 24,000 kWh/year (84 MMBtu/yr), are located to minimize turbulence as well as site disturbances. A 45 kW photovoltaic (PV) array, predicted to produce 43,000 kWh/year (146.9 MMBtu/yr), is located on south-facing roofs. Although when compared to PVs, the wind turbine system was less economically viable, the team and client were interested in proceeding with a wind turbine system both as a test case for wind turbines and as a way of diversifying the source of renewable power for the building.

A Different Approach for Life Cycle Cost Assessment [8]

The LBC net-zero energy goals altered the approach to life cycle cost assessment (LCCA). The cost benefit of conservation approaches was measured against the cost of on-site renewables, rather than against the cost of cheap, grid-provided electricity. This approach put an increased emphasis on conservation. The investment in insulation, triple-pane windows, ground-source wells, and so on, was cost effective given the items' ability to reduce the demand for photovoltaics. An LCCA was used to validate HVAC system selection by comparing the VRF system used against a more conventional ground-source heat pump. The energy savings from the VRF system eliminated the need for USD $15,000 of additional photovoltaics.

Some strategies, like rainwater harvesting, did not prove to have economic justification, but rather were adopted to catalyze change within the building and regulatory spheres. LBC material requirements often limited competition, escalating project costs. Approaches that could not be economically justified had to be justified for their potential to impact greater ecological awareness. Excluding site work costs and the premium to elevate the building above the flood plain, Brock's construction costs were just over USD $4,300/m^2 ($400/ft^2) including on-site renewables.

10.3.4   Innovations

Brock Environmental Center is the first building in the United States to receive a commercial permit for drinking treated rainwater in accordance with federal requirements. Two standing seam metal roofs capture rainwater, filling two 6,000 l (1,650 gal) cisterns—enough to withstand 5 to 6 weeks of drought. The rainwater is filtered (four log filters) and treated with ozone and ultraviolet disinfection, and supplies all water uses within the center. Composting toilets reduce water demand while also treating waste on site. Solid compost is used on site, while leachate is stored and sent to a local struvite reactor and converted into commercially available fertilizer. Gray water from sinks and showers and excess roof runoff is piped to a rain garden that treats the water. All landscaping is native to the region, negating the need for dedicated irrigation systems. Figure 10.9 illustrates Brock's zero water strategy.

Meeting the LBC's strict criteria for responsible and locally sourced materials (within a 500 km radius for dense materials), no Red List chemicals, and full transparency of material components has enhanced the overall scheme. Whenever possible, natural materials from the U.S. southeast (wood, uncoated metals) were selected to reinforce a sense-of-place and biophilic goals, while reducing chemical constituents. As the first LBC project in the region, the criteria on material sourcing was challenging and led to alternative solutions. For example, after finding that the only drywall that could be sourced within the radius was made of coal ash with traces of mercury, the manufacturer supplied a special custom edition made from natural gypsum. Salvaged building products were used extensively and celebrated within the design: maple floors from a local gymnasium were repurposed into interior flooring; all interior wood trim was made from salvaged school bleachers (students' carvings/graffiti were preserved); and fixtures and fittings were salvaged from local demolition projects. The wood siding was milled from cypress "sinker logs" (remnants from 19th-century logging) that had been recovered from the bottom of rivers centuries later.

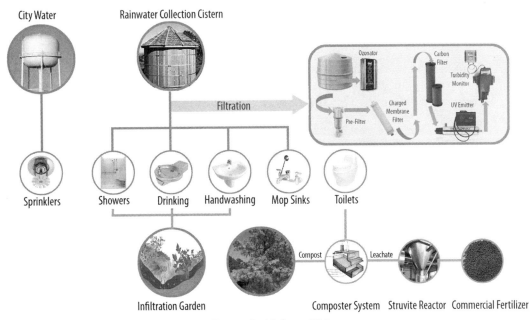

Figure 10.9   Brock's zero water strategy. (*Source:* SmithGroupJJR.)

Situated on a coastal site, the center's design anticipates the onset of sea-level rise and hurricanes. The building is set back 61m (200 ft) from the shore and sits on pylons 4m (14 ft) above sea level, anticipating the projected shoreline in 2100 when the sea level is expected to have risen by 1m (3 ft). The building's structural system is capable of withstanding 120-mph hurricane-force winds, and windows are capable of resisting windborne debris. External materials such as zinc shingles and thick, galvanized-coated steel resist corrosion from salt spray, and the cypress siding has a natural ability to resist rot.

The center's anticipated longevity necessitated considerations for flexibility. Workspaces and furniture can easily be reconfigured to accommodate growth and change. In the conference room, openable glass walls can expand the room to the outside deck, doubling its capacity for larger events. If the center's usage or population grows over time, roof areas and solar inverters can accommodate future PVs allowing the building to remain net-zero. Universal accessibility was a guiding principle for the center, with all spaces meeting the latest federal regulations for accessibility.

The center's design also anticipates its future disassembly. The use of uncoated, panelized materials like zinc shingles, standing seam roofing, panelized PVs, and fastener-attached assemblies can be disassembled to be reused or easily recycled.

During construction, all excavators, generators, and forklifts were fitted with "dry scrubbers," reducing fossil fuel use and emissions. Two mobile PV arrays powered building construction and on-site temporary offices. All new virgin timber was FSC certified, and 95.9% of all construction waste was diverted from landfill; it was reused on site where possible.

The environmental impact of construction and materials was carefully monitored, and offset through the purchase of 1,234 metric tonnes of carbon offsets through Sterling Planet to support a Landfill Gas to Energy project in Dartmouth, Massachusetts. The Greater New Bedford Landfill Gas Utilization Project diverts the landfill gas for use as fuel in four reciprocating internal combustion engine-generator sets that are specially designed for combustion of landfill gas.

The commissioning phase for the project was extensive and detailed, validating strict fabric infiltration limits and system performances to ensure that the optimal building operation required to meet strict LBC performance standards was achieved: requiring the building to produce more energy than it consumes for 12 consecutive months, with the project team remaining engaged in the monitoring process.

10.3.5 Post-Occupancy Evaluation (POE)

The POE involved interviews with occupants and post-completion charrettes with the design team to establish if the project had met its design ambitions. The key learning outcomes from this process were as follows:

- Wind speeds are far less predictable for a specific site than solar insolation. During the first year of operation, the wind turbines actually produced 99.6% of their targeted output, but the wind output varied dramatically from historic averages in actual versus predicted output from month to month. Using wind turbines certified for their output is important.

- The building management system (BMS) can be used along with a comprehensive submetering strategy to identify any abnormalities in performance compared with predictions during the commissioning process. For example, the factory controls on the wall-mounted VRF indoor units prevented fans from turning off whenever the system was considered enabled, and the BMS could not override this function, resulting in more fan energy being used than expected. The design team worked with the suppliers to identify solutions.

- Occupants reported using natural ventilation to much higher indoor temperatures than outlined in the ASHRAE Standard 55 thermal comfort recommendations. Providing users with several options for adjusting and fine-tuning indoor environmental conditions can dramatically expand perceptions of comfort.

- Diligently prepared building use and load profiles for each space covering gave the design team better comfort with right-sizing systems and understanding the energy consumption during the modeling process. It also allowed the owner to see how their decisions impacted building energy consumption and resultant renewable needs.

Sharing the story of the project has been important to transferring the lessons learned from the challenging process. The contractor, Hourigan Construction, kept all stakeholders informed through a live blog [9], updated with site progress photos and key project milestones, allowing community involvement in the process. The architects and MEP engineers, SmithGroupJJR, have published their substantial and exhaustively researched materials database, encouraging transparency in materials reporting and compliance with the LBC's Red List, enabling the industry's collective knowledge [10]. A real-time dashboard on the Chesapeake Bay Foundation (CBF) website tracks renewable energy generation, energy and water consumption, and information on key sustainability features of the building [11].

10.3.6 Endnote

The Brock Environmental Center is a testament to what can be achieved with collaboration and the openness of the entire project team to embrace new and unchartered methods. These are the key successes of the project; the concepts are increasingly well understood, but bringing them to life has taken a phenomenal effort that only comes from a combined focus toward the end goals. The result is a simple, elegant, and effortless building that embodies the environmental preservation ethos it preaches.

The sharing of information and lessons learned from the project serve to demonstrate the ambition of the project team, and challenge the industry both locally and worldwide to reevaluate their standard approach, no matter what size or scale of project is being considered. Despite regulatory, financial, industry, and perception barriers that still exist, it can, and should, be done. Developments like this influence and challenge the industry and supply chain to adapt to meet consumer demands.

10.4   Elmsbrook, Oxfordshire, U.K.

Nicole Lazarus, Bicester Eco-Town Project Manager for Bioregional, and Steve Hornblow, Project Director, A2Dominion

10.4.1   Context

Elmsbrook is a new community of 393 homes (see Figure 10.10) being built on the edge of an historic market town in the English county of Oxfordshire (see Table 10.4 for climate data). Its developer, A2Dominion, aims to set a new standard for large-scale, mixed-use development in achieving genuinely sustainable development across the board, bringing social, economic, and environmental benefits to the existing town of Bicester as well as to the residents of the urban expansion.

Construction began in 2014 and the first 91 homes were completed in 2016. Some 40% of the 51-acre (21-hectare) greenfield site is being retained as green space for people and nature. The development includes a primary school, community

Figure 10.10   Elmsbrook, the first phase of the North West Bicester eco-town. (*Photo:* Courtesy A2Dominion.)

Table 10.4   Key Climate Data for Oxfordshire, U.K.

Altitude	79m (259 ft)
Climate	Temperate
Average Monthly Maximum	20.4°C (68.7°F) dry bulb 14.2°C (57.6°F) wet bulb 88.3% RH
Average Monthly Minimum	2.1°C (35.8°F) dry bulb 0.4°C (32.7°F) wet bulb 75.6% RH

center, convenience store, and business center and is the largest true zero-carbon development in the United Kingdom. Elmsbrook is the first phase of the North West Bicester eco-town, which will eventually grow into a settlement of some 6,000 homes with accompanying infrastructure, community services, and workplaces.

The origins of this project lie back in 2007, when the U.K. government proposed that several eco-towns should be built in England on the edge of existing settlements to meet the urgent demand for more housing. These new communities were intended to demonstrate how the environmental impacts of new homes on greenfield sites could be radically reduced while offering social and economic gains to both new and existing communities.

The government developed planning policy to support the concept, and proposals for several eco-towns were put forward by local councils working with developers. While the succeeding U.K. government did not favor eco-towns, the North West Bicester proposal has endured. This was because it was the most advanced of all of the eco-town proposals, with strong support from the local authority, the Cherwell District Council, and residential property group A2Dominion, lead developer of the eco-town with a long-term interest in North West Bicester. A2Dominion provides affordable, private, and social rented homes as well as homes for sale and shared ownership through its FABRICA by A2Dominion brand.

10.4.2   One Planet Community

Elmsbrook was planned and built in accordance with the U.K. government's original planning policy statement for eco-towns and the One Planet Living sustainability framework. This framework aims to enable residents to live a One Planet lifestyle, which is a lifestyle that our finite planet could support if everyone lived that way, given its abilities to furnish essential natural resources, maintain a stable climate, and handle wastes and pollution. One Planet Living was developed by the sustainability charity Bioregional out of its partnership role in creating the world-renowned BedZED eco-village of 100 homes in Sutton, South London.

Using the One Planet framework, A2Dominion and its stakeholders created a sustainability action plan based on 10 easily grasped principles. This covers the development's life cycle, from early design through use and refurbishment. It includes targets and key performance indicators (KPIs). Progress is regularly reviewed, allowing the plan to be updated. The ten One Planet principles set out to reduce environmental impacts from consumption of energy, water, food, and materials to One Planet levels, but they also cover health, happiness, culture, prosperity, and social justice, aiming to make sustainable living attractive and affordable for all.

The One Planet action plan for Elmsbrook was signed off on by A2Dominion and Bioregional in late 2012 [12]. The new community, still on the drawing board at that stage, then became part of a small but growing number of endorsed One Planet communities across the globe. The action plan coordinates with a wide range of plans, consents, agreements, and conditions between the developer and local authorities setting out how Elmsbrook is to be built and managed. It had its first review in 2015 [13], showing good progress against the framework.

10.4.3   A True Zero-Carbon Community

The action plan for Elmsbrook delivers net-zero carbon emissions from people oc-cupying and using its buildings, making it the United Kingdom's first true net-zero carbon housing development of significant size. This goal encompasses all of the energy used to heat and power the homes and nondomestic buildings.

The true zero carbon in use strategy (see Color Plate 27) relies on the following:

- Extensive deployment of rooftop PV panels, giving a total capacity of 2,047 kW peak output across the entire development with an average of 3.7 kW peak per home.
- A grid-connected natural gas-burning combined heat and power (CHP) sta-tion that supplies hot water for a district heating system while generating electricity. This CHP plant's running hours will increase to meet demand as the wider NW Bicester eco-town is developed. The plant can generate 844 kW of electricity and 865 kW of heat.
- High levels of fabric energy efficiency in all of Elmsbrook's buildings (the fabric energy efficiency target is <40.39 kWh/m^2 per annum).

Key design targets are as follows:

- Average dwelling carbon emission rate: 2.87 kgCO$_2$/m^2 per annum,
- Space heating: <28.9kWh/m^2 per annum,
- Hot water: <15.9kWh/m^2 per annum,
- Lighting and appliances: <27.9kWh/m^2 per annum, and
- Cooking (electric): <2.9kWh/m^2 per annum.

The electricity generated by the CHP plant and its associated carbon emissions are regarded as exports to the national electricity grid. This power substitutes for electricity that would have been generated elsewhere in the system, with similar carbon emissions. The hot water, which circulates to provide space heating and domestic hot water, is then considered as a net-zero carbon on-site heat source.

The total quantity of PV panels at Elmsbrook has been sized to match its elec-tricity demand. There will be sunny periods when almost all of the solar electricity has to be exported because it exceeds on-site demand, and times when no solar power is being generated and all of Elmsbrook's electricity has to be imported. Over the year, however, on-site solar generation should cover total electricity con-sumption leading to net-zero carbon emissions associated with the new commu-nity's electricity use (see Figure 10.11).

10.4.4   Zero Waste

The aim is for zero landfill wastes to be generated from the construction of Elms-brook. Once occupied, 80% of the municipal waste generated by residents should be composted, recycled, or reused, compared to an average across the Cherwell District Council area of 55% in 2014–2015. There is also a 2020 target for each household to produce no more than 200 kg of residual waste per annum destined for landfill or incineration with energy recovery, compared to a district average in 2014–2015 of 445 tonnes. Every home with a garden will be offered a composting bin, and all kitchens will have segregated recycling bins, including bins for food waste, collected by the local authority.

10.4.5   Sustainable Transport

Green, fossil-fuel-free transport is a challenge for Elmsbrook given its edge-of-town location and relatively low densities. Relying on the car for commuting and other journeys has long been the norm for this type of development. Elmsbrook has a target for at least 50% of all journeys to use sustainable transport modes by 2026. From the beginning residents have had a bus service to the town center every half hour. The development's layout and road hierarchy with dedicated cycling paths will encourage walking and cycling, and a free loan scheme for folding Brompton commuter bicycles was one early initiative.

Given that residents will continue to want to use cars, the plan favors ultra-low-emission vehicles. An electric car club with two vehicles began operating in Elmsbrook soon after the first residents moved in, with incentives for households to join it. There is a target for 10% of residents with cars to have switched to electric vehicles by 2018 with free home charging units on offer to households within the first 2 years of moving in.

10.4.6   Sustainable Water

Rainwater will be collected from roofs across Elmsbrook and used for toilet flushing, washing machines, and garden irrigation. There is a target for average treated drinking water consumption per resident to be only 80 l/day, achieved through rainwater harvesting and by installing water-efficient appliances and plumbing. Problems caused by runoff resulting from heavy rainfall will be avoided by installing green roofs on the car garages and by creating sustainable urban drainage systems with new ponds, swales, and soakaways on the site.

10.4.7   Endnote

Other elements of the One Planet action plan cover the sustainability of Elmsbrook's material use and food consumption, enhancing local biodiversity, and its contribution to culture and community, equity and local economy, and—last but not least—the health and happiness of both its new residents and those of people living nearby. This is a community for all income levels, with 30% of the homes either for affordable rent or shared home ownership.

Before it was named and marketed as Elmsbrook, the first phase of NW Bicester was called "The Exemplar." It aims to provide an example of how one of the most controversial and environmentally damaging forms of development—the sprawl of low-density new housing across greenfields and the extra road travel this causes—could instead become a sustainability success story. With the first homes now occupied, Elmsbrook has now become a practical, real-life example of what can be achieved and how problems can be overcome (see Figure 10.11).

Figure 10.11   New homes at Elmsbrook. (*Photo:* Courtesy A2Dominion.)

10.5   Park 20|20, Amsterdam, The Netherlands

William McDonough + Partners

10.5.1   Context

Park 20|20 (located close to Schipol Airport, Amsterdam; see Table 10.5 for climate data) is a model for sustainable master planning, guided by the Cradle to Cradle (C2C) philosophy [14] developed by architect William McDonough and chemist Michael Braungart [15]: creating closed-loop cycles for materials, energy, waste, and water whereby all outputs have the potential to be reused, composted, or recycled back into industry. These principles are applied at masterplan infrastructure through to building level, resulting in a development that increases its output as more assets are created (see Figure 10.12).

A collaborative effort by planners, landscape architects, and architects developed conceptual planning alternatives to explore the relationship of several key development aspects [16]:

- Integration of optimum solar and wind orientation (to reduce energy demand) for building within the context of the tight urban block and the

Table 10.5   Key Climate Data for Amsterdam, The Netherlands

Altitude	−3m (−10 ft)
Climate	Maritime, humid
Average Monthly Maximum	20.7°C (69.3°F) dry bulb 15.9°C (60.6°F) wet bulb 94.7% RH
Average Monthly Minimum	1.3°C (34.3°F) dry bulb 0.4°C (32.7°F) wet bulb 74.4% RH

Figure 10.12   Park 20|20 masterplan. (*Source:* Delta Developments Group.)

development program requirements by adjusting the building massing to ensure solar access in winter.

- Integration of regenerative landscape strategies respectful of the "cultural
  landscape" and the distinct planning template of the "polder grammatical"
  (narrow lots and orthogonal roads, vegetation, and canals) by introducing a
  more ecologically diverse plant palette, by using the landscape standards in
  exterior planting and creating more biologically robust interior gardens, by
  connecting the interior gardens to regional ecology with landscape corridors,
  and by creating additional landscape areas on roof surfaces and parking
  decks.

- Implementation of effective district-scaled sustainable infrastructure approaches by aligning scale and types of land uses (i.e., hotel demand for hot
  water with office waste water treatment output of biogas fuel for heating)
  and creating a centralized treatment facility for waste water, energy, and
  stormwater on site.

- Implementation of C2C agenda of waste-free design by treating waste water on site, capturing energy and soil amendments, and eliminating sewage
  discharge.

Cradle to Cradle is characterized by three principles [17] derived from nature:

1. *Everything is a resource for something else.* In nature, the "waste" of one
   system is food for another. Buildings can be designed to be disassembled and safely returned to the soil (biological nutrients), or reutilized as
   high-quality materials for new products and buildings (technical nutrients)—as illustrated in Figure 10.13. Conventional building systems and

infrastructures (for example, waste water treatment) can be redesigned to become nutrient management systems that capture previously discarded resources for safe and productive reuse.

2. *Use renewable energy.* Living things thrive on the energy of current solar income. Similarly, human constructs can utilize renewable energy in many forms, such as wind, geothermal, and gravitational energy—, thereby capitalizing on these abundant resources while supporting human and environmental health.

3. *Celebrate diversity.* Around the world, geology, hydrology, photosynthesis, and nutrient cycling, adapted to locale, yield an astonishing diversity of natural and cultural life. Designs that respond to the unique challenges and opportunities offered by each place fit elegantly and effectively into their own niches.

10.5.2 Applying Cradle to Cradle

The diversely designed Park 20|20 buildings offer identity for their tenants, while the use of a common design team introduces efficiency into the design and construction process without losing focus of the overall design philosophy. They also meet BREEAM certification requirements. They incorporate reconfiguration and disassembly, allowing the adaptation to accommodate future changing needs or new tenants. For example, floor designs are chosen that allow the repositioning of internal staircases, or ceramic cladding tiles that can simply be removed and returned to the supplier. The value is in the building elements providing longevity, that is, the shell and core, and the flexibility to change the internal use if desired.

The sustainable and biophilic design and indoor environmental quality (IEQ) aspects ensure the buildings themselves are high performance, providing attractive working environments. Specific materials have been selected for use that achieve C2C certification; those that did not were challenged by Delta Development Group to innovate and provide solutions, thereby stimulating the market. A database was maintained that detailed the materials used, the certification levels achieved, and their reuse potential through biological or technical cycles.

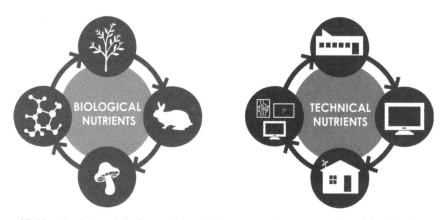

Figure 10.13   Nutrient metabolisms. (*Source:* McDonough Braungart Design Chemistry.)

The innovative development has required bespoke financial mechanisms to facilitate the process. One example is financial leases with material suppliers whereby the developer pays rent for the materials, with the supplier having the potential to recover the value of the material when the lease expires and take the components back if the building is disassembled. "This makes our up-front construction costs lower because we only invest in the use of the material. And it makes sense for suppliers because materials are valued on the expectation of rising commodity prices" [18].

10.5.3   Innovation

The masterplan optimizes passive design techniques by orienting buildings to take full advantage of solar heating and wind direction natural ventilation. Its buildings, like trees, harvest the energy of the sun, sequester carbon, make oxygen, distill water, and provide habitat.

At its core, is a closed-loop, fully integrated energy, water, and waste management system (see Figure 10.14 and Color Plate 28). Building waste water is directed to a solar-powered central treatment facility where it is purified and recirculated to buildings for use in toilet flushing. Heat generated in the process is used to create hot water for the area's hotel and in the on-site greenhouses to grow food for the restaurants serving the office facilities.

Park 20|20 has the capacity for continuously adding value as development continues: increasing solar energy generation, expanding its supply chain capacity of C2C certified products, developing mechanisms for shared rewards, and sharing knowledge. "Technology doesn't limit what can be achieved; it's conventional economic models and processes that do that" [19].

Delta Development Group has captured an opportunity to drive rental value, attracting (and retaining) tenants that benefit from increased worker productivity and well-being, providing longevity with low rates of depreciation. Indeed, CEO Coert Zacharaisse suggests that designing for disassembly can provide a positive residual value at end of life, because the value of the highly accessible materials is greater than the demolition costs [20].

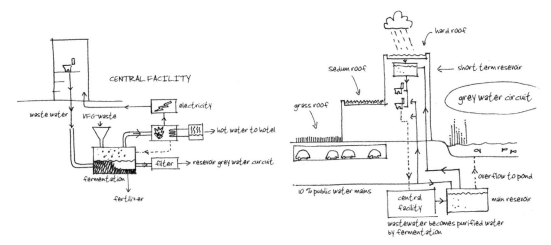

Figure 10.14   Integrated system process at Park 20|20. (*Source:* William McDonough + Partners.)

A model of holistic, closed-loop design, Park 20|20 will function as a dynamic environmental system that enhances the local community, its ecosystem, and its economy [21].

10.5.4 Endnote

Park 20|20 focuses on regeneration, rather than mitigation. It goes beyond the principles of good environmental design that are incorporated into the design of every new and unique building within the masterplan, to concepts that challenge the perceptions of how buildings should integrate with each other and their surrounding environment. It has flipped the notion that construction should follow the linear model of take–make–dispose and adopted a circular economy approach, in which the value of resources is retained.

Energy performance data for the completed buildings is not widely published, and therefore it is to be determined if the buildings live up to expectations in terms of energy and water consumption, or if this output has been compromised by the focus on C2C compliance, that is, through materials selection. Due to the integrated nature of the services, it is likely that the full potential of the operating performance will not be realized until after the final building in the current masterplan is completed in 2017. Nevertheless, this should not deter from the breakthroughs made in terms of the increased awareness of the impact, and benefits, of a cradle-to-cradle approach as an integral part of the business model.

10.6 Hotel Verde, Cape Town, South Africa

André Harms, Founder, Ecolution Consulting

10.6.1 Context

A design philosophy from the project's conception that embodies sustainable practices is the key to the success of four-star Hotel Verde at Cape Town International Airport (see Table 10.6 for climate data), completed in 2013 (see Figure 10.15). Dedicated and enthusiastic about sustainability, owners Maro and Annemarie Delicio have transformed what was initially just a sensible business proposition into a showcase for some of the most advanced environmentally conscious technological installations as well as construction and operation practices in the world [22].

Initially there were only two high-level targets: (1) Build Africa's greenest hotel and (2) showcase that luxury and sustainability are not mutually exclusive. This has transpired into a low-impact hotel facility that is challenging the industry to take note. Hotel Verde's *Thrivability Report* [23] develops that ambition and the outcomes of the Hotel Verde project into a model for hospitality development, based on the concept of thrivability as a regenerative and inclusive evolution to sustainability. The report states that nearly 11% of the capital investment of the project was allocated to the sustainable interventions of the hotel.

Hotel Verde was the first building in South Africa to achieve the LEED Building Design and Construction Platinum level, and the first hotel in the world to achieve double Platinum following certification under the LEED Existing Building Operations and Maintenance scheme in July 2015. Hotel Verde is also the first hotel

Table 10.6   Key Climate Data for Cape Town, South Africa

Altitude	46m (151 ft)
Climate	Mediterranean Maritime
Average Monthly Maximum	26.1°C (78.9°F) dry bulb 16.5°C (61.7°F) wet bulb 89.6% RH
Average Monthly Minimum	7.4°C (45.3°F) dry bulb 5.1°C (41.2°F) wet bulb 54.1% RH

Figure 10.15   Hotel Verde (*Photo:* Hotel Verde)

in South Africa to be awarded the highest accolade of a six-star rating under the Green Star South Africa (SA) Existing Building Performance scheme in June 2015, focusing on the efficient operations and management of the building in order to maintain optimal performance. Green Star SA is based on the Australian Green Star system and customized for the South African context, operated by the Green Building Council for South Africa (GBCSA).

10.6.2   Design Features

Ecolution Consulting was engaged as the lead sustainability consultant, along with other specialist firms, to develop the technical elements of the project. Advanced energy modeling enabled manipulation to evaluate and compare the performance of different design options, construction techniques, installations, and products to establish cost/benefit analyses against the project goals and to identify optimal solutions. This process was also used to ensure system integration and to accurately size the heating and cooling systems, ensuring efficient capital expenditures.

Quantifiable returns on investment from adopting these techniques include 5.35 years for water and sewerage systems and 9.7 years for energy-saving systems, future proofing the hotel against future utility costs. Other associated benefits, including increased PR exposure, staff productivity, lack of absenteeism, guest satisfaction, and repeat revenue, will significantly reduce the payback periods. Data from the first year of operation suggest that the hotel sustained substantially lower operating costs than an average Cape Town hotel room, up to 70% savings on utilities (electricity, water, and sewerage), and an EUI of 83kWh/m²/yr (26 kBtu/ft²) (see Figure 10.16).

An intelligent BMS actively and continuously monitors the performance of active systems within the building, optimizing efficiency and reporting any system malfunctions or inefficiently running equipment. Submetering throughout the building allows monitoring of any building areas or systems with abnormal usage, prompting intervention.

10.6.2.1 Passive Design Strategies

Passive design strategies adopted to reduce the heating and cooling loads include a well-insulated structure and services, spectrally selective double-glazed windows, airtight construction, natural ventilation where possible, indirect sunlight for natural lighting, shading and building layout to reduce direct sunlight, and use of light colors internally to reflect natural light.

10.6.2.2 Active Systems

Geothermal ground loops, incorporating 100 boreholes each approximately 65m (215 ft) deep, provide a total pipework length of 13 km coupled to heat pumps for central heating, cooling, and domestic hot water generation, thus providing a heat source in winter and a heat sink in summer.

Hot water is circulated throughout the hotel constantly to reduce wastage of water while guests wait for the water to heat up. Effective insulation on pipework for hot and chilled water systems minimizes losses. Limiting water pressure and

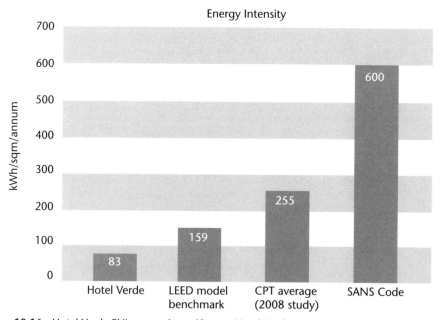

Figure 10.16 Hotel Verde EUI comparison. (*Source:* Hotel Verde.)

specifying aerators on water fittings reduce water consumption without compromising on functionality, while waterless urinals are expected to save close to 1 million liters of water per year.

Regenerative drive units on the three elevators allow for about 30% of the input energy to be recaptured and fed back into the building. Energy-efficient LED lighting with movement and light sensors, both for internal and external systems, ensure lighting is used only when required.

A total of 154 locally assembled Tenesol 240 Wp PV panels are installed on the north-facing roof. An additional 66 solar panels are positioned on the north façade to provide shading to hotel rooms exposed to direct sunlight, reducing heat gain in these spaces that would increase loads on the air-conditioning system. Energy generated from the solar panels is used within the building to charge the UPS battery and offset power from the grid.

Three vertical-axis wind turbines sit in front of the building, as a statement of the potential of wind energy as a renewable energy option. In the period from July 2015 to June 2016, 9.1% of the total electricity demand was met by on-site renewables: 0.5% from wind and 8.6% from solar PV.

10.6.2.3   Water and Landscaping Features

A gray water plant recycles water from showers and the few baths, as well as the condensate from HVAC fan coil units, for reuse in toilet flushing. The process uses a series of tanks to filter and aerate the water and uses ultraviolet light for sterilization, which saves up to 6,000 l of potable water per day. The hotel washing machines reuse the final rinse water from the previous cycle for the next load's prerinse cycle.

Rainwater is passed through a passive, self-cleaning mechanical Wisy screen filter, and stored in a 40,000 l rainwater harvesting tank in the basement partially beneath the water table, along with water collected from the subsoil drainage system. Collected rainwater is used in maintenance, car washing, and a drip-fed irrigation system. It is also linked to the gray water reticulation system, so that rainwater can be used to flush toilets in the future if desired.

A low-energy rainwater-fed aquaponics system (see Color Plate 29a) feeds species of plants such as lettuce, herbs, spinach, leeks, peppers, tomato, and spring onions for use in the hotel's kitchens. Other ingredients are responsibly sourced from suppliers within a 160 km radius of the hotel, wherever possible. The hotel's in-house water bottling purification and carbonation plant saves approximately USD $9,000 a year, as well as avoiding environmental impacts from manufacture and transportation.

External areas include restored wetlands, an eco-trail, outdoor gym, two beehives housing over 60,000 Cape honey bees, and an eco-pool. The eco-pool uses a living filtering system of plants and organisms, negating the need for harmful chemicals, salt, or chlorine. The result is a safe, clean, and inviting low-maintenance natural pool (see Color Plate 29b) that does not require energy-intensive filtration or pumps. The vegetated roof garden over the lobby area creates a habitat for biodiversity and thermally insulates the areas below, reducing the energy load on the heating and cooling systems.

10.6.3 Construction

Cobiax void formers were used to displace 1,279 tonnes of concrete within the concrete floor slabs (see Figure 10.17). Over 46,000 hollow plastic spheres made of recycled polypropylene ensure a lightweight structure, thereby reducing the foundation design while maintaining structural integrity, allowing larger floor spans and room heights and maximizing internal space. Further knock-on effects of this specification include reduced emissions associated with the energy-intensive concrete manufacturing process and transportation, reduced installation time, and less steel reinforcement.

Procurement policies for the sourcing of materials include recycled concrete content, bricks, and insulation to reduce the impacts associated with using virgin materials. Additionally, 50% of construction materials were sourced locally, reducing emissions associated with transporting materials and enabling ease of maintenance and replacement during operation.

Art installation and upcycling projects have created unique and unusual finishes, such as car tires for mirror frames and coconut shell tiles in the VIP lounge area. Ninety percent of construction waste was diverted from landfill as a result of an on-site waste minimization plan to encourage reuse of materials where possible.

10.6.4 Operational Impacts

All staff receive green induction training, and the in-house continuous development program, called Avanti, runs training and team-building events with an environmental and social focus. The environmental committee meets monthly to update staff on the hotel's performance against targets in energy, water, and waste and to

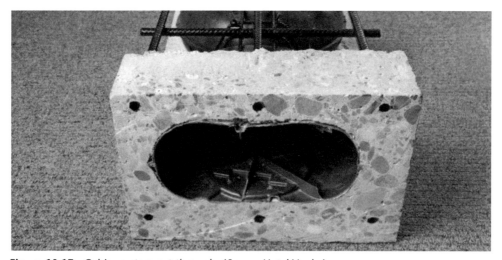

Figure 10.17 Cobiax system cut-through. (*Source:* Hotel Verde.)

discuss new ideas. This upskilling and awareness raising ensures that Hotel Verde's impact extends beyond the site boundary and into the local communities, along with numerous community engagement initiatives.

Building energy modeling, which is used to determine which rooms are the most energy efficient at specific times of the year according to the orientation of the sun, informs priority room filling by the reservations team (i.e., more efficient rooms are booked before less efficient rooms).

Guests at Hotel Verde are encouraged to follow their lead. Making choices for sustainable behavior during your stay may earn you "Verdinos," Hotel Verde's in-house currency, to redeem at the bar, to use toward your bill, or to donate to charity. Ways to earn Verdinos include the following:

- Choose not to switch on in-room air conditioning.
- Use the power-generating gym equipment.
- Reuse towels or bedding.
- Separate waste in the split bins for recycling.
- Take the stairs instead of the elevator when staying on the second floor or higher.
- Take a jog on the eco-trail.
- Use public transport, bicycle, electric vehicles, or carpooling to arrive at the hotel.

Hotel Verde celebrates Earth Hour once a week, by switching all noncritical equipment and lights off during dinner service, offering candle-lit dinners and food prepared without electricity, for example, wood-fired oven pizzas, with live music playing in the background. For International Earth Hour 2014, they held a night market showcasing local traders and produce.

Strategically positioned signage around the hotel offers guests insights into some of the sustainability interventions within the property, as well as thought-provoking facts and figures on, for example, energy generation versus energy consumption. A sustainability channel on the in-house televisions provides real-time data from the intelligent BMS to illustrate resource consumption and efficiency.

Through a partnership with impactChoice, Hotel Verde offsets the carbon emissions associated with their guests' stay or conference. The cost is absorbed by the hotel, demonstrating their commitment and ultimate responsibility for the carbon impact of guests staying at their hotel. The proceeds from carbon credit purchases go to the Kariba REDD+ project in Zimbabwe, which works with communities to reduce deforestation, provide training on responsible agriculture, and improve the livelihoods of local people. All transactions are confirmed through auditable micro carbon reduction certificates.

10.6.5   Endnote

Such initiatives enable the engagement and education of Hotel Verde's guests, to take their experience from airport hotel convenience into their everyday lives, encouraging a change in mind-set and challenging expectations. As an intrinsically transient facility—an airport hotel—Hotel Verde has a limited amount of time to make a lasting impact on its guests. However, the hotel succeeds in thoughtfully combining responsible development without compromising on luxury. It is an excellent example of selecting sustainable innovations that make commercial sense to the long-term operation of the business, and it is a model for responsible development beyond the hospitality industry.

Due to the pioneering nature of the project, options for responsible sourcing were limited and/or more expensive, and the more unconventional aspects of the project require additional commissioning and training to ensure optimum potential. These teething problems of introducing a new approach to development will lessen as the market responds to the demand for similar projects.

The success of Hotel Verde, stems from a desire to do everything better. Rather than settling for mitigation of the impact of the development, the project team have chosen to enrich the lives of everyone who engages with the facility, challenging perceptions of what is a normal hotel or business operations experience. The concepts and outcomes are replicable throughout hotel development and wider construction industries across Africa.

> We might have the slogan 'Africa's Greenest Hotel' right now, but we hope it won't be for long. We want to show the continent what can be done. We want to challenge the industry as a whole.
>
> —*André Harms, Ecolution Consulting*

10.7 The Sheikh Zayed Desert Learning Center, Abu Dhabi

Talik and Jaafar Chalabi, Principal Designers, Chalabi Architekten & Partner

10.7.1 Context

The Sheikh Zayed Desert Learning Center (SZDLC; see Figure 10.18) is an iconic and prestigious project in Al Ain Wildlife Park & Resort, Abu Dhabi (see Table 10.7 for climate data). The design is based on several innovative and interactive sustainable technologies designed to reduce water consumption, primary energy usage, and material usage.

The project was a significant opportunity to communicate the importance of designing buildings that are sustainable within a desert environment and region with no reliable water source and a high demand on nonrenewable energy sources, setting an example for future construction projects in the region.

From its conception, the SZDLC project received special attention from the stakeholders and government officials for its uniqueness and vision, which falls within some of the top priorities of the government agenda: sustainability, environment, tourism and education, leading to strong collaboration from an early stage.

The functional brief, together with the sustainable criteria for the building as defined through the pursuit of Estidama 5 Pearls and LEED Platinum accreditation, meant establishing a multidisciplinary collaborative approach. Regular design workshops and intermediate submissions of work during the design phases

Figure 10.18 Sheikh Zayed Desert Learning Center. (*Photo:* Chalabi Architekten & Partner.)

Table 10.7 Key Climate Data for Abu Dhabi

Altitude	27m (89 ft)
Climate	Desert Hot
Average Monthly Maximum	42.0°C (107.6°F) dry bulb 27.3°C (81.1°F) wet bulb 80.3% RH
Average Monthly Minimum	13.0°C (55.4°F) dry bulb 8.2°C (46.8°F) wet bulb 42.7% RH

allowed work to be independently reviewed and feedback provided to ensure follow-through for key decisions and objectives.

Important in the architectural design was ensuring that the building specifications described the minimum environmental benchmarks required to achieve the highest-level environmental ratings. Architectural drawings and details were important to describe material buildup, insulative qualities, material U-values, and sealant and material properties. The tectonics of how materials are put together in detail was an important consideration for not only selecting high-quality materials but also to ensure and demand the highest quality of craftsmanship in assembling materials to maximize the durable life of the project.

The building energy simulation was an important influence in design considerations for building services, such as the HVAC, electrical, renewable energy sources, water consumption, and building management systems. The firm iC consulenten ZT GmbH was commissioned to plan the energy systems and state-of-the-art building services, and also advised on building physics and energy-efficient operation. The design team employed an array of systems, some based on age-old practices and others based on state-of-the-art and innovative technologies.

Training for maintenance of new and unfamiliar technologies from system manufacturers, for example, for the PV systems, was important in order to ensure the equipment remains in its optimal state of operation over the life cycle. The ongoing training of personnel in order to manage the complex systems was a significant challenge in the transition from construction to operations.

10.7.2 Sustainability Innovations

SZDLC is largely self-sufficient in energy; with the aid of the sun's warmth, earth coupling, and photovoltaics, it can cover 80% of base load using renewable sources of energy, almost the whole time. Combining active and passive use of solar energy, and employing systems that conserve water and energy, has enabled the building to achieve high levels of performance.

Each feature has been evaluated against the project criteria, including the impact on the four Estidama pillars (environmental, cultural, economic, and social), feasibility, advantages and disadvantages, cost-benefit analyses, risks, integration, measurability, and maintainability/durability.

The building is oriented to minimize heat gain through window apertures yet maximize the daylight inside the building by having fewer and smaller windows facing south and west and having larger windows facing north and east. A very large overhang provides a shaded area at the building's main entrance to provide refuge for visitors from harsh summer sun.

The building fabric has been designed to minimize solar heat gain, reducing the heat load required to be serviced by the air-conditioning system. The building envelope comprises thick reinforced concrete walls and a 200 mm (8 in.) thick insulation layer covered with 40 mm (1.5 in.) thick stone with very high solar reflective index, which offers very high resistivity to heat gain from outside and heat loss from inside the building.

Reinforced concrete suspended floors have been constructed as bubble decks, a first for the UAE. Bubbles in the form of air-filled PVC spheres (300 mm in diameter) are incorporated into the suspended concrete slabs to improve their resistivity to thermal transmission (thereby helping to stabilize the thermal comfort inside the building) and reduce the weight.

The ancient practice of using high ceilings and lofty spaces to facilitate natural air circulation and reduce the volume of exchanged air volume led to an open spiraling design within the building, allowing heat loads generated from lighting, electrical equipment, and visitors to rise and be captured in the mechanical ventilation system.

Almost 10m (33 ft) of the building is subterranean (see Color Plate 30); the building uses the lower temperatures at depths below ground surface to precool the air supply to the air-conditioning system by drawing it through subterranean ducts buried 8m below the ground surface before this air enters the mechanical air-handling units. This *geothermal air heat exchange* is an ancient principle that has been adapted in a new technology, reducing cooling energy consumption by about 20%.

A portion of the energy demand of the building is met by renewable energy generated from an array of PV solar panels installed on the roof, which are capable of generating and contributing at peak approximately 149 kW of electricity daily to the building.

Concrete core activation (CCA) in the SZDLC design was considered a feasible application in combination with the high thermal mass; 1,100 m^2 of high-performance hot water solar thermal collectors drive a single-stage absorption chiller with a nominal capacity of 350 kW to produce 579.8 MWh/yr of thermal cooling energy (see Figure 10.19). The chilled water is circulated through pipes within the concrete floor, thereby stabilizing internal temperatures. Since the indoor air is dehumidified mechanically, no condensation results. The peak cooling demand in summer coincides with peak solar radiation availability; therefore, payback for the system is very short. The cooling strategy eliminates the need for traditional air-conditioning systems with uneven air distribution and high-maintenance ductwork.

10.7.3   Water Usage and Minimization

Water demand minimization is essential to the sustainability of the project. A sophisticated water-saving and gray water treatment strategy, along with an efficient recooling system, works in an adiabatic mode without the requirement for chemical additives.

The sanitary systems feature waterless urinals that reduce consumption per flush to 1.0 l, and flow fixtures limiting flow duration to 10 seconds. All gray water is collected, together with stormwater and condensate from HVAC equipment, and treated on site using filtration and treatment methods for reuse in cistern flushing

Figure 10.19   SZDLC concrete core activation. (*Photo:* Chalabi Architekten & Partner.)

and cooling tower heat rejection. Potable water consumption has therefore been reduced to supplying the showers and basins only.

10.7.4 Building Management System

The building management system installed for SZDLC provides advanced control and monitoring features of HVAC equipment, which is critical for ensuring energy-efficient performance of the cooling plant and for prioritizing renewable energy sources. Control of the indoor environment must be based on an energy management strategy that minimizes energy consumption, and therefore energy costs, while maintaining suitable comfort conditions for the occupants. An energy management strategy was defined in the design stage to reach the comfort conditions of 23°C (73.4°F) and 40% relative humidity within the building.

10.7.5 Endnote

The basic engineering challenge for this project was the newly (for the region) adapted sustainability standards, which set the mark for the equipment and system specifications. The design incorporated several highly sophisticated systems that are all integrated into an overall management system for monitoring, adjusting, and achieving the most efficient operating point for the building, while maintaining internal comfort levels.

The building seamlessly integrates within the natural environment. The application of the Estidama criteria has ensured that the project pursued integrated system design solutions to facilitate efficient operation (and cooling) of a large building in the heat of the desert.

10.8 Khoo Teck Puat Hospital, Singapore

Tan Shao Yen, Managing Director, CPG Consultants

10.8.1 Context

A truly sustainable healthcare development can benefit the community, enhance patient experience, improve patient health, and improve the environment. Healthcare organizations will also be able to reap economic benefits through lower utility expenses when the goals of sustainable initiatives are met [24].

The challenge in producing a well-designed sustainable healthcare development lies in negotiating the complexity of healthcare facilities, with a diverse range of functions and specialized requirements to cater to the medical and supporting systems (e.g., life support, telecommunications, space comfort, and hygiene) and with sophisticated systems (e.g., for infection control and thermal comfort) that consume high quantities of energy. Hospitals are also large producers of waste that needs to be comprehensively managed.

Khoo Teck Puat Hospital (KTPH) in Singapore (see Table 10.8 for climate data), completed in 2010, illustrates how an integrated design process (IDP) can match the vision and sustainable objectives set for the project, and the challenges faced in the process of design (see Figure 10.20).

Table 10.8   Key Climate Data for Singapore

Altitude	0m (0 ft)
Climate	Equatorial/tropical hot, humid
Average Monthly Maximum	32.1°C (89.8°F) dry bulb 25.9°C (78.6°F) wet bulb 96.3% RH
Average Monthly Minimum	24.3°C (75.7°F) dry bulb 22.6°C (72.7°F) wet bulb 71.1% RH

Figure 10.20   Khoo Teck Puat Hospital. (*Photo:* CPG Consultants Pte Ltd.)

10.8.2   IDP at KTPH

The vision of KTPH was translated through the brief of the project before the formation of the project team. Wellness philosophy is advocated in KTPH's holistic model of care through the hospital design brief for a hassle-free, patient-centric hospital with emphasis on "adding to, not subtracting from, neighborhood" that flows with the community and not as a "stumbling block." The planned hospital supplements the pre-hospitalization and post-hospitalization (promoting wellness) stages in the patients continuum of care [25].

KTPH's integrated design team comprised the core project team, along with subconsultants, clinicians for user work groups, the hospital planning team (HPT), and regulatory authorities. KTPH's CEO, Liak Teng Lit, was the de facto leader in championing sustainability issues during the visioning and objectives setting. The CPG architectural team as lead consultants led the building professionals in engaging the HPT and the user representatives, as well as the building authorities, while the HPT coordinated the user work group discussions, hospital department workshops, and internal hospital HPC meetings (see Figure 10.21).

A comprehensive sustainable objective focus was established by the KTPH HPT together with the consultant team, and the specific measurable goals were set using the prevailing Singapore building performance rating, Green Mark, as the benchmark. The highest rating of Green Mark Platinum was targeted. Establishing the objectives in collaboration with the client and project team was critical to setting the direction in which the design would evolve and eventually crystallize.

The process for design iteration started from the design brief. Once the client engaged the consultant team, workshops for design charrettes were conducted throughout the visioning, master plan, schematic design, value engineering, and design development stages. Medical professionals and building professionals contributed their respective knowledge domains, for example: the medical professionals offered the notion of a healing garden as informed by their practice of the same in their previous premise, Alexandra Hospital (AH); building professionals advocated a bioclimatic, resource-efficient green building design approach. Through the integrated design process, these ideas contributed to the eventual design outcomes in KTPH. The key design systems required close collaboration between disciplines and specialists to optimize integration and efficiency (see Table 10.9) [26].

10.8.3 Healing Environment

The design objectives established at the start of the project leaned toward a healing environment or a biophilic design, in the belief that sustainable design should go beyond the technical systems of the building and extend deeply into the sensorial experiences within. The biophilia hypothesis suggests that there is an inborn affinity

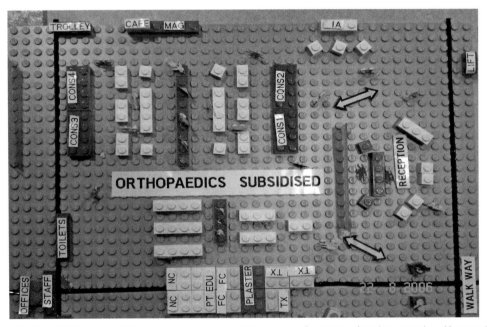

Figure 10.21 KTPH's early IDP process used Lego bricks as part of a space planning exercise. (*Source:* Alexandra Health System.)

Table 10.9 Key Design Systems

Categories	*Description*
1. Interdependency of façade system, thermal comfort system, daylight/lighting system	Study of air movement led to the integration of a wind wall on the façade of the naturally ventilated subsidized ward tower. Light shelves were used to reduce artificial lights.
2. Interdependency of air-conditioning system and natural ventilation system	To support the idea of enhancing the thermal comfort of roof terraces and to facilitate their use as an outdoor social space, detailed design of the spot cooling design was tested using CFD simulation (the efficiency of the chilled water system was found to be 33% [27]).
3. Interdependency of the built environment and natural systems	By discharging rainwater into Yishun Pond, and utilizing the pond water for irrigation and outdoor washing, the use of potable water was reduced, also reducing the carbon footprint in the process.
4. Resource efficiency within each M&E system design	Finally, energy-efficient system and resource-efficient system design is carried out for M&E engineering design.

within humankind with nature and living systems, including plant life, animals, and climatic elements [28], and that human wellness is encouraged through biophilic architectural designs by means of positive distractions for mental restoration and stress management. These qualities encourage the sensorial reconnection with nature that helps reduce stress and improve perceived physical and mental health. Research has also shown that stress and psychosocial factors can significantly affect patient health recovery.

Design strategies in KTPH are reviewed against the total building performance qualities and supported by the comprehensive research from *14 Patterns of Biophilic Designs* by Terrapin Bright Green [29] on the benefits of biophilic design. Many of the design strategies in KTPH demonstrate patterns in combinations. "Patterns in combination tend to increase the likelihood of health benefits of a space. Incorporating a diverse range of design strategies can accommodate the needs of various user groups from differing cultures and demographics and create an environment that is psycho-physiologically and cognitively restorative" [29].

Through a post-occupancy survey, KTPH was described as having "provided for natural and social environments well to a reasonably large extent" above a Green Mark Platinum certified green building. The survey reported that the integration of nature into the KTPH premises was found to be the most well-liked feature. It was also deemed to be the most important among all the features. In addition, the survey also found that "people prefer the positive feeling that nature offers, rather than manicured gardens" [30].

Circulation routes draw visitors through the building, experiencing greenery as they pass (see Color Plate 31). The landscaped courtyard is the heart and lung of the design. Designing around a central courtyard helps to orientate the patients and staff within this large development. With the hospital's main circulation route facing the courtyard, staff and patients experience this visual connection to the lush landscape during their transition from function to function. This supports the biophilic design objective of facilitating at least 5 to 20 minutes per day of visual connection to nature for the eyes to relax.

Even at high levels, naturally ventilated wards have visual access to views of plants at the shared central windows. Windows are lowered so that patients can still enjoy the view outside while lying on their beds. These large expanses of windows also benefit the staff servicing the patients by "shift(ing) focus to relax the eye muscles and temper cognitive fatigue" [29] from their directed attention during work.

The view of the calm water in the rejuvenated Yishun Pond provides a therapeutic distraction to the users of the hospital. "A good prospect condition imparts a sense of safety and control, particularly when alone or in unfamiliar environments. Images of nature that include aquatic elements are more likely to help reduce blood pressure and heart rate than similar imagery without aquatic elements" [29]. The community benefited from the pond cleanup and the users of the hospital benefited from the pond—a large calm body of water—being within view and providing an unobstructed area for wind generation. The stigma of a clinical hospital is removed and the hospital is the enabler.

The community rooftop farming space "offers colorful sights of the crops and great views of the surroundings to the patients and visitors. Some crops also emit fragrant scents which are therapeutic to occupants. In addition, the flora absorbs carbon dioxide and releases oxygen to improve air quality. Thriving birds and insect species provide sounds of nature to patients and staff, which contribute to a healing environment" [31]. Siting of the food court near the hospital border with Yishun Park invites the external community into the hospital for healthy food, dietary education, and promotion. Healthy hospitals are not intended merely to treat illness but to support and sustain human wellness; serving to connect, engage, and be enjoyed by its neighborhoods and communities.

The subsidized ward tower façade has solar screens to provide shade and wind walls to induce air movement (see Figure 10.22). It is positioned furthest away from the main road to mitigate traffic noise pollution. The naturally ventilated wards are complemented by ceiling-mounted fans that enhance wind speed to mitigate the discomfort of the tropical humid climate in Singapore. A post-occupancy study conducted on the thermal comfort of KTPH wards compared to existing hospitals in Singapore found that there was an insignificant difference in the satisfaction level between patients in the naturally ventilated wards and the air-conditioned wards [32]. This finding validated that, with thoroughly considered bioclimatic design, it is viable to design healthcare wards using natural ventilation only, enhanced by localized control to accommodate individuals' needs.

The large courtyard draws fresh air into the naturally ventilated spaces via prevalent wind directions. "Thermal comfort is a vital bridging component between biophilic design and sustainable design, especially in the face of climate change and rising energy costs. When thermal and airflow variability is implemented in a way that broadens people's perception of thermal comfort, it may also help reduce energy demands for air conditioning and heating" [29].

With the right selection of plants, biodiversity can be attracted back into the urban landscape. It is through the flora and fauna that stochastic and ephemeral connections with nature are most appreciated. "Humans perceive movement in the peripheral view much quicker than straight ahead. The brain also processes the movement of living things in a different place than it does of mechanical objects, whereby natural movement is generally perceived as positive, and mechanical

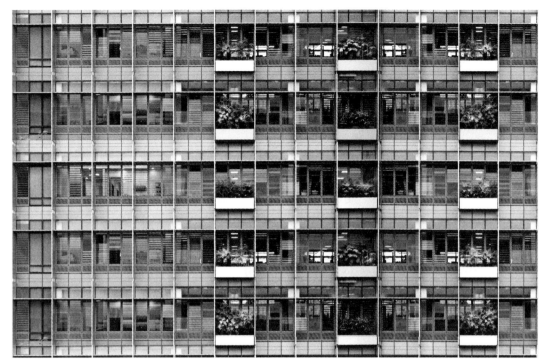

Figure 10.22   KTPH ward tower façade with greenery. (*Photo:* CPG Consultants Pte Ltd.)

movement as neutral or even negative. As a result, the repeating rhythmic motion of a pendulum will only hold one's attention briefly, the constant repetitive ticking of a clock may come to be ignored over time, and an ever-present scent may lose its mystique with long-term exposure; whereas, the stochastic movement of a butterfly will capture one's attention each time for recurring physiological benefits" [29].

10.8.4   Endnote

Khoo Teck Puat Hospital has adopted an approach to sustainable hospital design that combines the concepts of clinical, pathogenic treatment and the emerging recognition of the psychological recovery benefits of salutogenic treatment: focusing on health and the promotion of well-being. Through the use of biophilic design principles, these two trains of thought for treating illnesses are combined to great effect, benefiting the patient and wider community and encouraging the use of passive ventilation and cooling techniques that will benefit the facility's operation.

Post-occupancy studies, as earlier referenced, have cited concerns with "unanticipated and unintended challenges of KTPH's sustainable design" [32] strategies. For example, there are some operational and maintenance implications of some of the design strategies, such as wet open floors during rainy periods (cleaning, safety, and transportation issues), cleaning of the vast glazing, etc. Dealing with these concerns could benefit from involvement of a representative from the maintenance team of a similar facility to advise on operational issues, avoiding increased operational costs or to retrofit solutions to adapt to future needs.

10.9 Council House 2, Melbourne, Australia

The City of Melbourne

10.9.1 Context

Completed in 2005, Council House 2 (CH2; see Figure 10.23) in Melbourne, Australia (see Table 10.9 for climate data) was heralded as Australia's greenest office building for its ambitious, innovative, and holistic approach to sustainability—and rightly so. The project team set out to achieve "a revolutionary building that harvests sunlight, cool night air, water, wind and rain—creating a lasting landmark for one of the world's most liveable cities" [33]. In addition, specific council environmental and social strategies created a challenging brief that also sought to achieve Green Star certification, promote staff well-being and effectiveness, and create low risk with a high return on investment over 50 years [34].

Despite the building achieving the country's first six-star Green Star Office "As-Built" rating from the Green Building Council Australia, "no overt attempt was made to create a green looking building. The approach was taken that sustainable design should equal good design" [35].

Figure 10.23   Council House 2 timber shutters. (*Source:* Jonathan Lin, Council House 2, CC By-SA 2.0.)

Table 10.10   Key Climate Data for Melbourne, Australia

Altitude	10m (33 ft)
Climate	Maritime temperate/Humid
Average Monthly Maximum	24.0°C (75.2°F) dry bulb 13.8°C (56.8°F) wet bulb 89.9% RH
Average Monthly Minimum	5.6°C (42.1°F) dry bulb 3.3°C (37.9°F) wet bulb 63.7% RH

10.9.2   Design Development

An early 3-week charrette involving all project consultants and stakeholders allowed brainstorming and design development by pooling expertise and building a collaborative team. The process cost USD $127,000 (AUD $170,000), and resulted in a 6-month reduction in the design time, clarification of goals and objectives, and resolution of 70% to 80% of the building design and systems, including a major breakthrough decision to use water instead of air for cooling and numerous other outcomes [36]. The collaboration continued throughout the rest of the project program, resulting in a building with highly integrated systems and quality of space.

The design and development process is well documented on the City of Melbourne CH2 website [37] through design documentation and reports, along with case studies and research papers. Design "snapshots" capture emerging themes and focus areas such as biomimicry, people, indoor environment quality, and innovative features and also provide detailed information on the energy and water systems, including lessons learned from each process.

The energy-efficient design elements and systems that comprise the HVAC services include passive design techniques (thermal mass, night purging, ventilation stacks, natural daylighting), active systems (displacement ventilation, chilled beams and ceiling panels, phase-change materials, shower towers), and renewable energy technologies (cogeneration, roof-mounted microwind turbines, and solar PV panels). The cooling and ventilation strategy is a complex and interrelated system (see Color Plate 32).

Measures to enhance indoor environmental quality (IEQ) were adopted with the intention to improve the health, well-being, and productivity of staff in the building; recognizing the cost to the City of Melbourne through absenteeism. These include natural daylighting and ventilation, task lighting, low-toxicity materials for all furnishings and finishes, extensive use of planting, layout of workstations to promote collaborative working, and external spaces. The striking recycled timber louvres on the western elevation provide shading to workspaces and are designed to track the sun's movement via daylight sensors and the BMS. While improving user comfort, this integrated strategy also ensures that the internal lighting and cooling levels are appropriate for the daily solar/heat gain profile. An external stairwell encourages staff to use the stairs rather than the lifts to move between floors, getting fresh air at the same time.

10.9.3   Post-Occupancy Studies

POE surveys were carried out in the years following completion via physical IEQ measurements, occupant questionnaires, and focus group interviews. These are summarized in a 2008 report [38] as follows:

- The perceived productivity rating showed a significant improvement over the previous office location, CH1.
- Thermal comfort was generally considered good based on both physical measurements and occupant feedback; however, ventilation was rated poorly with air flow being perceived as too still.

- Measured pollutant levels showed excellent air quality provided through 100% fresh air, with formaldehyde levels much lower than in typical office buildings.

- Occupant feedback recognized a positive effect on their productivity of improved air quality.

- The ambient noise levels and reverberation times measured were considered ideal; however, occupants reported low satisfaction, possibly accredited to the unfamiliar open plan layout.

- Lighting levels were considered satisfactory; however, the integration with task lighting in the overall lighting strategy resulted in some complaints that it was too dark.

- Concerns over lighting levels, ventilation, and user controls were expected to be resolved through the commissioning and fine-tuning of systems over time.

In further studies, employees reported that "CH2 makes them feel healthier; they are relatively more productive at work; and the building provides a strong image of environmental intent" [39].

In 2012, the City of Melbourne invited Exergy to conduct a review of the building's energy efficiency performance. The findings were published in the *Council House 2 (CH2) in Review* report [40]. The main aims of the project were to:

1. Quantify the existing performance of the building against NABERS Energy benchmarks,
2. Identify issues impeding energy efficiency performance (focusing on core systems),
3. Detail measures to improve the NABERS energy rating, and
4. Identify lessons that can be learnt from CH2.

"At the time of CH2's construction most of these technologies were far from common within Australia's commercial building industry. And while chilled beam technology and trigeneration systems have since become more widespread, features such as the shower towers and phase-change storage tanks are still relatively uncommon among Australia's commercial building stock.

The complexity of CH2's design, coupled with the industry's general lack of familiarity with its features has proven to be one of the key challenges for the building's operation" [40].

The study found that the energy performance, 7 years after completion, did not meet the high standards expected of its design. Analysis found the base building to be performing at 3.24 stars (under the NABERS system), approximately 68% greater than the industry standard for good performance.

An investigation into the building operations and data outputs included site inspections over a course of several months at various times of the day and night to observe the building in its different modes of operation. A Sankey diagram was produced to represent energy flows through the building and identify problem areas (see Figure 10.24). The key issues were found to be in the cooling strategies operating inefficiently after hours, commissioning of HVAC controls, and optimization of system setpoints to accommodate variable demand conditions.

10.9.4   Lessons Learned

CH2 is currently performing well below its potential due to the anomalies identified with the HVAC controls. It appears that the complexity associated with the building's web of relatively unfamiliar subsystems has led to a range of flawed strategies and operational issues.

The building is an excellent illustration of the importance of optimizing control strategies and commissioning control behavior for subsystems, not only individually but also in their operation as a whole system and under numerous scenarios. Additionally, a key issue highlighted is the loss of knowledge of a building's systems over time, particularly through staff turnover.

Following a further study on the effect of the passive systems within the building, it was evident that there had been some loss of recognition of the importance of the relationship between the passive systems, a significant element of the building's energy efficiency strategy, and the interface with the building management system, such as:

- The setpoints in the BMS for the night purging were not being seasonally adjusted.
- The prioritization of the cooling modes in the BMS controls were not factoring in the passive systems (thermal mass, night purge) to be utilized primarily before the active systems (chilled panels), resulting in higher than required operation.
- The chilled ceiling panels were activating too early and too frequently, driven by BMS setpoints not aligned with the thermal mass properties of the building.

Upgrading of the building's submetering system, combined with a staged process of implementation and measurement, is necessary not only to optimize the building's operation but also to inform the industry on the performance of its more experimental technologies. This review marks the beginning of a project from which much more will hopefully be learned regarding the performance of its many features.

10.9.5   Endnote

Throughout the project life cycle, the client has maintained a commitment to share knowledge about the experience to facilitate learning and development in the industry. The willingness to share both the successes and shortcomings is commendable. The building design and systems installed have introduced unmanageable complexity, beyond the capabilities of the BMS to detect alone. The initial performance gap was identified through abnormalities in audit findings; these mechanisms along with continuous performance monitoring and fine-tuning are invaluable to ensuring that buildings perform optimally.

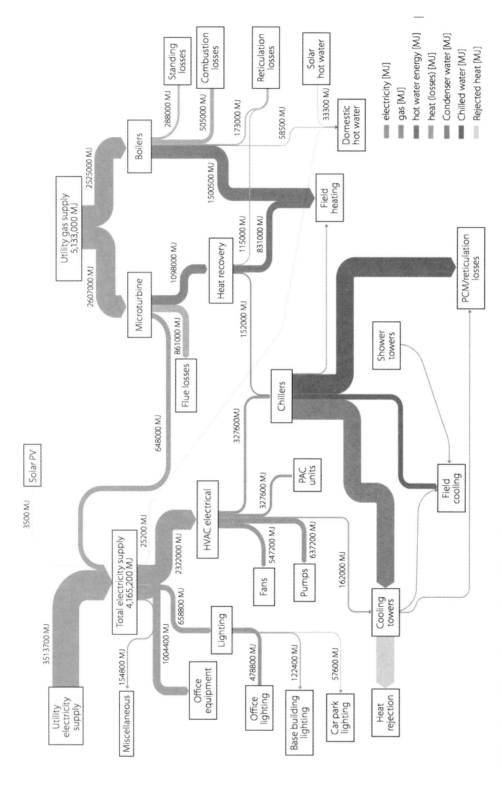

Figure 10.24 Council House 2 energy flows. (*Source*: Exergy.)

However, the POE studies carried out reflect three different forms of review: occupant, active systems, and passive systems. Only by aligning the findings of all studies can the issues be truly addressed; in isolation the systems are working against each other.

From a design target EUI of 55 kWh/m² (17 kBtu/ft²) [41], the latest published performance data from 2011 [42] suggest an operating EUI of 183 kWh/m² (58 kBtu/ft²); the difference is expected to be largely due to the shortcomings identified earlier. Based on an occupancy of 540 people, the 2011 energy consumption equates to 1.59 kW/Occ., placing it in the "Fair" quotient on the office performance spectrum (see Figure 2.8). The City of Melbourne council is taking the right steps toward understanding the reasons for the performance gap and also taking the necessary actions toward closing it.

CH2 was a catalyst for future change; a demonstration of what can be achieved by considering a building as a living system, rather than distinct processes. The City of Melbourne is incorporating the key POE findings to ensure that the building achieves the performance, longevity, and well-being that it also hopes to provide its occupants.

References

[1]   Key climatic data courtesy of Sefaira based on U.S. Department of Energy EPW weather files and weather analytics data.

[2]   Bullitt Center, *Waterless Waste*, http://www.bullittcenter.org/building/building-features/water-less-waste.

[3]   *Seattle's MEETS Coalition*, http://www.meetscoalition.org.

[4]   *Personal Comfort Systems*, http://www.personalcomfortsystems.com.

[5]   Lovins, A., *Reinventing Fire*, 2011, Boulder, CO: Rocky Mountain Institute.

[6]   *RMI IC: Thermal Comfort*, http://www.rmi.org/innovationcenter_thermal_comfort.

[7]   *The Chesapeake Bay Brock Environmental Center*, May 2016, http://trimtab.living-future.org/case-study/brock-environmental-center

[8]   Coffield, B., S. Lappano, and G. Mella, "Brock Environmental Center: Virginia Beach, Va.: Strong Through the Storm," *High Performance Building*, Summer 2016, http://www.hpbmagazine.org/Case-Studies/Brock-Environmental-Center-Virginia-Beach-Va.

[9]   *Hourigan Construction: Live Blog*, http://cbf.houriganconstruction.com/press-room/blog.

[10]   SmithGroupJJR, *Transparency*, http://www.smithgroupjjr.com/info/transparency.

[11]   *Chesapeake Bay Foundation: Brock Center Environmental Dashboard*, http://www.cbf.org/about-cbf/offices-operations/brock-center/dashboard.

[12]   North West Bicester, *One Planet Action Plan*, http://www.bioregional.com/wp-content/uploads/2014/09/BioRegional-NW-Bicester-One-Planet-Action-Plan-2013-high-res.pdf.

[13]   North West Bicester, *One Planet Action Plan Review*, http://www.bioregional.com/wp-content/uploads/2015/06/Bicester-Opap-review.pdf.

[14]   Cradle to Cradle® and C2C are registered trademarks of MBDC, LLC.

[15]   Braungart, M., and W. McDonough, *Cradle to Cradle: Remaking the Way We Make Things*, New York: North Point Press, 2002.

[16]   American Society of Landscape Architects, *2010 ASLA Professional Awards: Honor Award—Park 20/20: A Cradle to Cradle Inspired Master Plan*, https://www.asla.org/2010awards/612.html.

[17] William McDonough + Partners and M. Braungart, *Toward a Cradle to Cradle: Park 20|20—The Work Benefits, the World Benefits*, http://dev.nl.epea-hamburg.org/sites/default/files-nl/10_1115%20Park%202020%20booklet.pdf.

[18] Scott, L. *Park 20|20, Amsterdam: Born to be Recycled*, 2014 http://urbanland.uli.org/sustainability/park-2020-amsterdam-born-recycled.

[19] Ibid.

[20] Cheshire, D., *Is the Circular Economy the Way Forward?*, May 2016, http://www.building.co.uk/analysis/comment/is-the-circular-economy-the-way-forward?/5081762.article.

[21] William McDonough + Partners, *Park 20|20 Masterplan*, http://www.mcdonoughpartners.com/projects/park-2020-master-plan/#big-image.

[22] *Africa's "Greenest" Hotel Takes Shape in Cape Town*, January 2013, http://www.sapropertynews.com/africas-greenest-hotel-takes-shape-in-cape-town.

[23] Hotel Verde, *Thrivability Report*, http://www.hotelverde.com/static/thrivability-report; see also "What Makes a Green Hotel," *Simply Green*, No. 2, pp. 113–120, https://issuu.com/sgdigital/docs/sg0216/113; "Hotel Verde," *Architect and Builder*, Vol. 64, No. 6, November/December 2013, pp. 22–33, http://archibuild.businesscatalyst.com/assets/architect-and-builder-november-2013_hotel-verde.pdf.

[24] Health Research & Educational Trust, *Environmental Sustainability in Hospitals: The Value of Efficiency*, May 2014, Chicago, IL: Author, http://www.hpoe.org/Reports-HPOE/ashe-sustainability-report-FINAL.pdf .

[25] Liak, T. L., "Planning for a Hassle-Free Hospital: The Khoo Teck Puat Hospital," paper presented at *6th Design and Health World Congress 2009*, Singapore, 2009, http://www.designandhealth.com/Events/Singapore-Congress-2009.aspx; see also Liak, T. L., "From Vision to Reality: The Case of Khoo Teck Puat," paper presented at *Design and Health World Congress 2012*, Kuala Lumpur, June 2012, http://www.designandhealth.com/upl/files/121982.

[26] Tan, S. Y., *The Practice of Integrated Design: The Case Study of Khoo Teck Puat Hospital*, 2012, Master's dissertation, BCA Academy, University of Nottingham, Singapore.

[27] Nirmal, T. K., *Greening Asia, Emerging Principles for Sustainable Architecture*, 2012, BCI Asia Construction Information Pte Ltd, Singapore.

[28] Wilson, E., *Biophilia*, 1984, President and Fellows of Harvard College, USA.

[29] Terrapin Bright Green, *14 Patterns of Biophilic Design: Improving Health and Well-Being in the Built Environment*, 2014, http://www.terrapinbrightgreen.com/report/14-patterns.

[30] Sng, P. L. M., *In What Way Can Green Building Contribute to Human Wellness in the Singapore Context?*, 2011, National University of Singapore.

[31] Council on Tall Buildings and Urban Habitat (CTBUH) Research paper, *Beyond Skyrise Gardens: The Potential of Urban Roof-Top Farming in Singapore*, Wai Wing Tai Donald, Alexandrea Health Pte Ltd, 2011. http://global.ctbuh.org/resources/papers/download/882-beyond-skyrise-gardnes-the-potential-of-urban-roof-top-farming-in-singapore.pdf.

[32] Wu., Z., *Evaluation of a Sustainable Hospital Design Based on Its Social and Environmental Outcomes*, May 2011, Master's thesis, http://iwsp.human.cornell.edu/files/2013/09/Ziqi-Wu-2011-19cxn60.pdf.

[33] City of Melbourne, *CH2 Design Snap Shot 01: Introduction*, http://www.melbourne.vic.gov.au/SiteCollectionDocuments/ch2-snapshot-01-introduction.pdf.

[34] City of Melbourne, *CH2 Design Snap Shot 02: The Business Case*, http://www.melbourne.vic.gov.au/SiteCollectionDocuments/ch2-snapshot-02-business-case.pdf.

[35] City of Melbourne, *CH2 Design Snap Shot 03: The Design Charrette*, http://www.melbourne.vic.gov.au/SiteCollectionDocuments/ch2-snapshot-03-design-charrette.pdf.

[36] City of Melbourne CH2 website, http://www.melbourne.vic.gov.au/building-and-development/sustainable-building/council-house-2/Pages/council-house-2.aspx.

[37] Webb, S., *Environment Design Guide: The Integrated Design Process of CH2*, February 2005, http://www.melbourne.vic.gov.au/sitecollectiondocuments/ch2-case-study.pdf.

[38]   Paevere, P., and S. Brown, *Indoor Environment Quality and Occupant Productivity in the CH2 Building: Post-Occupancy Summary*, March 2008, Report No. USP2007/23, Commonwealth Scientific and Industrial Research Organisation, https://www.melbourne.vic.gov.au/SiteCollectionDocuments/CH2-post-occupancy-summary.pdf.

[39]   Leaman, A., et al., *Occupant Survey of CH2*, 2008; cited in Yudelson, J., and U. Meyer, *The World's Greenest Buildings: Promise Versus Performance in Sustainable Design*, 2013, New York and London: Routledge.

[40]   Hoogland, M., and P. Bannisert, *Council House 2 (CH2) in Review*, 2014, Exergy Australia,https://www.airah.org.au/imis15_prod/Content_Files/EcoLibrium/2014/March14/03-14-Eco-005.pdf.

[41]   Department of the Environment and Heritage, Australian Government, *ESD Design Guide for Australian Government Buildings—Edition 2*, February 2006, http://www.apcc.gov.au/ALLAPCC/GPG%20-%20ESD%20Design%20Guide%20for%20Australisn%20Government%20Buildings%20Edition%202.pdf.

[42]   Yudelson, J., and U. Meyer, *The World's Greenest Buildings: Promise Versus Performance in Sustainable Design*, 2013, New York: Routledge.

About the Authors

Professor David Strong graduated from Bath University with a B.Sc. in building engineering; he went on to be awarded a doctorate by Oxford University in 1980 for his development of a patented gas-fired domestic heat pump. Since 2002 he has been an honorary visiting professor at the University of Nottingham, School of Architecture & the Built Environment, and in 2013 he was also made a visiting professor at the Oxford Institute for Sustainable Development. David is currently a director of David Strong Consulting Ltd. and chairman of REAL Assurance Ltd.

Previously, he was CEO of the sustainability consultancy Inbuilt and chairman of the United Kingdom's Energy Efficiency Partnership for Buildings. Prior to this, he was managing director of the Building Research Establishment (BRE) Environment Division, where he was responsible for five centers of excellence: BREEAM, Sustainable Development, Housing, Sustainable Energy Centre (formerly BRECSU, with responsibility for delivering the U.K. government's Buildings Energy Efficiency Best Practice Programme), and Environmental Consultancy. Previous roles include executive director of: EA Technology (formerly the Electricity Research Centre, Capenhurst), Emstar (formerly Shell's contract energy management company, now Dalkia/Veolia), and W. S. Atkins & Partners.

In 2007 he was presented with the Building Sustainability Leadership Award for establishing the U.K. Green Building Council.

Victoria Kate Burrows graduated with a B.Sc. in architecture and environmental design from the University of Nottingham, and prior to this achieved the international baccalaureate diploma at The Henley College, United Kingdom.

Victoria is currently working as head of sustainability for a major international contractor, advising on value-adding practices from strategic to site level. Her work as a consultant in sustainable development and green building rating systems has spanned Europe, South East Asia, China, and parts of the Caribbean and North Africa as director of Sustainable Development Solutions Ltd., specializing in low-impact hospitality developments. Previous appointments have included The GreenAsia Group, Inbuilt Consulting (taking much of her inspiration from the late sustainability champion Mel Starrs), and the Building Research Establishment for the development of BREEAM schemes and certification of buildings.

At the time of writing, Victoria was a finalist for Building's "Woman of the Year" award for 2016.

Contributing Authors

Jerry Yudelson, P.E., LEED Fellow, Sustainability Consultant & Author

Thomas Hartman, Principal, The Hartman Company

Jane Anderson, Principal Consultant, thinkstep

Martin Cook, DQM Solutions

Derek Clements-Croome, Professor Emeritus in Architectural Engineering, University of Reading

Kathryn Bourke, Managing Director, Whole Life Ltd.

Bill Bordass, The Usable Buildings Trust, U.K.

Michael Pawlyn, Exploration Architecture

Gary Grant, CEnv FCIEEM, Green Infrastructure Consultancy Ltd.

John Newton, Founder and Managing Director, The Ecology Consultancy

Rob Bolin, P.E., Syska Hennessy Group

Rajat Gupta and Adorkor Bruce-Konuah, Oxford Brookes University

Alan Johnson, Honeywell, Energy & Environmental Solutions

Tim Dwyer, Visiting Professor, Building Services Systems, UCL Faculty of the Built Environment

Andrew Corney, P.E., Product Director, Sefaira

Kemi Adeyeye, University of Bath, U.K., Kenneth Ip and Kaiming She, University of Brighton, U.K.

Jane Shields, Director, Living Water Ecosystems Ltd.

David E. Claridge, Ph.D., P.E., PCC, Director, Mitch Paulus, Charles Culp, and Kevin Christman, Energy Systems Laboratory, Texas A&M Engineering Experiment Station

Case Study Contributors

10.1   Paul Schwer, President, PAE and Sara Calabro

10.2   John Breshears, President, Architectural Applications

10.3   Greg Mella, Vice President, SmithGroupJJR

10.4   Nicole Lazarus, Bicester Eco-Town Project Manager for Bioregional, and Steve Hornblow, Project Director, A2Dominion

10.5   William McDonough + Partners

10.6   André Harms, Founder, Ecolution Consulting

10.7   Talik and Jaafar Chalabi, Principal Designers, Chalabi Architekten & Partner

10.8   Tan Shao Yen, Managing Director, and Vanessa Yang, CPG Consultants Pte. Ltd.

10.9   City of Melbourne

Index

Recent Titles in the Artech House Integrated Microsystems Series

RF MEMS Circuit Design for Wireless Communications, Héctor J. De Los Santos

Understanding Smart Sensors, Third Edition, Randy Frank

Wafer-Level Testing and Test During Burn-in for Integrated Circuits,
  Sudarshan Bahukudumbi Krishnendu Chakrabarty

A Whole-System Approach to High-Performance Green Buildings, David Strong and
  Victoria Burrows

Wireless Sensor Network, Nirupama Bulusu and Sanjay Jha

For further information on these and other Artech House titles, including previously considered out-of-print books now available through our In-Print-Forever® (IPF®) program, contact:

Artech House
685 Canton Street
Norwood, MA 02062
Phone: 781-769-9750
Fax: 781-769-6334
e-mail: artech@artechhouse.com

Artech House
16 Sussex Street
London SW1V 4RW UK
Phone: +44 (0)20 7596-8750
Fax: +44 (0)20 7630-0166
e-mail: artech-uk@artechhouse.com

Find us on the World Wide Web at: www.artechhouse.com